Austria

Susan Roraff & Julie Krejci

Graphic Arts Center Publishing Company
Portland, Oregon

In the same series

Argentina	Egypt	Korea	Spain
Australia	Finland	Laos	Sri Lanka
Austria	France	Malaysia	Sweden
Bolivia	Germany	Mauritius	Switzerland
Borneo	Greece	Mexico	Syria
Britain	Hong Kong	Morocco	Taiwan
Burma	Hungary	Myanmar	Thailand
California	India	Nepal	Turkey
Canada	Indonesia	Netherlands	UAE
Chile	Iran	Norway	Ukraine
China	Ireland	Pakistan	USA
Cuba	Israel	Philippines	USA—The South
Czech Republic	Italy	Singapore	Venezuela
Denmark	Japan	South Africa	Vietnam

Barcelona At Your Door
Chicago At Your Door
Havana At Your Door
Jakarta At Your Door
Kuala Lumpur, Malaysia
 At Your Door
London At Your Door
New York At Your Door

Paris At Your Door
Rome At Your Door
San Francisco At Your
 Door

A Globe-Trotter's Guide
A Parent's Guide
A Student's Guide

A Traveller's Medical
 Guide
A Wife's Guide
Living and Working
 Abroad
Working Holidays
 Abroad

Illustrations by TRIGG

© 2001 Times Media Private Limited

This book is published by special
arrangement with Times Media Private Limited
Times Centre, 1 New Industrial Road, Singapore 536196
International Standard Book Number: 1-55868-591-X
Library of Congress Card Number: 00-110096

Graphic Arts Center Publishing Company
P.O. Box 10306 • Portland, Oregon 97296-0306 • (503) 226-2402

Printed in Singapore

To our beautiful children,
Natascha and Benjamin,
who motivate us with their boundless energy
and inspire us with their unending curiosity.

CONTENTS

INTRODUCTION

Austria! You've just found out that you are moving to Austria. Beautiful images pass through your mind ... the Vienna Boys' Choir, classical music, *The Sound of Music* and *The Blue Danube*, Baroque churches and ornate palaces, the Spanish Riding School, skiing in the Alps, and so much more. Everyone you know is envious and you are excited at the prospect. Then it suddenly hits you that this is not a two-week vacation, but the next few years of your life! How will it be to actually live in Austria? What are the day-to-day realities? Will you like it?

Relax. It will not be that difficult, and if you keep an open mind and welcome new experiences you will find yourself crying when the time comes for you to leave. Austria is a lovely country that is full of possibilities. After you learn what is expected of you, and become well versed in the local etiquette and customs, you will do just fine. The main problem with being an expatriate is that you don't always know why people do what they do, and in turn, you are uncertain as to what you should do. You don't want to appear rude or do something embarrassing, but it happens to just about every new arrival. This book will help you understand the little things as well as the major points about Austrian society so that you can start off on the right foot.

There are a few things you can do before you leave home. Probably the most important is to become familiar with basic German. Most Austrians in the major cities and quite a few in smaller towns speak very good English (besides other European languages), so knowing German isn't vital, but it will help damp the culture shock. Being able to read some of the signs and advertisements, or understanding the weather report on the radio will help you feel at home in Austria. If your departure is somewhat sudden, there are plenty of excellent and not too expensive places to learn German in Austria. Studying there will also provide you with an excuse to get out and about in your new home and allow you to meet people who are in similar situations.

Meeting new people is the second major weapon in the fight against culture shock. If you are heading to Austria with a job or are already enrolled in a school or university, you will have several opportunities to socialize. However, if you are giving up your job or studies and your social life back home to accompany your spouse or partner, it is essential that you make new friends and build your own life in Austria. Obviously, meeting people from your home country through clubs and organizations is the easiest path to follow, but why stop there? Although opportunities to meet and socialize with Austrians do not jump out at you every day, it is not impossible to make good friends and enter into the society. It can be very easy to isolate yourself from your host country and its people, but if you do you'll find that something is missing. Seek out Austrian friends and your efforts will be well rewarded.

Finally, staying busy will help keep homesickness at bay. Austria is an outdoor lover's paradise. You don't have to be an excellent skier to enjoy the fresh air. In fact, the most popular pastime is *wandern* (hiking). If that's too much exercise for you, the cities are bursting with museums, shops, concerts, opera, and theater. Learn about the rich history of this land and take advantage of all that it offers. Do as much as you can and your time in Austria will fly by. If you follow this simple advice, we believe that your stay in this wonderful country will be as pleasant as ours has been.

ACKNOWLEDGMENTS

The authors recognize that this book could not have been written without the help of many people. Our heartfelt thanks go to Julie's husband Gary, the Schwanzer family, Adele Jibidar, and Brian Roraff, for contributing valuable information, answering endless questions, and/or reviewing the manuscript. We would also like to thank Lisa Boucher, Carol and Robert Roraff, the Zanetti family, Pilar Peikoff, many teachers at the American International School in Vienna, and the students of Central University of Iowa for their comments and insights. We are indebted to the many Austrians who have made us feel welcome in their country and who have shared their historically rich culture with us. We would like to thank Jitka Dvořáčková for keeping Benjamin smiling and Suzanne Kuhnard for entertaining Natascha while their mommies worked. Finally, we recognize that any errors are the sole responsibility of the authors.

AUSTRIA

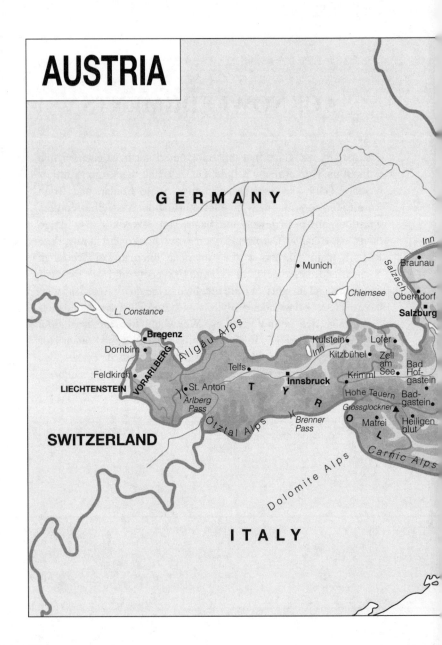

GERMANY

Munich

Inn

Braunau

Salzach

Chiemsee

Oberndorf

L. Constance

Salzburg

Bregenz

Allgäu Alps

Dornbirn

Kufstein

Lofer

VORARLBERG

Inn

Kitzbühel

Zell
am
See

Bad
Hof-
gastein

Feldkirch

Telfs

St. Anton

Krimml

LIECHTENSTEIN

T

Innsbruck

Y

Hohe Tauern

Bad-
gastein

Arlberg
Pass

R

Grossglockner

Ötztal Alps

Brenner
Pass

O

Matrei

Heiligen
blut

SWITZERLAND

L

Carnic Alps

Dolomite Alps

ITALY

N

CZECH
REPUBLIC

SLOVAKIA

Passau
Schärding
Mühlviertel
Danube
Freistadt
Greiner Wald
Krems
Tulln
Kloster-
neuburg
Gänserndorf
Linz
Melk
VIENNA
Bratislava
Hainburg
UPPER
AUSTRIA
Amstetten
Wachau Valley
St.
Pölten
Vienna
Woods
Perchtoldsdorf
Gmunden
Steyr
LOWER
AUSTRIA
Baden
Mödling
Bruck an der Leitha
Attersee
Mondsee
Traunsee
Ebensee
Mariazell
Wiener Neustadt
Eisenstadt
Rust
Neusiedlersee
St. Wolfgang
Bad Ischl
Bad Aussee
Hieflau
Admont
Mürzzuschlag
Semmering
Pass
Sopron
Hallstatt
Enns
Eisenerz
Kindberg
Deutschkreutz
Salzkammergut
Schladming
Erzberg
Mürz
Leoben
BURGENLAND
SALZBURG
Murau
Mur
STYRIA
Güssing
HUNGARY
Graz
CARINTHIA
Wolfsberg
Bad St. Leonhard
Deutschlandsberg
Spittal
Drau
Ossiachersee
Magdalensberg
Villach
Wörthersee
Klagenfurt
Karawanken

SLOVENIA
Ljubljana

CROATIA

Zagreb

NOTES TO THE READER

The chapters that follow may be read in any order. Chapter Eleven gives a simple overview of the provinces for those less familiar with the geography of Austria.

Terms are explained when first mentioned, and frequently used terms may also be found in the Glossary at the back of the book.

Chapter One

THE HISTORY OF THE AUSTRIAN EMPIRE

Throughout its long history, Austria has often been right at the center of events in Europe, not only politically but also in the arts and sciences. Living in Austria, one is constantly reminded of its former glory. Having a sense of this history helps one understand the Austrians of today.

EARLY HISTORY

Present-day Austria has been inhabited since prehistoric times. The Venus of Willendorf, a remarkable 20,000-year-old figurine in the shape of a woman symbolizing fertility, was unearthed in the Wachau valley. As early as 2000 BC, the area was populated by the Illyrians, early Iron Age miners who reached a high degree of civilization between 1700 and 700 BC. The Celts were next to populate the area and remained until the first century BC. Their kingdom, known as Noricum, thrived on salt mined from the Salzkammergut and iron ore from the Styrian mountains. The Celts were the first to settle in present-day Vienna, which they called Vindobona.

Vienna became an important settlement thanks to its location. The Amber Route, which ran from the Adriatic Sea to the Baltic, crossed the Danube River here. Bronze weapons and pottery from the south and amber and whale tusks from the north were traded along the route. By the year 15 BC, the Romans had extended their realm into the region, establishing a military camp on the banks of the Danube at present-day Vienna that was to stand for 400 years. Other Roman settlements at this time included Iuvavum, presently Salzburg, Brigantium at Bregenz, and the largest, Carnuntum, a major city with approximately 20,000 inhabitants located east of Vienna. Eventually, the Romans were overtaken by their enemies and withdrew from the area in the fifth century AD, leaving Austria to the so-called Dark Ages. During this time Austria was at the center of shifting populations which included Germanic tribes, Teutons, Huns, Slavs, Magyars, and Avars.

Between 791 and 796, the Frankish ruler Charlemagne founded the Holy Roman Empire to succeed the Roman Empire. Austria became the eastern border of the empire, and was referred to as Ostmark or the Eastern March. At the end of the 9th century this area succumbed to the Magyars. The region remained under Magyar control until their defeat by King Otto the Great. In 976 his successor, Otto II, presented the province to Margrave Leopold von Babenberg.

THE BABENBERG DYNASTY

The Babenberg family ruled the Ostmark for 270 years, gradually expanding their territory. The Babenberg holdings increased when Leopold V obtained the duchy of Styria in 1192. Vienna was granted a city charter in 1221 and cultural life at the Babenberg court flourished. Under its leadership, Austria became one of the richest duchies in the Holy Roman Empire, and Vienna the second most important city. In 1246 the dynasty ended suddenly when Duke Friedrich II, who was childless, was killed in a battle against the Magyars.

A dispute erupted as to who would rule the duchies of Austria and Styria. King Ottokar II Przemysl of Bohemia had the support of the Austrian nobility and assumed power. Rudolf of Habsburg, a minor count from Switzerland, was elected Holy Roman Emperor in 1273 by the German princes, who assumed erroneously that he could be controlled. Instead, they helped create a powerful dynasty that would rule Austria for over 600 years. Rudolf of Habsburg challenged King Ottokar's rule over Austria. King Ottokar was killed in 1278 in the Battle of Dürnkrut, and Rudolf assumed power.

THE HABSBURG DYNASTY

The Habsburgs consolidated their rule in the early 14th century. In the mid-14th century, Rudolf IV, later known as Rudolf the Founder, took the throne. He moved to establish Vienna as one of the premier cities of Europe. During the 14th and 15th centuries the Habsburgs gained Carinthia, Tyrol, Vorarlberg, Slovenia, and Trieste. Friedrich III raised the duchy of Austria to that of an archduchy within the Holy Roman Empire and consequently, from 1438 until its dissolution in 1806, the Habsburgs were the hereditary emperors of the empire.

Marriage Diplomacy

In the late 15th and 16th centuries, the Habsburgs peacefully obtained by marriage more lands than they ever could have won in battle, gaining Netherlands, Burgundy, Naples, Sicily, Sardinia, and large territories in the Americas. The line split when Emperor Charles V's son, Phillip II, took possession of the Spanish and Dutch lands, while Charles's brother, Ferdinand I, became regent not only of the

15

German-speaking lands but, through shrewd marriage policies of his own, also gained Bohemia and Hungary. This practice led to the famous saying, "Let the strong fight wars; thou, happy Austria, marry: What Mars bestows on others, Venus gives to thee."

THE 16TH AND 17TH CENTURIES

The Turks

The Ottoman Empire was also interested in expansion. The Turks set their sights on Vienna in 1529 but, thwarted by the city's strong defenses and the approaching winter, failed in their siege. Although they did not take Vienna, they maintained control of Hungary and remained a powerful and ever present enemy on Austria's doorstep.

The Thirty Years War waged from 1618 to 1648, pitting Catholics against Protestants, and left Austria somewhat weaker for the ordeal. The situation was compounded by the Plague, which devastated Vienna in 1669. Thus Vienna seemed easy prey to the Turks, who once again laid siege to the city in the summer of 1683. Prince Eugene of Savoy, a clever military commander, proved instrumental in the struggle against the Turks, who were finally firmly defeated, and consequently gave up control of Hungary (which included present-day Romania) and Croatia to Austria.

THE 18TH CENTURY

War of the Spanish Succession

In 1700, the Spanish line of the Habsburgs died out. The War of the Spanish Succession erupted as the Austrian line of the Habsburg dynasty attempted to reclaim its former territories. Ultimately, Austria lost the Spanish possessions, but was able to regain control of Italy and the Netherlands.

The Baroque Period

With the Turks no longer a threat, and with the end of a second plague

Holy Trinity columns were erected in towns all over Austria in the late 17th century to give thanks for the end of the Plague epidemic.

in 1713, new life was breathed into Vienna. As the Habsburgs and the accompanying nobility moved into the city, it became an imperial melting pot of Czechs, Poles, and Hungarians, among others. During the 18th century the population doubled to 200,000. No longer needing the protection of walls, the city overflowed into the suburbs. Economically, the region surged forward. The arts were summarily promoted and there was a frenzy of creative activity in literature, music, and architecture. Austria enthusiastically entered the Baroque period, which reached its highest point under Karl VI.

Maria Theresa (1740–80)

In 1713 Karl VI, who had no male heir, changed the law to allow daughters the right of succession, and thereby ensured that his daughter Maria Theresa would take the crown after his death. However, upon Karl's death in 1740, Maria Theresa faced challenges to her rule: Austria lost Silesia in the Silesian War, also known as the War of the Austrian Succession (1740–48), and an attempt to regain it in the Seven Years War (1756–63) was unsuccessful.

In 1745, Maria Theresa's husband, Franz Stephan of Lorraine, was crowned Holy Roman Emperor, Franz I. Although her father's edict had allowed her to become ruler of Austria, gender prevented Maria Theresa from becoming the Empress of the Holy Roman Empire. When her husband died in 1765, she named her son, Josef II, co-regent, in effect retaining power. She was respected and popular because of her reforms, which included making general education compulsory and building an efficient centralized administration, albeit at the expense of local governance. Yet one of her most impressive feats was not political at all. While concerned with the affairs of the empire, she gave birth to sixteen children, one of whom, Marie Antoinette, would lose her head during the French Revolution.

Josef II (1780–90)

When Josef II came to power following his mother's death, he began to institute his own reforms. Influenced by the Enlightenment, he issued the Toleration Patent in 1781, granting freedom of religious worship. He also set out to curtail the powerful Catholic Church. In addition, Josef II abolished serfdom, made the aristocracy liable to taxation, and opened the Prater, the imperial hunting grounds, to the public. More famously, he allowed vintners to sell their own "new wine" or *Heurige*. The government was unable to keep pace with the reforms, and following his death, many of them were repealed.

THE 19TH CENTURY

The Napoleonic Years

As was true for many European monarchies, the Habsburgs were threatened by the ideals of the French Revolution and the subsequent rise of Napoleon. Fighting erupted in 1792 when France declared war on Austria and most of Europe. In 1804 Napoleon crowned himself Emperor of France. To compensate, Franz II raised Austria from an archduchy to an empire and named himself Emperor of Austria as Franz I. In spite of his efforts, Franz was forced to renounce his crown as Holy Roman Emperor when Napoleon consolidated his own power. Vienna was occupied by French troops in 1805 and 1809. In yet another attempt at marriage diplomacy, Franz's daughter Marie Louise was married to Napoleon in 1810. This marriage produced a son, who, after Napoleon's downfall and exile, was closely guarded at Schönbrunn until he died at 21 from tuberculosis. Austria eventually took up arms again as part of the coalition comprising England, Prussia, and Russia that finally defeated Napoleon in 1814.

The Congress of Vienna (1814–15)

At the Congress of Vienna, 200 delegates from across the continent met to reestablish the traditional balance of power. Borders were redrawn and Austria regained lands lost to France. The Congress was more famous, however, for its extravagance as the delegates spent more time at dinner and balls.

The imposing Schönbrunn palace and gardens, originally on the outskirts of Vienna, was the summer residence of the Habsburgs.

Vormärz

The period between the Congress of Vienna and the revolution of March 1848 is known as the *Vormärz* (the period before March). Prince Metternich, chancellor during the reign of Franz I, was in charge of government policy. Metternich was extremely conservative, and employed harsh repression and censorship to uphold the absolute power of the monarch. As a result, many people turned inward, focusing on family life instead of venturing out under the careful gaze of the secret police. Among the upper and middle classes culture replaced political and economic activities, ushering in the *Biedermeier* period. Music, literature, and the other arts flourished during this time.

Revolution of 1848

The police state could not restrain the demands of a society entering the industrial age. The middle class led calls for increased freedoms, and the working class wanted better living and working conditions.

On March 13, 1848, a large group of students and workers protested, precipitating Prince Metternich's flight to England. Emperor Ferdinand eventually agreed to set up a parliament, and the first deputies took office in July. By October 31, after 2,000 people had died, the rebels were finally subdued.

The regions of Hungary and Bohemia were anxious to secure their independence and saw their opportunity in this unrest. The Bohemians were brought under control first, but the Hungarians proved a formidable enemy. Only with the help of Russian troops was the Hungarian revolt finally suppressed. On December 2, 1848, Emperor Ferdinand, who was epileptic and not in full command of his faculties, abdicated in favor of his nephew, Franz Josef.

Franz Josef (1848–1916)

Only 18 years of age when he became emperor, Franz Josef was a popular monarch, closely associated with the memories of imperial Austria. Under his rule, the second half of the 19th century came to be known as the *Gründerzeit*, or Founder era, and Vienna shone as one of the jewels of Europe. Yet Franz Josef also ruled during a time when the Austrian Empire began to break apart. Austria lost Lombardy in 1859. Following the Austro-Prussian War of 1866, Austria lost dominance among the German states and ceded Venice to Italy.

Meanwhile, the Hungarians were still demanding independence. Given their military losses, Austria agreed to negotiate. In 1867, the Austro-Hungarian dual monarchy was created. Each state would be autonomous, and a separate parliament was established in Budapest. In return, the Emperor of Austria would also be crowned King of Hungary and the two states would share the same defense, foreign, and economic policies.

Civilian Government

By the end of the 19th century, three main political parties had been formed in the Austrian part of the empire: the Austrian Social

Democratic Party, the Christian Social Party, and the German National Party. Austria enjoyed a relatively free press. Universal male suffrage was granted in 1907, and the first general elections were held for the imperial parliament, although Franz Josef remained in firm control. There were growing concerns within the empire: the working class was demanding better pay and working conditions; nationalistic tendencies among the many ethnic groups were on the rise, but the German-speaking Austrians were reluctant to grant them more rights; and tensions were running high. The emperor was also plagued by personal problems: while Franz Josef had survived an assassination attempt in 1853 by the Hungarian Janos Libenyi, his wife, Empress Elisabeth (better known as Sissi), was killed in Geneva in 1898 by an Italian anarchist. His son, Crown Prince Rudolph, committed suicide after killing his lover, Baroness Maria Vetsera, in Mayerling in 1889.

THE 20TH CENTURY

World War I
On June 28, 1914, Crown Prince Franz Ferdinand and his wife were assassinated in Sarajevo, Bosnia-Herzegovina (which had come under Austro-Hungarian rule in 1878), by the young Serbian nationalist, Gavrilo Princip. About two months later, Austria declared war on Serbia, and the latter's Russian allies came to its defense. Russia's allies, France and Britain, joined in and World War I was under way. Austria, aided by Germany, was unable to claim victory on the battlefield. Emperor Franz Josef died in 1916 and his successor, Kaiser Karl I, tried unsuccessfully to keep the empire intact. Austria eventually signed an armistice treaty on November 3, 1918. Eight days later, Karl I renounced participation in the government, although technically not the throne. South Tyrol was lost to Italy, Galicia went to Poland, and Yugoslavia was formed, encompassing some of the former Habsburg possessions. Hungary finally received its long-awaited independence, as did the Czechs and Slovaks. Austria was

reduced to one-eighth its former size with one-ninth its former population, primarily German-speaking areas of the former empire.

The First Republic

Delegates to parliament proclaimed the Republic of German Austria on November 12, 1918. Like many citizens, especially those in the Alpine provinces, the three major political parties were all favorable to a union with Germany. However, this would not have been in the best interests of Austria's World War I adversaries and thus any merger was expressly forbidden by the treaty ending the war. So the country was called merely "Austria" and in February 1919, the Social Democrat Dr. Karl Renner was elected the first state chancellor. The coalition that had brought Renner into power broke down the following year. The conservative Christian Social Party won elections in October 1920 and, in essence, ran the federal government until 1938. The inter-war years were marked by economic crisis, inflation, unemployment, hunger, and violence.

Red Vienna

Constitutional reform in 1922 granted Vienna special status as a *Land* or semi-autonomous province. The Social Democrats governing Vienna introduced a number of important social reforms, which ushered in the period known as Red Vienna. They instituted a massive housing program, building about 63,000 apartments for workers between 1923 and 1933. These complexes were quite innovative for their time in that they included amenities like indoor plumbing and community facilities such as kindergartens, cooperative food stores, medical services, meeting halls, libraries, and green courtyards.

Growing Tensions

While the Socialists had a lock on Vienna, the Christian Socials ran the federal government. The two were constantly at odds. Political tensions were heightened by the existence of paramilitary organiza-

Red Vienna produced a large number of public housing complexes, but the Karl-Marx-Hof in the 19th district is the most famous.

tions linked to the political parties whose ranks swelled as unemployment grew. In July 1927, a strike was called to protest the acquittal of three right-wing men accused of killing a man and a boy who had been marching in a Socialist parade. Clashes between demonstrators and the police in Vienna left 91 dead.

Civil War

The country was heading for civil war. By the late 1920s, the Nazi movement had entered Austria through the western provinces. By 1932, Austrian Nazis had begun to hold elected positions. The Christian Democrat Engelbert Dollfuss became chancellor. He took advantage of the resignation of the Speaker of the House and his two deputies following an impasse in parliament and quickly imposed an authoritarian regime. His right-wing government was hostile to both Social Democrats and the Nazis, a position that would ultimately lead to his downfall and the disappearance of Austria as a political entity. Instead of aligning with the Social Democrats against the threat of the Nazi government in Germany (Hitler had risen to power in May 1933), he faced both enemies simultaneously.

On February 12, 1934, civil war finally broke out, pitting the Social Democrats against the federal government, led by the Christian Socials and supported by the police and the army. The Social Democrats were summarily defeated and their hold on power was broken. The party was outlawed and the leaders were either exiled or imprisoned.

The End of Austria

In July 1934, the Austrian Nazis attempted a coup, and Dollfuss was assassinated. His successor, Dr. Kurt Schuschnigg, allied himself with Italy's Mussolini, as Dollfuss had done. When Hitler and Mussolini became friendly, Schuschnigg was forced to enter into the Austro-German Agreement of 1936, which recognized Austria's sovereignty on the grounds that Austrian Nazis be pardoned and included in the government. As the Austrian Nazis grew more powerful, Schuschnigg tried hard to secure true independence from Germany. This resulted in Hitler demanding the chancellor's resignation. Schuschnigg looked to the international community for help, but received none. On March 11, 1938, he resigned, stating that he did not want fighting to erupt. The next day, German troops marched into Austria, which put up no military resistance. Hitler was greeted by cheers in Linz and Vienna. After a hefty dose of propaganda, he held a plebiscite on April 10th and the *Anschluss* (annexation of Austria) was approved by 99.73 percent. Austria ceased to exist and the region became known as Ostmark, a province of the German Reich.

The Jews

Systematic persecution of the Jews began immediately. Jewish property was quickly Aryanized, or expropriated by non-Jews without any sort of payment rendered to its rightful owners. Jews were harassed and forced to wear the yellow Star of David. November 10, 1938 saw the infamous *Kristallnacht* take place. Throughout the German Reich, synagogues and Jewish stores and homes were destroyed. Only one synagogue in present-day Vienna dates from before 1938. Penniless and denied entrance visas by most countries, Jews found it very difficult to emigrate. By 1941, the government banned all Jews from leaving the country and shortly thereafter began to send them to concentration camps. Mathausen, near Linz, was the largest camp in Austria.

Anti-Semitism was not new to Austria. Persecution of Jews began with their expulsion from Vienna in 1421. About 200 who were unable to flee were burned at the stake. Jews returned to the city eventually, but periodically faced more repression, culminating in further expulsions. Empress Maria Theresa was an outspoken anti-Semite on religious grounds, but she chose to overlook the fact that many of her financiers were Jewish, as was Josef von Sonnenfels, one of her most important advisors. Dr. Karl Lueger, the Christian Social mayor of Vienna from 1897 to 1910, was also famous for his anti-Semitic rhetoric. Because of his harsh comments and policies, he was prohibited three times from taking his post by Emperor Franz Josef. One of Lueger's admirers was Adolf Hitler, who praised him in *Mein Kampf*. While most high-ranking Nazis were German, Hitler himself was Austrian.

World War II
Austria was spared most of the fighting until near the end of the war. The Allies carried out a massive bombing raid that culminated with the damage of the State Opera House, National Theater, and St. Stephen's Cathedral on March 12, 1945. The Battle of Vienna between the Germans and the Soviets (April 4–13) was the worst seen on Austrian soil. The Soviets finally "liberated" the city, and were initially welcomed by the hungry and distressed Viennese.

Susan Roraff

Flak towers, like this one in the Augarten, were built in Vienna by the Nazis to protect anti-aircraft artillery. They cannot be destroyed without damaging nearby buildings due to their 10-feet thick concrete walls.

Post-World War II

By 1945, Austrians had come to dislike the Nazis, but soon the Red Army was hated even more. Often drunk, the soldiers terrorized society, raping women and looting. The country and the capital were divided into four zones (just as Germany and Berlin were), to be occupied by each of the Allied nations. The inner city was declared an international sector and kept intact. Patrols consisted of one soldier from each of the four nations, so the post-war period was described as "four in a jeep." In November 1943, the Allies had stated in the Moscow Declaration that Austria was a victim of the Nazis and as such should be reestablished as a free and democratic state. Thus, international borders were reestablished using January 1, 1938 maps.

27

On April 27, 1945 Austria reemerged as its own nation and the Second Republic was established under the leadership of Dr. Karl Renner. Elections were held in November 1945 and the electorate was split between the SPÖ (Social Democratic Party of Austria) from the left and the ÖVP (Austrian People's Party) from the right, the new incarnation of the Christian Social Party. A coalition government was set up with Dr. Renner (SPÖ) as president and Leopold Figl (ÖVP) as chancellor. Initially, it was a very difficult time. Hunger was widespread and a black market flourished, but with substantial aid under the Marshall Plan from 1948 until 1953, the situation gradually improved.

Independence

In 1955, the Allies finally reached agreement on Austria. The Cold War was well under way and the East and West had already established their zones of influence. The Soviet Union agreed to withdraw from Austria on condition it remained neutral, did not join NATO, and refused foreign military bases. On May 15, 1955, the State Treaty granting Austria independence was signed. Foreign Minister Leopold Figl waved the State Treaty out of the window of the Upper Belvedere to the crowds below and yelled, "Austria is free!"

— Chapter Two —

TODAY'S AUSTRIA

With the withdrawal of occupying troops in 1955, Austria was once again a free and independent nation, but one that sat squarely in the middle of the Cold War. The newly established Second Republic faced severe domestic problems, including hunger and a shattered economy. At the same time, the country needed to find its place within the international community. Austria has been successful in addressing both areas. Today, it boasts one of the highest standards of living in the world, is a member of the European Union, and its capital Vienna hosts the headquarters for several important international organizations, including the United Nations.

THE SECOND REPUBLIC

The Second Republic was founded in 1945 by three parties from the pre-World War II era. A fourth party, the Austrian Nazi Party, was forbidden by the occupying forces to participate in politics. The Christian Social Party reemerged as the Austrian People's Party (ÖVP). The Social Democrats became the Social Democratic Party of Austria (SPÖ). These two parties, the biggest in the country, joined the Communist Party of Austria (KPÖ) to set up a provisional government headed by Karl Renner, a Socialist.

The 1920 constitution, amended in 1929, was reinstated in May 1945. The federal government holds most of the political and economic power, while the nine *Länder* (provinces) have their own local governments, which have authority over other areas. The president is elected for a six-year term, but is primarily a figurehead. It is the chancellor who runs the federal government. Parliament consists of two houses, the *Nationalrat* and the *Bundesrat*. The *Nationalrat* is the upper house and has greater powers, including the mandate to pass legislation. Its 183 members are directly elected by the population for four-year terms. The *Bundesrat*, or lower house, is mainly concerned with safeguarding the rights of the provinces. Its 65 members are selected by the provincial legislatures. The number of representatives per province is based on the size of its population.

The first postwar elections were held in November 1945. The ÖVP and the SPÖ won most of the seats in parliament, with the communists, who had never had a strong following, winning only four seats. The two main parties formed a "grand coalition," which would govern Austria for most of the rest of the century.

THE SPÖ AND ÖVP

The Socialists (SPÖ), founded in 1889 by Viktor Adler, have always spoken for the working class. Thus, much of their support has come from the cities. They were in power for most of the postwar years, either on their own or at the head of a coalition government. The more conservative ÖVP is backed by businessmen, farmers, and, unofficially, the Roman Catholic Church. It promotes greater individual freedoms and less bureaucracy. From 1986 until 1999, the ÖVP was the junior member of a SPÖ–ÖVP coalition government.

PROPORZ

In an effort to avoid the internal conflict that led to civil war in 1934, the new Austrian government unofficially established the *Proporz* system, whereby the two main political parties agreed to divide among themselves jobs in the government bureaucracy, nationalized businesses, and public services. Although this system might be illegal in other countries, it has only recently begun to face opposition from other political parties and the general populace.

SOCIAL PARTNERSHIP

The First Republic had been torn apart by political infighting and civil strife. To avoid repeating earlier mistakes, the *Paritätische Kommission* (Parity Commission) was created in 1945. The Commission is part of a mechanism, referred to as "social partnership," that brings together organized labor, businesses, and government to discuss and settle labor and economic issues, especially wage and price increases. It has no legislative powers, but wields considerable influence nonetheless. Labor conflicts are often settled quietly through negotiation and compromise, although not always in the best interest of the general public. On the other hand, the level of cooperation is such that Austria does not suffer from paralyzing strikes. In fact, time lost by strikes per person is counted in seconds, not hours.

INDEPENDENCE

In its new form, Austria turned outward in an effort to recapture some of its previous importance in global affairs. Because of its history, geographical location, and neutrality, Austria was a logical place for East-West relations to develop during the Cold War. Known to be a hotbed of spying activity, Vienna also made more honorable contributions to East-West relations. As security issues were of premier importance, Vienna became the headquarters of the International Atomic Energy Agency (IAEA) in 1956. One year later, OPEC, the Organization of Petroleum Exporting Countries, located its permanent secretariat in the capital as well. The city also hosted two key East-West summit meetings: between President John F. Kennedy and Premier Nikita Khrushchev in 1961, and between President Jimmy Carter and Premier Leonid Brezhnev in 1979.

COLD WAR REFUGEES

Austria's geographical location and neutrality also made it a transit point for many immigrants from the East. Hungarians were welcomed following the Soviet invasion in 1956, as were Czechoslovakians after the 1968 uprising. Poles made their way to Austria when the Solidarity movement was banned in 1981. Hundreds of thousands of Soviet Jews passed through Vienna, the bulk coming during the 1970s. When relations between the two superpowers were good, a great many refugees flooded into Vienna. When tensions were high, few would arrive at the train station.

BRUNO KREISKY

Between 1945 and 1966, the SPÖ and ÖVP jointly ran the Austrian government. In 1966, however, the Socialists were forced into opposition when the ÖVP won an absolute majority and formed a one-party government. The Socialists, under Bruno Kreisky, made a strong comeback and governed Austria alone from 1970 until 1983. During his term as federal chancellor, Austria prospered amidst political and social stability, and he became affectionately known as Emperor Bruno.

Kreisky strove hard to strengthen Austria's role in international affairs. He argued that Vienna should be home to as many international organizations as possible because this would help prevent it

Susan Roraff

By hosting international organizations such as the United Nations, Vienna sought to remake its image as a world-class city.

from ever again falling victim to aggression by a larger country, as it had to Hitler's Germany. In 1979, Austria was chosen as the site of the third major United Nations headquarters, following New York and Geneva. In addition to the IAEA and the United Nations Industrial Development Organization (UNIDO), which had been established in Vienna in 1967, the city continued to attract more agencies, among them the UN International Drug Control Program (UNDCP), the Comprehensive Nuclear-Test-Ban Treaty Organization (CTBTO), the UN Office for Outer Space Affairs (OOSA), the UN Commission on International Trade Law (UNCITRAL), and the Organization for Security and Cooperation in Europe (OSCE).

THE FPÖ

In 1983, the Socialist government lost its clear majority in parliament and entered into a coalition government with the Freedom Party of Austria (FPÖ). This far right party was founded in 1955. When Jörg Haider was elected party leader in 1986, the Socialists called an end to the coalition and the following year once again joined forces with

The ascent of the rightwing FPÖ party to a ruling coalition government once again brought the sensitive issue of racism to the fore.

the ÖVP. They ruled together for the next 13 years. The FPÖ is an ultranationalist and populist party that has garnered severe criticism and rejection by virtue of its leadership. Haider has been severely criticized for making pro-Nazi and anti-immigrant remarks. He was elected governor of Carinthia province in 1989 but was forced to resign in 1991 after having praised Nazi employment policies. Yet he did not disappear from the political scene.

THE WALDHEIM AFFAIR

It was also around this time that another Austrian stirred up controversy. Kurt Waldheim, who had been secretary-general of the United Nations from 1972 until 1982, ran for the presidency of Austria in 1986. This time, however, his involvement in public life led to an international backlash as accusations of his participation in Nazi-era crimes surfaced. During the war he had served as a lieutenant in the

German army in the Balkans, at a time when the Nazis were deporting Jews from Greece, rounding up slave laborers, and carrying out reprisals on Yugoslavs and Albanians. Questions arose as to just how much he knew about such atrocities, and whether or not he had been involved. In spite of, and to some extent in defiance of, the international uproar, Austrians elected him president. The United States later declared him an undesirable alien and put him on its watch list, which prevented him from visiting U.S. territory. The Austrian government set up an international commission to investigate Waldheim's past. It found no proof of his direct involvement in any war crime. However, it noted that he had lied about his past and that he had known about what was taking place, although his ability to prevent war crimes was limited. While there were some protests and calls for his resignation, he remained president and Austria was ostracized by the international community for the duration of his six-year term.

THE END OF THE COLD WAR

Soon after the fall of communism Austria sought closer ties with Western Europe. In 1989, it applied for membership to the EU, and negotiations were completed in 1994. A national referendum was held, and Austrians voted overwhelmingly in favor of membership. On January 1, 1995, Austria joined the EU. The country maintains its permanent neutrality status. As such, it cannot join NATO, but in February 1995 it entered into the NATO Partnership for Peace. Militarily, this means Austria can only take part in humanitarian and peacekeeping missions, as it did with conflicts in the Balkans.

"BLACK AND BLUE" COALITION AND INTERNATIONAL SANCTIONS

National elections were held in October 1999. Polls indicated that the FPÖ party, led by Jörg Haider, was gaining popularity. This raised concerns within Austria and in the international community. Peaceful anti-Haider and anti-racism rallies were held in the country. Foreign governments warned that an FPÖ government would not be accepted.

The electorate ignored the international threats. The Socialists won the elections but did not get an absolute majority. The FPÖ did very well, winning 27 percent of the votes, up from 5 percent in 1986. The ÖVP dropped to third place, although it won the same number of seats in the *Nationalrat* as the FPÖ. Political analysts argue that the FPÖ did so well not because of Haider's populist comments, but rather because Austrians were fed up with the two main parties. During the campaign, Haider had spoken out against the *Proporz* system, the large number of immigrants in Austria, and EU expansion to the east, while promoting the need to restructure the social security system. These were all highly sensitive issues. Not only did the party do well in the conservative Alpine regions, as was expected, but its popularity in Vienna grew as well.

The head of the Socialists, Viktor Klima, said that his party would refuse to form a coalition government with the FPÖ, and so entered into negotiations with the ÖVP, which dragged on for months. Finally, in January 2000, the Socialist Party informed the president— who was opposed to an ÖVP-FPÖ coalition—that it could not form a government. The ÖVP immediately entered into talks with the FPÖ, and an agreement was reached quickly. On February 4, 2000, the new ÖVP-led coalition government assumed power, with the ÖVP ("Blacks") responsible for running the political portfolios, and the FPÖ ("Blues") managing financial and social issues. Many Austrians peacefully showed their discontent with the coalition: in February 2000, Vienna saw its largest postwar rally with approximately 200,000 demonstrators.

INTERNATIONAL REACTION

International reaction was swift and harsh. The other EU members imposed bilateral diplomatic sanctions; all diplomatic contact was to be kept to a minimum and there would be no support for Austria in international forums. France and Belgium were the staunchest opponents. Austria considered EU sanctions "unjust and exaggerated." Other countries including Israel and the United States also showed disapproval. Economically, only the tourism and conference sectors were marginally affected.

The Austrian government faced the immense task of legitimizing itself. President Thomas Klestil agreed to accept the ÖVP-FPÖ government on condition the party leaders signed a statement that promised to reject discrimination and intolerance, uphold European values, respect ethnic and religious minorities, accept Austria's role in Nazi crimes, and promote EU expansion. This was achieved, but critics were not appeased. The government tried to fight the sanctions but met strong resistance. Finally, it was agreed that the president of the European Commission on Human Rights would name a group of "three wise men," who would monitor the "political nature" of the FPÖ and the conduct of the Austrian government towards minorities and immigrants. The commission's findings, although critical in many aspects, did not find the situation in Austria worse than in other European countries. The sanctions were lifted, but links between Austria and the other EU members, particularly France, will take time to recover.

Haider, who was once again elected governor of Carinthia in 1999, stepped down as head of the FPÖ at the end of February 2000. His comments and actions as governor still have a strong impact on how the party is perceived.

DOMESTIC ISSUES

The new Austrian government faces a number of important domestic and international issues. Particularly pressing is the need to reduce the budget deficit. In order to meet EU criteria for the Euro, the common currency established by the Maastricht Treaty, public debt must be kept low. An increase in privatizations and cuts in the civil service and social security benefits are anticipated.

Social Security

Every Austrian is covered by a comprehensive social security system that ranks among the best in the world. In addition to welfare benefits, a pension plan, and health, unemployment, and disability insurance, the system provides well for families by way of family allowances and extended maternity leave and allowances. Due to the budget deficit, entitlements are likely to be trimmed back.

Working Hours

One issue on which Austrian labor unions remain immovable is the duration of the work week. Austria has some of the most limited business hours in all of Europe. Many big businesses are pushing for longer hours, in order to be able to operate on evenings and Sundays. Currently, stores close around 6:30 pm weekdays, 5 pm Saturday, and all day Sunday. Opponents argue that extended business hours would reduce employees' flexibility and time with family, and would hurt small family-owned businesses. Even though most Austrians say they would probably shop on Sundays if possible, three-quarters of those polled do not think business hours should be lengthened.

Immigrants

One reason that there have been increased calls for tighter regulations on immigration is the fact that the number of foreigners living in the country has more than doubled during the 1990s, from 345,000 to 750,000. Austria has one of the largest proportions of foreigners in the EU. Estimates place the current number at 1 million, which is considerable given that the population of the entire country is only 8 million. Most of this immigration is from neighboring non-EU countries and the Balkans. During the war in Bosnia, Austria accepted the highest number of refugees per capita in all of Europe. More refugees arrived during the Kosovo conflict. While some would like to see immigration reduced, others argue that Austria needs immigrants to offset its flat population growth. It is these new workers who will support the extensive social security system, which will be burdened heavily as the Austrian population ages. Furthermore, many foreigners are employed in low-paying jobs that the average Austrian refuses to perform. Calls to raise the quota for skilled immigrants were not successful.

Environmental Issues

Austrians are very concerned with environmental issues, and have strongly supported progressive policies. In 1975, Austrians voted in a plebiscite against the use of atomic energy, launching the first such ban in Europe. Critics, however, argue that even though Austria does not produce nuclear energy, it buys it gladly from its neighbors. Yet, Austrians oppose the operation of "unsafe" nuclear power plants by their former eastern bloc neighbors. In some instances, protestors have blockaded border crossings to the Czech Republic.

INTERNATIONAL ISSUES

EU Expansion

Austria is a committed member of the European Union. In spite of the sanctions imposed after the 1999 elections, the majority of Austrians would not consider withdrawing from the organization. There is, however, some disagreement on the terms and pace of EU expansion towards the east. Officially, the Austrian government favors EU expansion. First, it is believed that it would promote security and stability in the region. Moreover, proponents say that Austria could be one of the main economic beneficiaries of EU expansion because of its existing presence in eastern markets.

Those who do not favor EU expansion fear the loss of Austrian jobs, as firms move operations to countries with lower wage floors. They also warn of an influx of cheap labor, which would upset the stability of the domestic labor market. Thus labor unions are demanding that a country's wage level reach 80 percent of that of the EU before being allowed membership. Others are concerned about the impact on the environment, the availability of lower priced agricultural products, and the danger posed by the nuclear power produced by the eastern countries. They want new members to first comply with EU standards on social and environmental issues.

Austria's Military Role

Austria, a vital neutral presence during the tense days of the Cold War, wants to continue to be a key player between East and West. Yet, after so many years of neutrality, Austria must answer difficult questions regarding its involvement in multilateral security structures. This issue was brought to the forefront during the Kosovo crisis and the NATO bombing of Yugoslavia.

Having retained its neutrality, Austria can only participate in UN and EU humanitarian and peacekeeping missions. Yet, being outside of NATO prohibits Austria from fully participating in an EU mission if sensitive NATO material is used. As a consequence, Austria is not considered an equal partner in EU security policy. The Socialists and the Greens are strongly opposed to joining NATO, as are a majority of Austrians. The ÖVP and FPÖ are, in general, pro-NATO. Membership, however, would require a constitutional amendment revoking permanent neutrality.

COMPENSATION FOR NAZI CRIMES

Slave Labor

On October 27, 2000 an agreement was finally reached regarding compensation for 150,000 slave laborers under the Nazi government. Payments will be made to the victims, the majority of whom are from Central and Eastern Europe, from a special reconciliation fund of 6 billion Schillings (US$415 million). Half of the funds will come from the Austrian government and the other half from private businesses. The highest payments will be paid to slave laborers in concentration camps. Smaller payments will be made to other categories of victims. In return, Austrian companies will be safe from future lawsuits.

Stolen Assets

On January 17, 2001 an agreement was reached on the difficult subject of Aryanized property. A General Settlement Fund will be established by the Austrian government and Austrian companies. The bulk of the fund will be designated for property claims. The balance will be used for interest payments, insurance claims, social benefits, the restoration and maintenance of Jewish cemeteries, and to expedite the return of works of art. In return for quick payments, the claimants will drop their lawsuits.

THE ECONOMY

Austria's economy was in shambles following World War II. The Marshall Plan pumped much-needed money into the country, and eventually the economy took off. Forecasts predict that the economy, already strong, will grow at an even faster pace in the first few years of the 21st century. Key economic indicators like unemployment and inflation are better than those found in the rest of Europe. However, this does not mean that Austria is free of economic problems.

Following its entrance into the European Union in 1995, the Austrian economy has become integrated with the other markets of the region. On January 1, 1999 the single currency of the EU was launched. The Austrian Schilling will be replaced by the Euro in January 2002. Although the Euro will not be in circulation until then, all bank accounts are held in Euros and prices are listed in both currencies to ease consumers into the change. The Austrian Schilling is tied to the Euro at an exchange rate of ATS 13.7603 to 1 Euro.

In order to comply with the stability program for the Euro, Austria must reduce both its total debt and its budget deficit. The costs of maintaining the extensive welfare state also need to be brought under control. There is a general consensus that budget cuts are needed, although there is disagreement on what areas should be hit, and to what degree. With the minimum retirement age, pension amounts, and health care at stake, the issue has been heavily politicized.

The privatization of government-owned firms has also been targeted as a budget reduction measure. Not unlike other European nations with a very strong public sector, Austria boasts a large number of publicly owned companies and heavy regulation of the economy. Traditionally, monopolies and oligopolies have run the economy. Various associations and chambers make decisions, instead of letting them fall to the "free hand" of the market. This is evident at all levels of the economy, from the big state-run tobacco monopoly to the Association of Pharmacists that decides when and where a new pharmacy is needed. However, in order to be competitive, the economy must liberalize. The telecommunications sector already allows private sector competition, and prices are falling fast as a result. The electricity market will also open to competition in the near future.

International Trade

Austria's main trading partners are its fellow countries in the EU. In fact, over 60 percent of exports are to EU members, with Germany receiving the lion's share. Important non-EU trading partners are Switzerland and Eastern European countries, with Hungary topping the list. Outside of Europe, a significant amount of trade is conducted with the United States and Japan. Almost half of all exports consists of machines and transport equipment; manufactured goods make up another quarter; and consumer goods, chemicals, foodstuffs, tobacco, raw materials, and energy make up the rest. Environmental technologies are also an important aspect of international trade.

Austrian businesses are taking part in the globalization process, particularly in Eastern Europe. In the first few years following the collapse of communism, about 40 percent of direct foreign investment in these countries came from Austria. That percentage has since declined as other countries (mainly from the EU) have headed into these markets, with the exception of Slovakia and Slovenia, where Austria remains the dominant investor. About two-thirds of Austrian total direct foreign investment is in Hungary and the Czech Republic.

Not only are Austrian firms venturing out into neighboring markets, but foreign firms see Austria (most notably Vienna) as the best base for their forays into these same markets. A significant number of important multinational corporations, headquartered in the United States and in EU countries, have set up offices in Vienna to oversee their expansion into the former eastern bloc. In addition to the obvious benefits of living in Vienna, foreign executives can rely on a valuable labor force that has close links, both cultural and linguistic, with these markets.

ECONOMIC SECTORS

Agriculture

Agricultural production is an important part of the Austrian identity. A drive through low-lying areas reveals farms, orchards, vineyards, and grazing and pastureland. Practically all farms are family operated, and over half are small-scale enterprises. In spite of EU subsidies, only about a third of farmers earn enough from farming to cover living expenses; the rest must seek additional sources of income.

About two-thirds of agricultural products are derived from animals, with an emphasis on dairy yield. The main crops cultivated are corn, barley, wheat, rye, potatoes, and sugar beets. In the east there is a significant number of vineyards and orchards where apples, plums, apricots, peaches, and pears are grown.

Forestry

Almost half Austria's surface is covered with forests and woods, and about 12 percent of its exports are timber, timber products, and paper. After years of exploitation, reforestation efforts are being made, and new techniques, such as controlled thinning, have been introduced.

The Schwechat refinery meets almost all of Austria's oil and gas needs.

Industry

Industry and mining combined account for about a quarter of GDP. The main industries in Austria are foodstuffs, beverages, tobacco, mechanical and steel engineering, electronic products, chemicals and plastics, transportation equipment, construction, and textiles. In general, most manufacturing outfits are small. The few exceptions include iron and steel plants in Linz and Styria, which produce enough material for the entire country, and an aluminum plant near the border with Germany that is one of the largest in Europe.

Austria is famous for crystal, porcelain, leather, and ski equipment. The country produces ski lifts and is the largest exporter of skis in the world. In fact, one half of all skis in the world are manufactured in Austria.

Mining

Important minerals have been mined in this region since prehistoric times. The key minerals found in Austria are iron ore, lignite, gypsum, salt, limestone, and magnesite. Aluminum, lead, and copper are also produced in Austria.

Energy Resources

Austria lacks major energy sources and must import more than 80 percent of its oil and natural gas. Most of the latter is piped in from Russia. While small reserves of oil can be found north of the Alps, it is mainly imported from the Middle East. Near the airport on the outskirts of Vienna is the Schwechat refinery, one of the largest in Europe. Most of the power produced within Austria comes from hydroelectric power stations located in mountain areas, the Alpine foothills, and on the Danube River. Nuclear power is not generated in the country.

Services

The entire service sector accounts for the largest percentage of GDP, ringing in at about 60 percent. Financial services represent a key sector of the economy and have made significant inroads into Eastern Europe. Yet, it is the tourist industry that dominates the sector, bringing in substantial revenue. Tyrol leads the provinces, welcoming the highest number of both international and domestic tourists. In the winter months, ski resorts across the country are packed. Germans make up the largest group of foreign visitors by far, and an overwhelming majority of tourists are European.

— Chapter Three —

AUSTRIAN FOLK

The Austrians are an interesting but complicated people. Their day-to-day life is conservative and quite regimented. They are deferential to a fault, dress neatly and properly depending on the venue, and are always punctual. Frugal and moderate, they enjoy their children and retain close connections with family, and like to meet their friends at the local coffeehouse. For leisure, they enjoy the outdoors and related sports for each of the four seasons. But that's just the tip of the iceberg.

The Austrian personality is a paradox. Austrian humor and grumpiness are tied into one. Whether at home or at work, they complain about most things: colleagues, neighbors, their children, and their health. However, they also yearn to make good and to be accepted, and their pliancy helps them achieve this. This manner of being leads them to be contradictory and inconsistent, and they end up saying yes and no to everything and everybody. Some believe that this ambivalence, which some psychologists would identify as early neurosis, has roots in Austria's landscape, ethnic mix, history, attitude toward religion, and mature civilization.

Their sense of humor is not obvious. Austrians rely on wit and irony, rather than on pun. The wit shines through in their use of wonderfully vivid names. Nestroy, a comedian and playwright, employed the word *Lumpazivagabundus* in many of his works, as a label for a scoundrel and vagabond. Irony, known as *Weltanschaung*, is where the Austrian tends to see the whole world in himself. Self-deprecation is a form of humor realized from the day-to-day world: it's much easier to see the negative and expect it than the other way around.

The bureaucracy may have a hand in the personality of the people. On the one hand, Austria has a well structured social security system which takes good care of everyone's health, job security, and pension; on the other hand, the government system can be extremely oppressive in that it keeps everyone mired in bureaucratic procedure.

A very good reason for Austrians' automatic compliance with rules dates back to the Metternich era (1814–48), when those who did not obey and conform were penalized in some way. In fact, it was in this period that spying on the general population to keep it in line was rampant.

One shouldn't forget, however, that Austria is divided into nine federal provinces and that each province has its distinct personality and pride. Salzburg, for example, feels itself to be more German, whereas Vorarlberg and Tyrol think of themselves as more Swiss. The Carinthian is very macho and hot-blooded, and supposedly still dreaming of a greater Germany. The Burgenländers are farmers, and life in their part of the world tends to be simple.

All said and done, Austria is a wonderful place to live in. In a poll conducted at the end of 1999, Austria ranked highest in Europe in having the best political and economic situation, environmental standards, health and social security system, and cultural and leisure activities. These standards do give a vivid account of life in Austria. The people are proud of their country and, in turn, try and maintain its beauty.

THE FAMILY

The family is important to Austrians. Parents try to establish a safe place for their children. Moving from town to town is quite unheard of and the children grow up knowing one town and the same people and friends their whole lives. The mother and father usually take equal share in the care of the children and do many activities with them. They often go to the many different parks, woods, or mountains together. In turn, the children grow up with a considerable awareness of the natural environment. Austrian parents, although frugal, spend more money per capita per child on toys than parents in any other European nation.

School System

Even the school system is geared to having the children spend time at home. From kindergarten until about the 4th grade, children come home at around noon. The mother or grandmother is at home waiting to serve them lunch. After lunch they go out to play, attend team practice, study another language, or learn to play an instrument. The latter two activities are seen as a sign of good education and culture.

In Public with Mom and Dad

In public, children are well behaved; in fact, one doesn't hear a peep from them. To an outsider, it seems a little harsh that the children cannot just "be children." Strict but loving upbringing molds them to fit neatly into society.

Having Fun Together

Parents also do many sports with their children—ice-skating, soccer, cycling, tennis, horseback riding, and swimming. Skiing is by far the most popular sport; having the Alps beckoning at the doorstep makes it the natural sport of choice. Children put on skis as soon as they learn to walk. By the age of 7 or 8, they start resembling speeding bullets going down the ski slopes.

Getting to Know Everyone in the Family

The children grow up knowing each member of the extended family, including their grandmother and grandfather, or *Oma* and *Opa*. *Oma*, especially, takes on an important role. She is the one who baby-sits the children, takes them for walks, and, of course, spoils them silly. On Sunday afternoons, most families get together at *Oma* and *Opa's* in the afternoon for an early dinner followed by cake and coffee a little later on. This is a good time to catch up on the past week's happenings, but more importantly, it is a time to relax and enjoy each other's company.

The Weekends

The weekends are sacred to the average Austrian family. They value spending their time off with their family and don't believe in working after hours. That is why you will often find all stores closed on Sundays, and it is only in the last couple of years that stores have stayed open until 5 pm on Saturday. There is a great debate as to whether stores should ever open up on Sunday. Many feel that this would cause the breakdown of the family.

Special Holidays Together

Many families love to celebrate special occasions, especially birthdays, Saints' Days, Easter, and Christmas. Each celebration is a time for a nice family dinner, the opening of gifts, having friends over, and making merry.

THE ELDERLY

A great percentage of the Austrian folk are over the age of 60. You often see white-haired men and blue-haired old ladies on trams or doing their weekly shopping. Many are good-natured and friendly, especially if you have a baby or dog in tow, but some can seem grumpy and unhappy with you if you don't appear to be following the rules of good behavior.

The social system is so good and the family situation so close that the elderly are very well taken care of by their immediate family. They usually enter nursing homes only when close medical supervision is required.

GETTING AWAY

Garden lots

Garden lots or small gardens (*Schrebergärten* or *Kleingärten*) became popular after World War I as a private source of vegetables in times of shortage. Later on, the garden became a summer retreat and a means of escaping from the crowds of the city.

Today, the garden lot has become a second home for many, who build small houses on the lots and either live in them permanently, or on weekends or in the summer. In most of the outer districts of Vienna alone there are approximately 35,000 garden lots.

Inheriting a House

Many Austrians are lucky enough to inherit an apartment, house, or farmhouse. The house can become the permanent home or, if it is located outside the city, the country home. Families tend to stay in one place all their lives, which makes the passing on of a house or apartment more common than in more mobile societies.

Vacations

All Austrians believe in their vacation time, which is usually about

The much-loved Kleingärten (garden lot) is visited frequently in the summer or lived in year-round.

five to six weeks a year. Depending on their interests, many go skiing for a week in February, go away for a week to ten days during Easter, take two to three weeks during the summer, and perhaps a week or so at Christmas time. Those with families tend not to leave Austria for their vacations. They would rather go skiing locally and spend the rest of their vacation time at their second home in the countryside or in the mountains. Of those who do travel, many go to the seaside in Italy, Croatia, or even Spain (popular spots include Mallorca and the Canary Islands), especially in the summer. Other popular destinations include Greece, Tunisia, and Turkey.

Singles and couples usually travel far and wide, from the Americas, to Australia, Asia, and Africa. They enjoy the exotic culture, new language, and different food. One often sees billboards advertising documentaries on faraway lands, enticing people to travel more.

SAVING FOR THE FUTURE

Saving is a virtue in Austria. There is little debt, and credit cards are used wisely. Many Austrians save to buy a car, go on family holidays, and, most importantly, build a home. When it comes to homes, parents' longer-term savings are usually needed, and fortunate are the children whose parents help them in times like these. Julie is married to an Austrian and they are in the midst of building a house. If it weren't for her in-laws they could not afford it.

FRIENDS

Friendships are extremely important to Austrians. They value their friends and believe in staying in touch on a regular basis. Many, unless they have moved from the country to the big city, have had the same friends since childhood. They meet their friends in their homes or at a restaurant, *Heurige* (wine tavern), coffeehouse, or *Beisel* (bar).

A jolly Austrian shows off his felt hat with Gamsbart.

It is often easier to meet and befriend non-Austrians than locals. Austrian reserve hinders them from making friends easily, and should you make a move to talk to them in a class or meeting, they will usually be friendly but introverted.

If you work among Austrians, you will get to know them eventually although you may find that many Austrians who work together don't necessarily go out together. Studying in Austria makes it much easier to get to know Austrians, as students are more carefree and uninhibited. If you are neither working nor studying in Austria, being open and chatting with your neighbors and local shopkeepers will help you feel more relaxed and at home. Other ways of meeting people include joining art or exercise classes or groups such as the American Women's Association (AWA), which is open to all nationalities, going to church, and just being outgoing yourself.

THE ESOTERIC SIDE OF THE AUSTRIANS

Although reserved, many Austrians are drawn to the esoteric during their leisure time. Many love to take dance lessons not only to enjoy the ball season but also to add another dimension to their lives. Samba, mambo, cha-cha, tango, rumba, fox trot, waltz, jive, and jitterbug are but a smattering of the dances taught at the many dance schools. Indian dance and belly dancing are popular among women, and country-and-western is popular among couples, with quite a few locations featuring live bands playing music for the two-step.

AUSTRIAN WOMEN

The Austrian woman is a very strong-minded individual. She takes care of her household, the budget, and the raising of her children.

Many more women are going to work today than previously. About half the workforce is made up of women as more and more are going back to work after childbirth to improve the family's standard of living. Children are well taken care of by the state. Women cannot work within eight weeks of giving birth; this gives them a compulsory

4-month break from work. After this period, either the mother or father (or both, in alternation), get 18 months' paid leave from their work (more time if employed as a civil servant) in order to raise their child. And until the child is done with school, there is an additional payment from the government to help defray the cost of child rearing.

Single motherhood is also on the rise in Austria. The state takes such good care of the mother and child that many women choose single motherhood over abortion, adoption, or marriage—a not unreasonable choice when one considers that half of all marriages in Austria today end in divorce.

Even with all the incentives to have children, the birthrate is equal to the death rate, resulting in a zero net birthrate. The implications of this statistic will be felt in years to come.

It is not uncommon to see Austrians dressed from head to toe in modern Trachten outfits every day of the year.

THE NEIGHBORS

Neighbors can be important to you. Most of them are friendly and will always greet you. They are a good source of information and advice during your stay, and will also help out during emergencies. They often keep an eye on their neighbors' homes when their neighbors are on vacation. Julie moved around a lot in Vienna and always found the neighbors extremely nice. Once, when there was a medical emergency, the neighbors really went out of their way to help out.

It is also a good idea to always invite the neighbors if you are having a large party. Not only is it a goodwill gesture, but if you are intending to make a lot of noise, there will be no one to complain. This would also avoid the inconvenience of having to end the party early or toning down the noise by 10 pm, which is the law! There have been instances where the police visited our friends, whose neighbors had complained of the noise level. Then again, there are neighbors who come out of courtesy, then leave at 10 pm and call the police on you. Figure that one out!

You might find your neighbors openly nosy. They seem to know everything that goes on in most of the neighboring households, and if they are walking by a house, will blatantly stare into the windows without a hint of pretense.

Remember that Sunday is acknowledged as a quiet day. So don't go disturbing your neighbor by mowing the lawn, working on the car, or doing carpentry work. All of this should be done on Saturday or on weekdays.

THE CELL PHONE

If at times the Austrian way appears old-fashioned and anachronistic, at others the cell phone or *Handy* has revolutionized the Austrian way of life. From moms pushing baby carriages, to people walking their dogs, horseback riders, *Fiaker* (horse-drawn carriage) drivers, businessmen at lunch or driving, and the public transportation rider, everyone is carrying one. Statistics at the time of writing show that more than half the population has a cell phone. In fact, Austrians have a cell phone penetration rate that is one of the highest in Europe.

FARMING COMMUNITY

Most of Austria is made up of mountains, beautiful lush forests, and, most importantly, farming land. The farmers produce a variety of plant and meat products, such as wheat, vegetables, fruit, wine, milk, eggs, pork, and beef. The dairy products, especially, are thought of as truly superior.

Farming is hard work, and everyone in the family contributes. Working hours on a farm (*Bauernhof*) are from sunrise to sunset, and the women work as hard as the men. Despite this, many farms, unless they are large, have difficulty making ends meet in spite of subsidies. They are great vacationing spots, as children enjoy learning about and interacting with farm animals. Fresh milk, cheese, eggs, and freshly baked bread are also available.

Generally speaking, farming people are much friendlier than city folk and much easier to talk to and laugh with. Certainly, the *Heurigen* (wine taverns) in the country are much more interesting because of the light-heartedness of the people. (Plus their wines are nothing to balk at!)

SAFETY

Austria is a very safe place to live and work in. One can walk the streets alone in the wee hours of the morning, whether in a small or large city, without fear of pickpockets, muggers, rapists, or the like lurking around the corner. One does hear of the occasional pickpocket in large department stores, and of home or car burglaries, but crimes are rare. Some petty crimes may be attributed to the migrant influx from the East since the fall of the Berlin Wall. Violent crime is, to all intents and purposes, nonexistent.

AUSTRIA'S UNCONVENTIONAL SIDE

Prostitution

If you think the average Austrian a bit too demure, take a drive late at night along the Gürtel or the Prater in Vienna, and you might be surprised at the scantily clad women waiting for customers. Prostitution is legal in Vienna and the rest of Austria. Legalizing prostitution could have begun with Emperor Franz Josef, as he did not have a blissful marriage and sought other women to satisfy his needs. Franz Josef also felt that prostitutes should be well taken care of and had a special health system instituted for them.

Saunas and Nude Bathing

Austrians are open and accepting toward nudity. Now and then, you will see nude or suggestive advertising. On warm summer days, many women go about braless. If you enjoy saunas, be prepared to wear just your towel. Some saunas have mixed days when men and women share the sauna. Along the same lines, there is nude swimming, usually on Sunday evenings, at certain pools; nudist swimming areas can be found around lakes and rivers in Austria. While cycling or strolling by the Danube, don't be surprised if you spot one or two people with nothing but their birthday suits on!

Sex

Austria seems to have no hang-up about sex. Prudery and chastity were never very fashionable. Most also ignore the Catholic Church with regard to contraception and abortion. The unmarried person in a steady relationship is referred to as the *Lebensgefährten* or *Lebensgefährtin* (life companion); a married woman's lover is referred to as the *Hausfreund* (friend of the house).

LOVE THOSE DOGS!

The down side of having so many dogs in Austria, especially in large cities like Vienna, is having to clean up the 15 tons of fecal matter every month, deposited by those sweet, loving canine pets. Dog owners don't feel in any way responsible for cleaning up after their pets as they pay a special dog tax. Helmut Zilk, a former mayor, tried to clean up the streets by hiring a French firm to vacuum up the waste using heavy motorized "shit collectors." The mayor even accompanied these trucks on their rounds. The citizens were not amused and the collecting machines were sent back to France. Therefore, until a street sweeper cleans up the mess on a sidewalk, one must tiptoe around it or endure messy, smelly shoes.

For all the love bestowed on these animals, the government has interesting ways of disposing of them once they are dead or out of the reach of their owners. Dogs cannot be buried. A law from 1919 states that all animal carcasses have to be collected and utilized, or burned. A pet owner has to call a special agency, TKW (*Tierkörperverwertung*), to remove its corpse; if he does not, a fine could result. Recently it was revealed that bodies of dogs, cats, and laboratory animals ended up being processed into animal feed for pigs and chickens. Many Austrians and environmental groups are aghast and are trying to make the Ministry of Agriculture change the outdated law.

Austria's Supreme Court upholds a new law that will fine drivers if they brake to avoid hitting smaller animals such as cats, lap dogs, puppies, hares, and hedgehogs. Only wild boar and deer have the law

Susan Roraff

Austrians revere their dogs and take them just about everywhere, not only for walks on the street but also to banks, stores, and restaurants.

on their side. Austria's animal rights groups are crying murder over the new ruling and some are even saying that the law gives drivers the legal right to murder animals on the roads. The government's Department for Traffic Safety holds that a driver should brake if the size of the animal endangers road safety but drivers cannot stop for smaller animals even after they have run over them.

RELIGION

The main religion in Austria is Roman Catholicism. The Habsburgs made it the religion of their empire and fought many wars in its defense. Josef II made many religious reforms in the late 18th century and gave Calvinists, Lutherans, and Jews more rights. He also gave Orthodox citizens the right to practice their religion and build churches.

Austria, and Vienna in particular, has always been at the cross-roads of many nationalities and their respective religions, yet not until Austria became a sovereign country after World War II did the

59

various nationalities openly practice their religions. As one drives through some of the larger cities, especially Vienna and Salzburg, one sees synagogues, mosques, and Buddhist temples.

Paying into the Church

Belonging to any church in Austria requires you to pay a certain percentage (approximately 1.5 percent) of your earnings into the church's account. A word of warning: if you don't wish to pay into a church, do not fill out the religion section of your initial police registration form (*Meldezettel*). You might then get a payment form (*Zahlschein*) and newsletters from the church, and you will be expected to pay. Getting out of this situation is extremely difficult and requires many phone calls and a letter or two in German stating why you do not wish to contribute toward that church.

The Catholic rituals are similar to those around the world, with a few exceptions:

Attending Mass

Only a small number of the 90 percent of Austrians who are Roman Catholic practice their religion and attend church. They have many beautiful churches to choose from, several fashioned in the Baroque style. There is usually daily mass. On Sundays there are three masses: early morning, late morning (where the priest gives a sermon, or *Hochamt*, and a choir performs), and late evening.

Wedding

An Austrian couple can choose to have either a civil court marriage or a church ceremony. The civil court marriage is quick, short, and inexpensive. Setting up a date and bringing all the necessary paperwork to the civil court is all a couple needs to do. If a couple chooses to get married in church, they first have to go to a civil court, register, and get the necessary paperwork. Then they need to talk to the priest of the church in which they wish to marry. If they have been paying into the church, they will have no problems. They pay a certain fee and then set a date for the ceremony.

At the wedding, the bride and groom usually have a bridesmaid and best man who stand by them during the ceremony. The exchange of rings is performed and the ring is worn on the ring finger of the right hand, which is believed to be closest the heart. Then there is a mass followed by an Agape (meaning love in Greek), where canapés are served with champagne and other drinks. A couple of hours later, close friends and family of the newlyweds will go to a restaurant or special hall to celebrate with dinner and music.

If you are invited to a wedding and don't know what to give, money is always acceptable (there is special stationery where bank-notes can be inserted). It is also appropriate to ask if the couple is registered with any store. There, one may choose to buy something on the couple's pre-selected list.

Baptism

The baptism requires a godmother only. If the godmother is part of a church there should be no problems in getting your child baptized. A fee will be paid to the church and a date set. On the day of the baptism, the child will be blessed on the forehead with holy water, a prayer said, and then a mass held.

Grandparents on both sides are invited, together with some uncles and aunts close to the family. Afterward, there is a small get-together for lunch at a nice restaurant, where the gifts for the baby are presented. Gifts vary from baby silverware to jewelry, and even money in a card or a savings account voucher.

Religious Classes for Children

Religious instruction is given at school for 12 years. Parents can elect to have their child not attend these classes, and instead opt to have the child take private religious classes during the week. However, these are expensive and not very popular.

PREPARING FOR DEATH

Most Austrians are practical and buy a graveyard plot when they are in their 30s or 40s, both as an investment (graves are extremely expensive) and to secure a gravesite. There is a general attitude that death is a part of life, not simply the end of it.

Many older Viennese who do not come from wealthy families belong to a death association (*Sterbeverein*), to which they pay monthly dues that eventually pay for a decent burial and gravesite.

Funeral

When there is a death, an official funeral announcement (*Parte*) is delivered immediately to family and friends before they have time to find out from a different source. It is usually on black-bordered stationery and gives details of the memorial service. Once the announcement is received, one can choose to go to either the church or cemetery service, or to both. The standard practice is to meet the grieving family, shake hands, and say *"Mein Beileid"* (my condolences). Then one would follow the mourners to the gravesite and cast a scoop of dirt onto the coffin as it is being lowered into the grave. Sometimes, three red roses may be cast along with the dirt. Today, instead of bringing or sending a special flower arrangement to the grieving family, it is common to make a contribution to the favorite charity of the deceased. This information is available on the announcement.

Elaborate funerals are also known as a beautiful corpse (*schöne Leich'*). At these, especially at the largest graveyard in Vienna, the *Zentralfriedhof*, members of the Vienna State Opera are often asked to sing at the departing soul's grave.

The Wake

There are also traditional wakes after the burial where family members and friends get together at a relative's home to mourn the passing of the loved one. It is customary to eat and drink at this event.

The Mortuary Service

The mortuary service in Austria is one of the biggest funeral enterprises in the world. There are approximately 500 employees arranging 30,000 burials a year. They provide wreath-carriers, grand hearses, and major paraphernalia. The cost is upwards of ATS 50,000.

The Zentralfriedhof

The *Zentralfriedhof*, in Vienna, is the second largest cemetery in Europe. It holds over 3 million people, or twice the population in Vienna. There are approximately 50 funerals a day. It has special Jewish and Muslim sections.

The cemetery is quite beautiful and reminds one of a park, with green grass and trees everywhere. In fact, many go there to unwind or take a stroll. On November 1st and 2nd, All Saints' and All Souls' Day respectively, the cemetery takes on a jovial atmosphere. *Würstelstände* (sausage stands) and *Maronistände* (chestnut stands) open up, friends and family gather, and the dearly departed are remembered.

The Japanese are especially keen on this cemetery. Some say that it is the first place they visit. Julie was very surprised to hear and see, one day, a chorus of Japanese women singing beautifully next to Johann Strauss's grave. The women were paying a most gracious homage to their favorite musician.

SUICIDE

At one point at the turn of the 20th century, it was commonplace to hear in Vienna of intellectuals dying by their own hand. The best known suicide at the time was that of Prince Rudolf, the son of Franz Josef, who after killing his mistress put a gun to his head. The suicide rate is still high, some 25 in 100,000, about double the US figure. The reason is not certain. It is speculated that some people believe that in death, they will achieve the recognition denied during life. It has also been said that the warm winds that occur in the fall, the *Föhn*, have debilitating mental effects, causing some to kill themselves.

THE JEWS

The Jews have always been in Vienna. In a commercial edict passed in AD 966, less than a century after the name Vienna first appeared on historic documents, the phrase "Jews and other legitimate merchants" shows up. In the 1300s, a contemporary observer remarked, "There are more Jews in Vienna than in any other German city familiar to me." Vienna had become known in the Jewish world as a center of learning, and rabbis and Hebraic scholars were often referred to as the "sages of Vienna" (*Vienna and Its Jews*, p. 29). The history thereafter is one of being exiled, then let back in, and so on and so forth. At one point, the Jews were the reason for the economic stability of the Austrian empire. Maria Theresa hated them and said, "I know of no greater plague on the state than this nation which, through deception, usury and cheating, brings people into beggary." She should have bitten her tongue, as her finance minister was a Jew. Her son, Josef, was a true son of the Enlightenment, and issued a Tolerance Ordinance in 1781 that protected many Jews.

The Jews came in great numbers to Vienna in the 19th century. In fact, at the close of the century, they accounted for 11 percent of the population. Jews held a variety of positions at differing economic levels and many were very successful. Many of those positions were in the retail and wholesale trade, banking, and in the press. In fact, 61 percent of the doctors, 57 percent of the lawyers, and 86 percent of the law clerks were Jewish.

At the turn of the 19th century, the population of Jews started dwindling. They were used as scapegoats during the 1873 stock market crash. Karl Lueger, Vienna's mayor from 1897 to 1910, was virulently anti-Semitic and caused approximately 120,000 Jews to flee even before the *Anschluss* in 1938. Over 65,000 died during the Holocaust. More left after World War II. In 1954 they numbered 11,224, and by 1986 their numbers had dwindled to 6,200.

Today, feelings toward the Jews have changed dramatically. Catholics have spoken in defense of Jews and groups of Austrian

Catholics have made pilgrimages to Israel. Parliament has disbanded organizations and limited events believed to have pro-Nazi overtones. A Sigmund Freud park was opened and the city has contributed generously to the maintenance of various Jewish institutions. Simon Wiesenthal set up a documentation center in the former Jewish textile quarter. The Jewish Welcome Center keeps in contact with emigrants all over the world. There is a new Jewish school, Lauder Chabad Campus, for 400 students. Finally, the Judenplatz is being totally redesigned. In addition to current excavations on the Or Sarua Synagogue, plans include an exhibit on the history of the square, memorial rooms in Misrachi House, and a Holocaust memorial.

The sheer size of the historical Jewish population is better understood after a visit to the Jewish section of the *Zentralfriedhof*. However, the oldest surviving Jewish cemetery, with gravestones dating back to 1540, is found in the 9th district on Seegasse 9–11. To visit it, one must go through the foyer of an old folks' home to the back of the building.

Eisenstadt, the capital of Burgenland, also has a large Jewish population and museum.

IMMIGRANTS

Immigrants, especially in Vienna and its suburbs, have always been a part of Austrian culture. In centuries past, Austria was a large empire with many different peoples interacting and trading within it. The turning point came toward the end of the 19th century when, under the dual monarchy, many Hungarian aristocrats and artists came to seek a new life in the cosmopolitan city of Vienna. Many other groups, including Turks, Greeks, Macedonians, and Rumanians, were also drawn to the metropolis, which was then at a major crossroads intellectually, artistically, and politically. Vienna was Austria's center, and it was a great mix of faces. A ditty was sung in the late 19th century epitomizing the mixture:

The Christians, the Turks, the Heathen, and Jew
Have dwelt here in ages old and new
Harmoniously and without any strife
For everyone's entitled to live his own life.

In fact, no Austrian today could trace his roots in unbroken lines to his great-grandfather. Today, most ethnic groups, except the Hungarians who formed part of the empire at one time, are not completely accepted. The Slavs, i.e. Czech, Croatian, Polish, or Slovakian, are especially unpopular. The Turks and Yugoslavians have been working in Vienna for over 50 years and are still seen as "guest workers" and often treated badly. Recently, the immigrant influx has been from the war-torn lands of the former Yugoslavia, Turkey, and Nigeria. Many migrants are illegal aliens: some have sought political asylum, and others have gone through the proper channels to obtain residency permits or citizenship.

Most immigrants have settled in Vienna. In fact, 10 per cent of Vienna's population is foreign. Most live in the 2nd–6th, 16th, and 22nd districts. Hungarians and Croatians live mainly in Burgenland, while Carinthia is home to many Slovenians. Muslim women from Bosnia or Turkey are easy to spot as they wear scarves and long dresses or long coats. They are often seen in the parks with their families, enjoying picnics or barbecues on warm summer weekends.

The immigrants are called *Gastarbeiter* or guest workers. Most of them are hardworking, pay their taxes, and contribute to the social system. In fact, the Employers' Federation is one of their main supporters. Immigrants fill a variety of jobs: they are manual or hard laborers working on construction sites, some are custodians and maids, others sell newspapers and flowers, open up restaurants (especially the Chinese, Turks, and Croatians) and shops, and yet more are taxi drivers. Some gain a good education and become professionals.

Many Austrians still deprecate Turks and other dark-skinned people because they look and act differently. Many are called

Tschuschen, which is an insulting term for the Balkan people. Some of Julie's dark-skinned friends have experienced bad treatment by Austrians in stores and other service-oriented areas.

The government has had to address immigration problems, and in 1986, Austrian politics became a rational zone of compromise rather than an arena of conflict. However, the right-wing, anti-immigration Freedom Party led by Jörg Haider reared its ugly head in the late 1980s when increases in Eastern European immigration followed the collapse of the eastern bloc. Concern even among moderates has been exacerbated by the recent influx of refugees from the former Yugoslavia. Austria is hoping to get help and support from the European Union regarding its immigration issues.

— Chapter Four —

SETTLING IN

Moving to a new country can be a tremendous enterprise unless you have traveled before or have an adventurous heart. Austria is easier to adjust to than some other countries, as many Austrians speak English, and there is an established international community in the larger cities which is a great source of information and help.

There are problems that cause frustration for newcomers, including short opening hours for stores, banks, post offices, and government offices; the bureaucracy and cranky civil servants; the limited selection of products in grocery stores; occasional chauvinism; poor to adequate service in some stores and restaurants (although changes have been noticed); and having to communicate in German.

Yet relocating to Austria means you can look forward to less stressful working conditions, a relaxed pace of life, a safe and family-oriented environment, a rich cultural atmosphere, good medical care, and an excellent public transportation system.

LOOKING FOR AN APARTMENT

If you are working for a consulate, embassy, or international organization, your employer may help you find a nice apartment or house, and bear the partial or full cost of your rent. If you are searching for an apartment on your own, look through advertisements in the Saturday editions of local newspapers such as *Kurier, Die Presse,* and *Der Standard.* The *Bazar* is an advertisement paper that contains listings not only of apartments and homes to rent, but also furnishings, cars, and other useful amenities. *Falter*, a paper for the trendy, lists entertainment events in addition to apartments.

In your search for an apartment, it is useful to know how the floors in a building are named. Generally, the first floor is the *Erdgeschoss*, and the second floor is the *erste Stock* (first floor). If you are in an old-fashioned building, you may encounter other floor levels including the *Mezzanine, Tiefparterre,* and *Hochparterre* floors before getting to the first floor! Large apartment complexes have different buildings or stairwells, known as *Stiege.* For example, if your address is Juliagasse 38/12/17, this will translate to: Julia Street, street number 38, building or stairwell 12, and apartment number 17.

Using a Realtor

If you have cash to spare, use a realtor (*Makler*). The cost can be alarming: for a rental of up to two years, the commission is one month's gross rent; for two to three years, it is two months' rent; and for leases of more than three years, the commission is three months. There is no harm in trying for a cheaper fee, so ask! There are also relocation services advertised in the Yellow Pages that help you not only in finding an apartment, but also with moving in.

Where to Live in Vienna

Vienna is the largest city in Austria. Some of the ritzier areas to live in are the 1st, 13th, 18th, and 19th districts. More affordable—and still central—apartments can be found in the 2nd to 9th districts. The farther away you get from the center, the cheaper the housing. Nevertheless, nothing in Vienna is really inconvenient, as public transportation is excellent. Furthermore, there are no slum or ghetto areas, so one feels safe all the time.

The Perfect Landlord

Having a good landlord is an advantage, but no matter how perfect your landlord, make sure you have a city approved rental contract. If the apartment comes furnished, inspect the furniture and fixtures and take pictures of anything that is marked or damaged, and be sure to append a list of such flaws in the contract. You can repaint the apartment and make changes only if the landlord agrees to it. There may be extra costs (*Ablöse*) before you move in, including renovation expenses and furniture left behind by a previous owner. If something breaks down, such as the fridge, oven, or heating, the renter is usually responsible (unless the contract says otherwise). Many of the older houses have only one phone line. It is wise to ask the landlord to install a second line in your apartment, especially if you intend to use a dialup Internet connection.

UTILITIES

Make sure that all the utilities are in your name and be prepared to put down deposits for them. Gas and electricity usage is billed quarterly. The total due may take you by surprise if it is based on the previous tenant's consumption—a shock if the previous tenant had six kids! Unfortunately, the meter is read only once a year, so wait for the yearly itemization bill or *Jahresabrechnung*. Either a credit or a debit will show up on the next quarter's bill based on your usage of gas or electricity, so don't despair.

Your phone bill comes bimonthly. There will be a base charge from *Telekom Austria* (which provides the telephone line), and an itemization of your calls by area from the telephone company of your choice. If you want a breakdown of the telephone numbers called, you will need to contact the telephone company personally.

A chimneysweep comes four times a year to clean out the gas or coal heating system. His schedule is posted in your apartment building or in your mailbox if you live in a house. You must be available to let him in one of the four times, or have an explanation handy for the fire police. The rat man usually comes every two months. If you merely say a few words to him be prepared to pay up to 15 minutes of his time; the price can be hefty. Instead, answer your door only twice a year with, hopefully, good news.

The electricity/gas man (*Strom/Gas*) will also send you notice of when you must be home to let him in to read the meter. Houses built after 1930 have the meter outside; for these, meter inspection does not require the presence of the occupant.

REGISTERING WITH THE POLICE

If you are living in an apartment or house, you should register with the police at a police station or municipal office within three days of arrival, by filling out a *Meldezettel* (registration form). If you are staying in a hotel or hostel for up to 60 days, the hotel or hostel reception will fill out the necessary forms; if you are staying longer than 60 days, you must register personally. A form can be purchased for ATS 10 at any *Tabak-Trafik*. (Originally a smoke shop or tobacconist, it now carries a variety of goods besides. See page 95.) Unless you read German, find someone to help you fill out the form, and make sure your landlord signs it too.

In the form, there is a section regarding your religion. If you don't plan on paying into a church, do not fill out this section, or write "O.B." (*Ohne Bekenntnis*).

Bring the form with your passport to the police station in your district (*Bezirkspolizeikommissariat*, signified by a blue and white shield on a map of your district). At the police station, look for a sign on the directory that says *Meldeamt* (registration office). Take a number and wait your turn. Remember to arrive between 8 am and 1 pm (the earlier the better), Monday through Friday. If you don't have a visa in your passport and plan on staying longer than six months, make sure you go back to the *Meldeamt* and show them your visa or residence permit when you get it.

VISA

If you plan on staying in Austria for a while, remember that a visa is not necessary if you are from an EU country or a European Economic Area (EEA). U.S. citizens need only apply for a visa or a residence permit (*Aufenthaltsbewilligung*) if they intend to stay longer than up to two three-month periods during one calendar year. Consult the Austrian consulate in your home country before departure; if afterwards, go to the local magistrate (*Magistrat*), district office (*Magistratisches Bezirkamt*), or regional district office (*Bezirkshauptmannschaft*). Once the six-month period is up, you are required to leave the country. For more information on all official documents, visit www.austria.org/govsite.htm on the Internet or contact your consulate or embassy.

RESIDENCE PERMIT FOR WORK

To get a job, a residence permit (*Aufenthaltsbewilligung*) is required. To obtain the permit, you must provide proof of health insurance (*Unfall- und Krankenversicherungsnachweis*), proof of accommodation (rental contract or *Mietvertrag*) and financial means, police record certificate (*Leumundszeugnis*), and working papers (*Arbeitsgenehmigung*) issued by the Labor Office (*Arbeitsmarktservice*).

Diplomats (United Nations, foreign embassy, and consulate employees) and their families are exempted from *Meldezettel*, visa, and residence permit requirements.

BANKING

Banking in Austria is as simple as pie. The hardest part is getting there while the bank is open, as the hours don't fit the working person's schedule. They are:

Monday–Wednesday and Friday	8 am–12:30 pm, 1:30–3 pm
Thursday	8 am–12:30 pm, 1:30–5:30 pm
Saturday–Sunday and holidays	closed

Vestibules open during banks' hours of closure allow you to withdraw cash, make payments, or get a statement reading. In the main cities, one has several banks to choose from, including Die Erste Bank, Bank Austria, Volksbank, Creditanstalt, Raiffeisenbank, Österreichische Postsparkasse AG (P.S.K.), and Bank für Arbeit und Wirtschaft (BAWAG). There are also regional banks in small cities.

Banking Services

Depending on the service you are looking for, you may have to go to a special counter or speak to one of the representatives (banks are one of the few places in Austria where the customer is king). If you are just changing money, go to the window labelled *Geldwechsel*; all other transactions are done at the *Kassa* window. Austrians have a tough time standing in line. That's why you'll often see footprints in yellow

73

on the ground more than 2 meters away from the window, signalling that the next person in line must wait at that point.

Standing Payment Orders

To make banking easy for yourself, open up as many standing orders as necessary. If you have fixed amounts to be paid on a certain date, the orders you want are called *Dauerauftrag*. If the amount and date vary from month to month, open an *Einziehungsauftrag*. Regular payments to doctors, dentists, etc. can be made using the *Erlagschein* (product of the postal bank) or *Zahlschein* (product of the regular banks), account-to-account transfer forms which will be given to you by the payee. You may also receive a letter from the payee (*Honorarnote*) with his or her bank's information. You can do all of these payments at the bank. There is an area set up, telling you exactly how to fill out and stamp the forms, and to put one in the box and keep the other for your records.

Bankcards

Bankcards, or debit cards (*Bankomatkarte*), and automatic teller machines are widely available in Austria. Some words you should know in order to use the ATM:

confirm amounts with the green button marked *BESTÄTIGUNG*
correct a mistake with the yellow button marked *KORREKTUR*
cancel the transaction with the red button marked *ABBRUCH*

Once you have your money (take the card first, then the money), don't wait for a receipt, as none will be given. You can withdraw up to ATS 5,000 a day, ATS 10,000 a week, and ATS 30,000 a month.

Bank Credit Cards

Bank credit cards give you a one-month grace period before the total amount you charged is due. They are not set up to charge a monthly minimum amount, so beware! They can be used in any teller machine with your PIN number for cash withdrawal.

Personal Checks

Personal checks are nonexistent. Instead, one can use Eurocheques, which are also valid in bordering Mediterranean countries. However, one must be extremely careful while using these checks, as there is no section marked for the payee. Once filled out, the checks are like cash. If stolen (banks only issue 10 at a time at a cost of ATS 25 for this reason), report the loss immediately to the nearest police station and then to your bank. If you do not, expect to be held responsible for 10 percent of the total amount, or a minimum of ATS 1,000.

Savings Accounts

Regular savings accounts, such as the simple savings book, earn very little (1.5 percent interest). Fixed deposits earn more, the percentage increasing with the investment duration. The anonymous savings account is extremely popular, as one declares only the interest earned for tax purposes, and not the principal. But limits will soon be set on the amount one can put into the account. The government is under pressure to make changes, in order to avoid international Financial Action Task Force (FATF) sanctions set up to combat money laundering. Such sanctions adversely affect the banking industry.

Monthly Statements

You don't have to wait for your monthly statement (*Kontoauszüge*) to come by post. You can get a daily reading from an account statement machine at your bank simply by putting in your bankcard and waiting a few seconds (a special ring binder to hold the statements is available from the bank). Another benefit is that you can overdraw up to twice your monthly income, if you request this facility. Be careful, as there is also a daily overdraft interest, charged on a quarterly basis.

On-line Banking

On-line banking is a great alternative if your time is at a premium. Your bank will provide you with the necessary information.

POST OFFICE

Post office locations and hours are listed in the White Pages. The hours are generally Monday–Friday, 8 am–noon and 2–6 pm (sometimes 7 pm at the main offices). Post offices located at major train stations are open 24 hours a day.

The post office experience can be quite daunting in the bigger cities. One may have to choose from between 10 and 20 different counters. The following terms should help you decide where to go:

Counters

Auf u. Abgabe	mailing of packages
Briefaufgabe	posting, mailing
Ein- und Auszahlungen	deposit and withdrawals
Fax	fax
Gebühren Eilsendung	cost for express item
Kleine Inlandspakete	small domestic packages
Massensendung	mass mailing
Pakete-EMS	express mail service
Postanweisungen	money transfer
Postlagernde	in care of general delivery
Produktverkauf	sales
Radio- und TV-Anmeldung	radio and television payments
Sondermarken	collector's stamps
Telegramme	telegram
Telekom/Mobilkom Beratung	advice on phone and mobile
Wertzeichen	postage stamp
Wertzeichnen Und Grossen	cost for bulky items
Zeitung	mailing newspapers

Terms

Absender	sender
Anschrift	address
Aufgabeschein	postal form

Bestimmungsort	destination city, country
Bezugszahl	reference number
Brief	letter
Briefmarke	stamp
Buchstaben	letters
Detaillierte Inhaltsangabe	detailed contents
Empfänger	addressee, recipient
Nachnahme	cash on delivery
Päckchen	small package
Postleitzahl	postal/zip code
Unterschrift	signature
Wert/Wertangabe	value
Ziffern	numbers

The cost of sending a priority letter weighing 20 grams or less is ATS 7 within Europe, and ATS 15 outside of Europe. Further postal rates or *Postgebühren* are listed in a small booklet called *Das kleine Postbuch*, which is left in your mailbox every December. Rates are also listed in the introductory section of the White Pages. When sending a small package (at the letter window), make sure that it is not sealed if going outside Austria, nor tied with a string, and that it does not contain a letter. Don't forget to fill out the appropriate forms for registered mail. Tape-sealed packages weighing more than 2 kilograms require a customs declaration form or international customs form (*Zollerklärung*). There are three categories of mail: Airmail (*Luftpost*) (10 working days), Surface Air Lifted Mail (SAL) (slower than airmail but faster than surface), and Surface Mail (*Gewöhnlich*) (up to 10 weeks).

Postal Codes

When sending mail within Vienna, remember that the city has 23 postal codes. When addressing a letter, make sure the postal code is written correctly; in the postal code 1010, for example, the first digit refers to Vienna, the middle two digits refer to the 1st district, and the last digit refers to the post office in that district. In the telephone book, however, the address is written with the district first; for example, "1, Fleischmarkt 8," which means door number 8, on Fleischmarkt Street, in the 1st district.

All other cities and towns within Austria have postal codes that are much easier to figure out.

Telegrams

Telegrams are sent through the local post office. The forms can be found at the *Telegramme* counter. You can also send a telegram by phoning 190. You can speak in English, making sure that your telegram is longer than seven words. Rates are listed in the White Pages under *Telegrammentgelte*.

TELEPHONE SERVICE

Applications for telephone service are found at your local post office at the *Fernmeldedienst* counter. You can also apply by phone, at 0800 100 100, or through the Internet, at www.telekom.at. There is a one-time installation fee of ATS 1,000 and a six-day waiting period for the line. It is much easier to take over the telephone number of the last tenant. This requires filling out a form entitled *Übertragung*.

Telephones at the Post Office

You can make international phone calls from the post office. At the telephone call (*Telefongespräche*) counter, you will be directed to a telephone booth. After your call, return to the counter and pay your charges.

Telephone booths are also conveniently located throughout the city. A booth accepting coins is usually placed beside one that accepts telephone debit cards (*Telefonwertkarte*) with ATS 50, 100, and 200 stored value. *Telefonwertkarte* may be bought at post offices and most *Tabak-Trafik*.

Telephoning Long Distance

Country and city codes can be found in the White Pages of the telephone directory.

Recently, the Austrian telephone monopoly was broken by companies such as Tele 2, Multikom Austria, Tele Ring, UTA, and Cybertron, which all offer cheaper services. Currently, the best value service can be found under the website www.SaveCall.at (they have contracts with the cheapest service providers).

Call-Back Telephone Services

U.S.-based call-back services for international phone calls are available. Once you have registered with a call-back service provider, you dial a phone number, hang up, and wait for a call back, which gives you an open U.S. line. The call made with that line is charged at U.S. rates. International companies such as Kallback (www.kallback. com) and Teleworld are recommended when traveling worldwide.

RADIO AND TELEVISION

If you own a radio or television, you must register them at the post office at the *Radio- und TV-Anmeldung* counter, and pay a bimonthly fee to use them. Many newcomers are unaware of this fee, and could be fined by the police if found out.

PUBLIC TRANSPORTATION

Austria's public transportation system is one of the best in Europe. It is safe, clean, reliable, reasonably priced, and, surprisingly enough in this day and age, practices the honor system.

Variety of Public Transportation

In Austria there are the underground (*U-Bahn*, found only in Vienna), buses, trams (*Strassenbahn*), and quick train (*Schnellbahn*, only in Vienna and its surrounding zones). The underground and bus systems are reliable, quick, and easy to figure out. There are also night buses, available only on weekends after midnight. The trams, though reliable, are slow and inconvenient for the handicapped or people with strollers. New trams are lower to the ground, making access much more convenient. The fast train is a bit of a misnomer: it is only fast if you catch it at the right time (usually four times per hour—the times are posted on each platform). The waiting time in between can be long, but the ride is quick, hence the prefix *Schnell*.

Honor System

Since the honor system is practiced on public transportation, no gates or turnstiles bar your entry. But remember to buy a ticket, to avoid the embarrassing and far more costly experience of having a plainclothes transportation officer check your ticket. If caught riding "black," there is an ATS 600 fee. If you do not have the money, you will have to show a photo ID, take a payment form (*Zahlschein*), and pay within three days. If you don't have a photo ID, you could be taken to the police station to sign a sworn statement. Either way, you must pay the fine within three days, or pay up to ATS 1,000 instead.

Myriad of Tickets

There are a variety of tickets (*Fahrschein*) to buy, depending on how frequently you will use the public transportation system. These are strictly for the 100 zone (center zone), the area within the city. If you travel outside the city, you pay a supplement. You can buy a one-way ticket (which does not have to be validated if bought on the bus) or a four-day or eight-day network strip ("*8-Tage*" *Umwelt Streifenkarte*). Remember that the ticket with a date and time, called a Time Ticket (*Zeitkarten*), is good only for the specified day. There are special tourist tickets for travel of up to three days in some of the larger cities. Anyone using public transportation regularly would want a weekly, monthly, or yearly pass that allows them unlimited rides in the specified period. The pass requires bank information and a picture, and is only available at a pre-sale ticket window or *Vorverkaufstellen*.

Tickets can be bought at a *Tabak-Trafik*, on the bus or tram (one-way tickets only), at an automatic dispenser found outside most metro stations, or at the pre-sale ticket window at the bigger metro stations.

Unless you bought your ticket on the bus or tram, don't forget to validate it in a cancelling machine (*Entwerter*). These small machines are usually found on the bus or tram, at the entrance of *U-Bahn* stations, and on the platforms of the *Schnellbahn*.

Children up to the age of 6 ride free year-round, and children up to the age of 15 can travel free on Sundays, public holidays, and national school holidays. Children over the age of 6 must always carry their student identification card (*Schülerausweis*).

Driving

Having your own car is a big plus if you intend to travel around Austria and Europe. Driving can be fun and delightful, but there can also be problems along the way.

Austrians have a tendency to get aggressive while driving, and will often go on the offensive. Some might get angry and flash their lights if they are made to wait behind you, or get flustered if you don't seem to know what you are doing. On the freeways, they will go exceedingly fast, even in rain, snow, and fog.

One of the scariest situations to be in is to be driving along a freeway and having a "ghost driver", or someone driving on the wrong side of the freeway, coming head-on. Austria, unfortunately, has one of the highest frequencies of ghost driving in the European Union. Often, the outcome of this type of driving is the tragic death of many innocent people. There are many reasons for ghost driving, but the most common factors are drunken driving and obscure traffic signs at the entrances and exits of freeways. The solutions are not simple. Some states have begun to put up fluorescent yellow warning lights at entrances and exits, and many traffic experts want the law changed to enable police to immediately withdraw the license of a ghost driver who has been driving under the influence of alcohol.

Gary Krejci

These large signs are posted in strategic locations to prevent the recurring problem of the "ghost driver."

Bringing Your Own Car

If you are importing your car from outside the EU, you must submit a permission form beforehand. Shortly after the car arrives, you should get the necessary inspections done. Your car must comply with Austria's environmental standards, which will likely cost you some time and money. In order to drive the car duty-free, it must have been in one's possession at least six months beforehand. Check with the Austrian consulate in your home country for further details.

Buying a Car

If you are a diplomat, you can buy a car tax-free, with the requirement that you will eventually be exporting it or selling it to another diplomat. If not associated with an embassy or consulate, you will be required to pay taxes on your new car.

Rental Cars

Car rental facilities (*Autovermietung*) are available at all international airports in larger cities, and in most major train stations (e.g. Bregenz, Graz, Innsbruck, Klagenfurt, Linz, Salzburg, Seefeld, Zell am See, and Vienna's Westbahnhof and Südbahnhof). Reservations at any of these stations can be made through any railway ticket office in Austria, or through a travel agency. All major international car rental firms have offices in Austria.

Automobile Clubs

There are two automobile clubs: Austrian Automobile, Motorcycle and Touring Club (*Österreichischer Automobil-, Motorrad- und Touring Club/ÖAMTC*) and Austrian Auto, Motor and Bicycle League (*Auto-, Motor- und Radfahrerbund Österreichs/ARBÖ*). Members receive free road service and towing, but even if you aren't a member and need such a service, you can call for help and pay for the membership on the spot.

Car Insurance

All owners of Austria-registered cars must have recognized third party or liability insurance. All EU countries have the same requirement so they don't need green insurance cards (except for Italy). The green insurance card is proof that you have insurance and must be specifically requested from your insurance provider. If you are travelling outside the EU, you are expected to present the green insurance card at the border. Further insurance can be bought. Full comprehensive insurance (*Vollkaskoversicherung*) adds collision and vandalism damage. A letter from your previous insurance company stating that you have had no recent liability claims may get you a discount of up to 50 percent on your premium.

If You Get Into an Accident

Accidents happen and it's always best to be prepared for one. Here are some basic tips:

1. Stop your car immediately, turn on your hazard lights and set up your red warning triangle 50 meters ahead of the accident area.
2. Administer first aid or call an ambulance if necessary (tel. 144 for ambulance, or tel. 133 for police).
3. Always exchange names, addresses, and telephone numbers.
4. Take note of details, such as the make and model of the car(s), license plate number(s), driver's license number(s), insurance company(ies) and policy number(s).
5. Don't claim responsibility. Instead, call and talk to someone from your insurance company.
6. Fill out the accident form (*Europäischer Unfallbericht*) provided by your insurance company.

Driver's License

If you need to get a driver's license and are not a diplomat, or a citizen of the European Union (EU) or the *Europäischer Wirtschaftsraum* (EWR, also known as European Economic Area or EEA), then you will need to have a lot of patience. It is conceivable to end up with an Austrian license, but many steps must be followed.

Once you arrive in Austria, you have six months from the date on your *Meldezettel* form to apply for a driver's license. You are allowed to drive for up to one year after arrival with a license from your home country. However, if you miss the six-month limit to apply for your license, you will have to take the driving test, which may cost upwards from ATS 10,000; you need a certain amount of hours for theory and practical class, and if you fail you must repeat the class and pay again.

If you are from the EU or the EWR (or EEA), you need not apply for an Austrian driver's license, as your license is acceptable.

Where to apply for a license in Vienna:
Bundespolizeidirektion Wien Verkehrsamt
Lichtenwerderplatz 5
1090 Wien
Tel. 01/313 34 0
Opening times: Monday–Friday, 8 am–12:30 pm

These are the steps to take:

1. If your license is not in German, go to an automobile club such as *ÖAMTC* or *ARBÖ* to have your license translated. The fee is likely to be less than that charged at your own consulate.

2. Go to the Department of Motor Vehicles (*Verkehrsamt*). Get an application form for a driver's license at the entrance.

3. Fill out the application form then go to room 3125 (if in Vienna), with the following documents: current driver's license, German translation of your driver's license, passport, police registration form (*Meldezettel*), two passport-sized photos, and proof of at least one year's driving experience (a letter in German from your company or a friend verifying that you have been driving for one year will suffice). Get a number, then wait patiently until your number is called.

4 Once your application has been accepted, you will be notified by mail as to where and when you will need to undergo a medical examination.

5. Once all the above is completed, you can pick up your license! Remember that you will have to give up your current license. (You will most likely get it back. However, you should get another one from your home country beforehand, just in case.) You will also have to pay a fee of ATS 660.

For more current information, go to www.help.gv.at, where there is a driver's license section entitled *Fuhrerscheinumschreibung*.

What to Bring with You in the Car

The following are extremely important items that you should have at
all times, either on your person or in the car:

1. Driver's license – on your person
2. Car registration (*Zulassungsschein*)—on your person. Be careful
   not to leave this in the car or glove compartment. Thieves can
   register your car, and insurance companies may invalidate your
   theft claim.
3. Automobile inspection sticker (*Pickerl*), plus documentation
   showing that this annual test has been performed. (The documentation, which is carried with you at all times, is required in order
   to show what minor damages need repair.)
4. Country identification sticker (*Internationales Autokennzeichnen*)
5. Road tax sticker (*Vignette*). Must be displayed while travelling
   on expressways or freeways (see below).
6. Insurance papers
7. Radio registration
8. First aid kit
9. Red reflective warning triangle (*Pannendreieck*)
10. Fog lights. Use only when visibility is low—turn them off when
    visibility improves or risk paying a fine.

Road Information

The roads in Austria are well maintained and very well marked. The
freeways (*Autobahn*) are all over Austria and lead to all surrounding
countries. Be careful when driving along the mountain roads, as there
are many turns and the grade is steep at times. Major border crossing
points are open 24 hours a day. Those served by minor roads are open
between 7 am and 9 pm, give or take an hour.

Austria's freeways and speed roads are subject to a road tax or
Vignette. The tax is paid through the purchase of a sticker, which has
to be attached to the middle of the windscreen. The annual road tax is
ATS 1,000 for automobiles and motor homes (up to 3.5 tons), and

ATS 220 for motorcycles. For vacationers, two-month (ATS 150) and one-week stickers (ATS 70) are available. Infringements of this tax regulation are punished with an additional charge of ATS 1,100 or an administrative fine. The road tax stickers may be purchased at automobile clubs (*ÖAMTC* or *ARBÖ*) in Austria and abroad, at petrol stations and stores close to the border, and at post offices (*Postämter*), tobacco shops (*Tabak*), and gas stations (*Tankstelle*).

Radars are becoming more and more obvious throughout Austria. They are large, grey metal boxes located on the side of the street. If you are going over the speed limit, a picture of your car is taken, the license plate number looked up, and a traffic ticket sent to you by mail. So if you are in a rush going through the city, make sure you smile!

Information on road conditions and the traffic situation is available in English daily including weekends from 6 am to 8 pm from the Austrian Automobile Club; call 71 19 97 in Vienna, or (01) 71 19 97 from anywhere else in Austria.

Rules of the Road

Traffic regulations are similar to those in other European countries.

- For driving during the winter months, winter tires are essential; in extreme cases, snow chains have to be used. These can be rented at all major border crossings.
- The minimum driving age in Austria is 18.
- Wearing seatbelts is compulsory. The driver is responsible for the safety of his passengers, and will be held accountable if anyone is injured while not wearing his or her seatbelt.
- Children under the age of 12, or shorter than 1.5 m, are not allowed to sit in the front seat. Infant seats are mandatory for babies under the age of 9 months. The seats must go in the back, as passenger side air bags pose a potential danger to babies and small children.
- Buses and trams always have the right of way. Always yield to a bus leaving a bus stop. Be careful not to block tram tracks as trams are silent, heavy, and will hit you, as they have nowhere else to go.

Some tramlines cross roads, and always have the right of way coming from the left. Always stop where trams stop (the stop is always in the middle of the road), to allow passengers to get on and off safely.

- The speed limit is 100 km/h on highways, 130 km/h on freeways, 50 km/h in built-up areas, and 30 km/h in residential areas.
- Drunken driving (the permissible alcohol limit is 0.5 percent) is punishable and can lead to confiscation of your driving license.

Parking

You can park your car on the street either in or against the flow of traffic. This can be handy if you are in a hurry and don't want to make a U-turn to get in the right direction.

Limited parking zones (blue zones) allow you to park for $1^{1}/_{2}$ to 3 hours. Read all parking signs. In some cities, such as Vienna, Graz, Linz, Klagenfurt, and Innsbruck, there is a charge for parking. You either buy parking vouchers from a *Tabak*, or display the receipt you get from a coin-operated machine located nearby (only in some parking areas). If you are parking for 10 minutes or less, you can get the required vouchers at *Tabaks*, banks, hotels, and some gas stations. Whatever your situation, display the vouchers or receipts clearly on the inside of the windscreen or risk getting a parking ticket.

Airports

Vienna is Austria's main air transport hub, but there are also international airports at Linz, Graz, Salzburg, Innsbruck, and Klagenfurt. The closest airport to Eisenstadt is the Vienna airport. Tyrolean Airways, the main domestic carrier, operates several flights a day between Austria's larger cities.

The airports are modern, well maintained, and easily accessible. Short- and long-term parking are available for a reasonable fee.

Taxis

With taxi stands throughout the city, it isn't usual to hail a taxi, although they have been known to stop if empty. Pay what the meter reads, based on a per kilometer charge and a small transportation levy. On Sundays, public holidays, and from 11 pm to 6 am, both charges go up. Tip 5–10 percent of the fare. If calling in advance for a taxi, the dispatcher will ask for the district (if in Vienna) and house address. If you are going away and have lots of luggage or have children, ask for a large wagon (*Kombiwagen*). If you are going to the airport, call a taxi service the night before and you will get a discounted rate.

Trains

Austria has excellent rail connections to major European destinations. Trains are efficient, safe, clean, and reliable. It is best to reserve a seat if you intend to travel on a holiday or in the summer.

Stops are usually announced via loudspeaker. Sometimes, especially when going through some mountain resorts, there is a chance your stop won't be announced. Julie was in such a situation, and had to run and throw herself and the bags out the door at her stop.

The Bundesbus (federal bus) network supplements the rail service, and is used for local trips, or to get to out-of-the-way places, rather than for long-distance travel. The Bundesbus travels to some ski resorts in Tyrol and Vorarlberg.

If you are going on a cycling trip, most trains have a compartment for bicycles. Check before your trip.

Boats on the Danube

Boat services on the Danube are slow and expensive, and geared to scenic excursions rather than functional transport. Fast hydrofoils skim between Vienna, Bratislava, and Budapest in spring and summer, but are not cheap. Steamers travel between Vienna and the German border town of Passau from May to late September.

SHOPPING

Shopping in Austria is quite an experience. First, shops are not open seven days a week, unlike in some other parts of Europe. Second, cash payment is still popular, although grocery stores and some shops have bankcard or debit machines. Third, one has the distinct feeling of being underdressed in jeans. Most Austrians "dress up" to shop; one does get better service when well dressed.

When entering or leaving small stores, it is customary to say hello or "*Grüss Gott.*" This is a sweet formality which makes one feel welcome. The owner or clerk will automatically ask if you need help. You can then ask for what you want, or if you are only browsing, say, "*Ich schaue nur.*" It is mainly in the smaller boutiques that the help can be a bit overwhelming, if you are not used to it. Of course, there are large department stores in most cities where you can browse to your heart's content without being followed about by a salesperson.

Clothing

Fashion in Austria is conservative and elegant. Some well known women's stores are Fuernkranz, Maldone, and Austrian traditional clothing stores such as Loden and Geiger. For men, there are Teller and Tlapa. For the teens and 20-year-olds, there are fun stores such as H&M, Schöps, Street One, Orsay, Turek, and Sisley. Children's clothing stores in the large cities are part of big chains like H&M and C&A, and of smaller ones like Dohnal, and Mary for Kids. The popular department stores for just about everyone in the family are C&A (budget), Gerngross, and Peek and Cloppenburg.

Specialty Stores

Austria produces its own ceramics in the town of Gmunden, in Upper Austria. The patterns are well known among Austrian households, but the most popular are green swirls or blue polka dots on a white background. Ceramics are sold in household stores.

The Augarten in Vienna produces fine china. The popular pattern

Julie Krejci

Pricey boutiques and souvenir shops line Vienna's premier shopping street, Kärntner Strasse.

is fine pastel flowers on white. The decoration is beautifully painted in a very delicate manner. Special tours can be arranged by contacting the Augarten factory.

The *Wiener Werkstätte* (WW) produces an assortment of objects for the kitchen and dining-room. Its heyday was at the turn of the 20th century during the Jugendstil period. The WW believed it could make anything a household could want. When the materials used proved to be too costly for the average family, it ended up making specialty objects for a select clientele.

Also popular is the Dorotheum, fondly called "Aunt Dorli's," an auction house, pawn brokerage, and store opened in 1707. The Dorotheum proper is located in Vienna's 1st district, but smaller branches are found throughout Vienna. One can get anything from furniture and china, to jewelry, paintings, and fur coats. Auctions are held almost daily, with a special viewing time before the event to allow prospective bidders to check out the merchandise.

Let's not forget the famous Flea Market, which borders the *Naschmarkt*. It is open every Saturday, from the wee hours until sunset. There is an assortment of everything from junk to real treasures. Mind your purse or wallet as the place is crowded.

Claiming a Tax Refund

If you are a nonresident and spend over ATS 1,000, you may claim a refund. The forms are available at most stores. When leaving the EU, customs officials at the airport or train station will validate your items. Cash your refund check at a refund office after you have cleared passport control. You may also be able to mail your validated refund check to an address provided at customs (if you can't find your receipt) and have your credit card account credited.

Food

Shopping at grocery stores (*Lebensmittelgeschäfte*) or supermarkets (*Supermärkte*) can be a shock if you are used to huge grocery stores.

Many stores are expanding, and it is common to find two stores of the same name a small distance apart, one selling food and the other, toiletries. The aisles can be extremely small and it requires a lot of patience and good humor to make shopping a good experience. The common grocery stores are Billa, Zielpunkt, Mondo, Merkur, Hofer, Spar, Eurospar, Interspar, Pam Pam, and Metro. Interspar, Pam Pam, Metro, and Merkur tend to be large but not very accessible, being found on the outskirts of large cities. Metro is extremely large and sells in bulk, but only to customers who have the membership or diplomatic card necessary to gain entrance. Zielpunkt, Mondo, and Hofer tend to be much cheaper as they are wholesale stores that also sell overstocked merchandise at low prices.

When you go grocery shopping, bring your own shopping bags or a shopping wagon, as shopping bags will often cost you a couple of Schillings. Once you are at the store, remember to have either an ATS 5 or 10 to get a cart. Withdraw the coin or token at the end of your shopping trip by attaching the chain at the end of the cart line to your cart.

The produce section usually carries a wide selection of goods, with more variety now than ever before, due to the trading ties within the European Union. A word of warning: always weigh the produce you buy if it is not sold on a per piece basis; with very few exceptions, this is not done by the cashier. It can be embarrassing when the cashier has to leave her register and weigh an item you have forgotten, while there are customers waiting behind you.

The meat and cheese section is wonderful, offering a great variety from all over Europe. Everything is priced by the kilogram. However, one doesn't break down the amounts by 100ths (100 gram) but by 10ths (decagram). So, if you want 200 grams of cheese, you say, "*zwanzig deca Käse, bitte*." ("Twenty decagrams of cheese, please.")

Many bottles and some plastics carry a deposit (*Pfand*). You usually go to the back of the store, where a conveyor belt will accept your empties, then spit out a credit receipt (*Flaschenzettel*). Present this ticket to the cashier when you check out, and she will credit the amount to your grocery bill.

Bankcards (*Bankomat Karte*) make it easy to pay for your groceries. You just insert your card and type in your PIN. Remember to keep your *Bankomat* card current.

The most shocking part about the grocery stores is the small area, sometimes nonexistent, in which to gather the groceries you have bought. This means that once the items have been checked through, one has to gather them all at Olympian speed, to put back into the cart. One then goes to a special packing counter to pack the groceries. If you go to the larger grocery stores with your car, you can bring the grocery cart to the car and unload it directly.

If you like the royal treatment, and have a penchant for fine foods and wine, go to Julius Meinl on the Graben in Vienna. The employees will greet you and make you feel quite at home. The ambience is refined and super-modern. There is also a cozy coffee shop on the first floor, and a gourmet restaurant located behind the store. The best thing of all, however, is that when you leave the store, someone will bag your groceries, even without you having to pay for the bags!

Some grocery stores are trying to make life a bit easier on the customer. Merkur, for example, has an order and delivery service available from 6 am until midnight.

Shopping Hours

The hours for shopping can sometimes be annoyingly inconvenient, but changes are taking place, and now stores are opening later and later. Generally, the hours at department stores and boutiques are Monday–Friday 10 am–6 pm, Saturday 10 am–5 pm. Grocery stores are open Monday–Wednesday 8 am–7 pm, Thursday–Friday 7:30 am–7 pm, and Saturday 7 am–5 pm.

Don't despair if you find yourself with nothing in the fridge on a holiday. The main train stations and gas stations carry a wide range of foodstuff and other necessary items.

primary school (*Volksschule*) at about age 6 and stay for four years. Then there is a choice between four types of schooling to create a well trained workforce of young adults.

1. Vocational school—five years regular secondary school (*Hauptschule*) followed by three years vocational training with salary.
2. Trade school (secretarial, bookkeeping)—four years upper-level secondary school (*Gymnasium*), then five years trade school.
3. Electronic school (*Höhere Technische Lehranstalt*)—four years *Gymnasium* or *Hauptschule*, then five years electronic study, followed by final exams for the diploma (*Matura*).
4. University path—8 years *Gymnasium* followed by final exams for the *Matura*.

Religion is taught in school for 12 years. However, the classes are not mandatory and some parents choose not to have their child attend.

More and more Austrian schools are providing bilingual teaching, or teach their students in a foreign language.

There are a number of private schools in Vienna. The American International School (AIS) provides an American-style education from pre-kindergarten up to 12th grade. The Vienna International School (VIS) provides an English-style education from kindergarten up to 12th grade. The Danube International School and the Vienna Christian School provide an education similar to an AIS one. There is also the *Lycée Français de Vienne*. Other private schools are the Japanese, Arab, and Swedish Schools.

German Classes

German classes for foreigners are easily available. In Vienna, most classes are held in the 1st district. In other cities, most universities and adult schools (*Volkhochschule*) have special German classes for foreigners. If you already know some German, you can take a placement test to ascertain the level you should start at. Classes meet once or twice a week. Intensive classes are available as well.

MEDICAL SERVICES

The medical services in Austria are good and efficient. Vienna has one of the biggest hospitals in Europe, *Allgemeines Krankenhaus* (AKH). Private doctors and specialists are also available throughout Austria.

These emergency telephone numbers are applicable throughout Austria:

Ambulance or *Rettung*	144
Police or *Polizei*	133
Fire or *Feuerwehr*	122

Pharmacies (Apotheken)

Pharmacies proliferate, as most drugs need a prescription, and common items such as aspirin and cough syrup must be bought at a pharmacy and not a drugstore (*Drogerien*).

Pharmacies take turns staying open during lunch and after hours. A notice of the next pharmacy open is posted on each pharmacy door. There is an extra charge for medicine purchased after hours.

Austrian National Health Insurance

The Austrian national health insurance is the *Krankenkasse* (KK). It is part of Austria's huge social security system. Health insurance is mandatory for all Austrian workers. Half the premium for coverage is a set percentage paid out of a person's salary; the other half is paid by the employer. Any permanent resident can become part of the KK by applying at the health insurance agency (*Gebietskrankenkasse*). You can also apply for self-insurance (*Selbstversicherung*) if you are self-employed, a student, or unemployed.

Once you have joined the KK, you'll receive a treatment voucher (*Krankenschein*) from your employer. There are three different *Krankenschein*, for visits to a dentist, a specialist, and a general practitioner respectively. Each voucher is valid for three months. If you forget to bring the voucher with you on a visit, you must pay between ATS 300 and ATS 500 as a deposit (*Einlage* or *Kaution*). Once you have found a doctor, expect a long wait as doctors are paid a minimum sum per patient, and the system is there to serve everyone. Be prepared with all of your questions ahead of time, and you will not be disappointed. If further consultation with a specialist is necessary, your doctor will give you a referral voucher (*Überweisungsschein*). If you are unhappy with your doctor, you may opt for a change after the end of the quarter. If your doctor is on vacation, you can obtain information from his or her office as to which doctors in your neighborhood have a similar practice.

The *Krankenkasse* is a wonderful system and protects you generously. Some of its highlights include maternity leave, annual physicals, paid sick leave, and treatment in other countries (make sure you have a certificate or *Auslandsbetreungsschein* for care in a foreign country to exercise this privilege).

Private medical insurance (*Nebenversicherung* or *Zusatzversicherung*) are for those who require special services in a hospital or treatment by doctors who do not have contracts with the *Krankenkasse*. There are numerous plans to choose from, some of which are available through your employer.

Doctors

You may find a doctor through your employer, private insurance provider, embassy, or consulate. The White Pages have a listing by district under *Ärzte*.

Once you have found a doctor, the chances are high that if you must disrobe, there will be no gown for you to wear.

Immunizations

Austrians are big on having both regular and incidental (for vacations) immunizations. An important shot for anyone living in Austria is the tick shot, which guards against *Meningoencephalitis*, an inflammation of the brain and meninges. The threat is especially great for

99

those living near the Vienna Woods, the Wachau, Burgenland, Styria, and Carinthia. The series of shots is given in the following sequence:

First injection   late winter/early spring
Second injection   after an interval of 2–8 weeks (protection starts)
Third injection   1–12 months later (protection complete)
Booster injection   every 3–4 years thereafter

Go to the District Health Office or *Bezirksgesundheitsamt* for your tick shots. They can be obtained cheaply at certain times of the year.

Chapter Five

AUSTRIAN CUISINE: *MAHLZEIT!*

It is an accomplishment if you leave Austria the same size as when you arrived. Not only are the main dishes hearty and filling, but the pastries are so delicious that you won't be able to refuse them. Main courses are meat-oriented, consisting primarily of pork, but chicken, veal, beef, and turkey are also eaten regularly. As if these large portions of meat aren't enough, potatoes, dumplings, or sauerkraut often accompany them, with green vegetables in short supply.

Austria's neighbors have heavily influenced its cuisine, although by now favorite dishes are considered truly Austrian. Regional influences become evident once you begin to look at provincial specialties. The food of Burgenland, for example, reflects the Hungarian taste for paprika and sour cream. *Gulasch* is perhaps Hungary's most important contribution to Austrian stomachs. Upper and Lower Austrian and Viennese dishes include many Czech staples. Bohemia, in the Czech Republic, is the birthplace of the dumpling, which Austrians have made their own. Sausages arrived via Germany and Poland. Italian, Slavic, Middle Eastern, and even Asian cooking have also influenced the Austrian menu.

REGIONAL CUISINE

While you can order certain dishes throughout the country, each region is particularly proud of its own delicious specialties. Vorarlberg, which in many aspects is closer to Switzerland than Austria, introduced the tasty *Gröstl* (fried potatoes and onions served with or without meat) to the rest of the country. Tyrol is noted for the heavy but good *Käsenockerln* or *Käsespätzle* (cheese egg noodles). *Speck,* ham that is cured high up in the fresh mountain air and found in a variety of dishes, is another trademark of the region. Salzburg is famous for the *Salzburger Nockerln*, a light dessert soufflé dusted with vanilla sugar. Carinthians love *Ritscher(t)*, a meat dish made with white beans, barley, vegetables, and herbs.

Upper Austrians have invented a number of different types of *Knödel* (dumpling). A favorite among the farmers are *Mühlviertler Hackknödel*, made with leftover meat. *Mostbraten*, pork marinated in *Most* (semi-fermented grape juice), is extremely popular. For something sweet, they like *Strauben*, fried dough. Lower Austrians prefer *Buchteln*, a sweet bun filled with plum marmalade and served warm with vanilla sauce. Styria is known for the hearty *Steirisches Wurzelfleisch*, beef cooked with carrots and other root vegetables. The not particularly healthy *Grammelpogatscherl*—fried pork fat baked in dough and served with sour cream—is a favorite in Burgenland. Of course, Vienna is known for its *Schnitzeln* and *Strudeln.*

ENTRÉES

If you find yourself living in Austria, you'd better be a fan of pork, because it is eaten everywhere. It comes as cutlets, ham, sausages, and pork chops, among others, and tends to dominate menus and the meat section at the supermarket.

Perhaps the most famous dish in Vienna is *Wiener Schnitzel*, a veal or pork cutlet that is pounded paper thin, dipped in egg, flour, and breadcrumbs, and fried. *Schnitzel* refers to the thinly pounded piece of meat. It is often served with potato salad. The menu will specify if the meat is veal, and if it doesn't say *Wiener Schnitzel von Kalb* (veal) it is most likely made with pork (*Schwein*). If you are dining in an upscale restaurant, it should be veal. After you've been in Austria a while, you should be able to guess which it is just from the price.

Putenschnitzel (turkey *Schnitzel*) and *Hühnerschnitzel* (chicken *Schnitzel*) are prepared in exactly the same manner as *Wiener Schnitzel*. *Pariserschnitzel* is *Wiener Schnitzel* minus the egg. Not all *Schnitzeln* are breaded: *Champignonschnitzel* is a thin slice of grilled pork served with a mushroom cream sauce and rice; *Rahmschnitzel* is covered in a thick gravy; and *Zigeunerschnitzel* (Gypsy *Schnitzel*) comes with mild to hot peppers in a spicy tomato sauce.

Tafelspitz, boiled beef served with potatoes and vegetables, was Emperor Franz Josef's favorite meal (he ate it every day), and its name translates as "the head of the table." *Schweinsbraten* is juicy roast pork.

Zwiebelrostbraten is a thin steak that is fried and then smothered with sautéed onions. *Gulasch* originated in Hungary but is a staple of Viennese fare. Served as a soup or stew, often with dumplings or bread, it is made with large pieces of meat in a strong paprika sauce. *Fiakergulasch* comes with a hardboiled egg and is said to be the favorite of drivers of *Fiaker*, the horse-drawn carriages seen throughout Vienna. *Laibchen* are tasty little meatballs, and *Fachiertes Fleisch* refers to ground beef. For the adventurous there is *Beuschel*, or lung. *Backhendl* is a young stuffed chicken that is breaded and fried.

Grammelknödel are delicious rich dumplings stuffed with pork and fried lard.

If you can't decide what to order, get *Bauernschmaus*, a sampler of smoked ham, roast pork, sausage, sauerkraut, and dumplings.

Fish

Freshwater fish comes from the lakes and rivers of Austria and is commonly eaten in towns and cities outside of Vienna. However it is prepared, the fish is usually very good. Commonly eaten fish are *Karpfen* (carp), *Kabeljau* (cod), *Scholle* (sole), *Heilbutt* (halibut), *Flunder* (flounder), *Zander* (perch or pike), *Lachs* (salmon), *Forelle* (trout), and *Thunfisch* (Tuna).

Vegetarian Food

Vegetarians do not have an easy time in Austria, although the situation is improving. Many menus list at least a couple of meatless entrées, like fried Emmenthaler cheese or dumplings. Some restaurants do offer large salads, although many are topped with chicken, tuna, or seafood. Other restaurants provide salad bars, but be advised that you are permitted one trip only. The number of vegetarian restaurants in the cities is steadily growing, however, and more options are becoming available. When traveling through rural areas, though, you'll have to make do with a limited menu.

SOUPS

Perhaps because winters can be so cold and long, soups are popular. One of the tastiest ways to start off a meal is with *Fritattensuppe*, a clear beef broth with thin slices of crêpe. Other clear soups are *Leberknödelsuppe*, with a large liver paté dumpling, and *Griessnockerl-suppe*, loaded with small gnocchi-style dumplings. *Hühnersuppe* (chicken soup) is always a safe and delicious choice, as are *Nudel-suppe* (noodle soup), *Knoblauchsuppe* (cream of garlic soup), and *Erdäpfelsuppe* (potato soup).

BEILAGEN

In most restaurants, *Beilagen*, or side dishes, are ordered separately. Unless the description of your entrée specifically mentions an accompaniment, it will come à la carte. The *Beilagen* section consists of a number of *Kartoffel* or *Erdäpfel* (both words mean potato) dishes. *Gröstl* or *Röstkartoffeln* are fried potatoes with onions. *Petersilkartoffeln* are parsley potatoes. The term *Pommes Frites,* borrowed from the French, is used for French fries. *Kartoffelsalat* is cold potato salad made with a vinegar and sugar dressing. *Reis* (rice) is another option, or you may choose the heavy but delicious large dumplings called *Knödel.* These are made from either bread or potato dough, and boiled.

You may notice that vegetables are lacking on the side dish menu. In fact, most meals are not accompanied by anything green. This can be traced back to medieval days when vegetables were in short supply and considered luxury items. Even though the price of vegetables is no longer prohibitively expensive, they have failed to become an integral part of the Austrian diet, with the exception of asparagus in season.

SALADS

If you are a big salad eater you'll have to alter your expectations while in Austria. Most salads, especially the *gemischter Salat*, are a combination of tasty marinated vegetables. These commonly include beets, green beans, cucumbers, sauerkraut, potato salad, carrots, and *Rettich* (a large white radish that is thinly sliced and mixed with vinegar and oil). If you prefer a lettuce salad, be sure to ask for a *Grünersalat* or green salad. This is a leafy salad with a number of different types of lettuce.

BREADS

If you enjoy eating bread with your meal, or even on its own, Austria is the place to be. There are so many different types of bread that it would be impossible to list them all here. What follows are just the highlights. For a better idea of what's available, visit your local bakery or the bread section at the supermarket. If the entire loaf is too much for your family, you may ask for a half (*Halbes*) or a quarter (*ein Viertel*). A *Semmel* is the average white roll. *Stangerl* are long rolls and come in different varieties like *Salzstangerl* (salted). *Hausbrot* (housebread) is a mixture of wheat and rye. *Roggenbrot* is rye bread and *Schwarzbrot* is black rye bread. Be sure to sample the bread when you travel around Austria because there are many different regional breads. Of course, if you must have white sandwich bread, that is available too.

DESSERTS

Pastries

The wonderful flavors of the pastries are difficult to describe. The best way to fully appreciate this aspect of life in Austria is to force yourself into a pastry shop and start eating. *Strudel* is the most popular dessert. Many layers of thick phyllo dough surround a warm filling, usually *Apfel* (apple) or *Topfen* with raisins. *Topfen* has been translated as sweet cream cheese or sweet curd, but it does not exist outside of this part of Europe. It should not be confused with cheesecake; *Topfen* is less sweet and has a delicious yet distinct flavor. A dash of lemon is sometimes added to heighten the flavor.

Sachertorte is Austria's most famous dessert. Sampled by practically every tourist, *Sachertorte* is chocolate cake covered in chocolate icing with apricot jam. Although it sounds heavy, it actually has a very delicate flavor. Herr Sacher, Prince Metternich's personal pastry chef, baked the first *Sachertorte* in the mid-19th century. The chef's son opened the Hotel Sacher in 1876, and the son's wife built up the hotel's reputation. This hotel claims to have the original secret recipe and legally won the right to spell it as one word. All other restaurants, cafés, and pastry shops must spell it as two words—*Sacher Torte*.

Linzertorte is made with apricot jam and almonds. *Esterhazytorte* is a delicious cake consisting of many very thin layers of dough with vanilla cream between the layers. *Mohntorte* is a poppy seed cake, and *Nusstorte* is walnut cake.

As you've probably guessed by now, *Torte* means cake. *Schnitte*—cut or slice—refers to a piece of pastry cut from a large sheet, the most famous being the *Kardinalschnitte* or Cardinal's cut. This rich but light dessert consists of meringue, yellow cake, and either chocolate, strawberry, or raspberry mousse. If you are lucky enough to find homemade *Kardinalschnitte*, you are in for a big treat. *Imperialschnitte* is a personal favorite of ours, and consists of chocolate and marzipan.

More Desserts

Kaiserschmarrn is an omelette/soufflé made from eggs and raisins. *Mohr im Hemd*, which means "Moor in a shirt," is a must for any chocolate lover; it is chocolate cake covered in warm chocolate sauce and topped with whipped cream. *Gugelhupf* is reminiscent of a bunt cake, but smaller. *Krapfen* are fried donuts filled with jam (often apricot jam).

Another big favorite is *Palatschinken*, a delectable plate of crêpe with a variety of fillings. *Marmaladepalatschinken* are filled with apricot jam, and *Schokonusspalatschinken* have walnut filling and are topped with warm chocolate sauce. The crêpe can also be filled with Nutella, ice cream, or fruit.

Ice Cream

As much as the Austrians love their pastries, Italian style ice cream (*gelato*) is savored as highly. Many people have their favorite *Gelateria* and intense rivalries have arisen. With a few exceptions, most ice cream parlors close from October to March. The opening of the local *Gelateria* in the spring is a day for celebration. Once you taste the creamy ice cream, you'll understand why. We promise that you'll return again and again to try each and every exotic flavor. If you want

more than a simple ice cream cone, the selection of ice cream dishes and sundaes is so broad that it'll take you at least one summer to sample them all. A popular dish is *heisse Liebe* (literally "warm love"), creamy vanilla ice cream smothered with warm raspberries and garnished with loads of whipped cream. Not to be missed!

Whipped Cream

If you love rich desserts, all of the above can and should be ordered with *Schlagobers*, or fresh whipped cream, on the side. No self-respecting Austrian would eat the light and airy pre-made whipped cream. *Schlagobers* is heavy unsweetened whipped cream that, in our opinion, is one of the advantages of living in Austria.

Chocolate

Although not literally a dessert, chocolates deserve mention. Austria is famous for *Mozartkugeln*, little round chocolate balls covering a nougat and marzipan center. Several boxes of these are all you need to take home as souvenirs! Not quite as well known, but every bit as delicious, are the candies named after Princess Sissi and Johann Strauss.

HEALTH AND DIET

The average Austrian diet, which is high on meat, fats, starches, and sweets, and low on fish and vegetables, may be blamed for the high rate of circulatory disorders and heart disease. It used to be quite common to compliment an overweight person by saying, "You're looking healthy." This attitude probably arose out of the years of hunger and hardship characterizing the world wars. Today, however, the younger generation is more concerned with body size, although not necessarily with their health.

MEAL SCHEDULE

Breakfast

Breakfast is usually eaten very early in the morning, between 6 and 7 am, as most Austrians are early risers. A typical breakfast consists of a few of the following: bread, butter, marmalade, cold cuts, paté, softboiled egg, cheese, yogurt, müsli, coffee, tea, and hot chocolate.

Gabelfrühstück

For many people who work, this is an important part of the day. Work schedules are such that many begin and end work early. For those who return home in the early evening, a big dinner awaits. Therefore, they pass up the afternoon coffee break with pastry. But rather than go a whole day without something sweet, around 10 am they stop for *Gabelfrühstück*, literally "breakfast eaten with a fork." This snack consisting of coffee and a pastry tides them over until lunch.

Lunch

Lunch can be a formal or informal affair, and is usually eaten between noon and 1 pm. For many busy workers, a quick bite from a *Würstelstand* (kiosk selling a variety of sausages), sandwich shop, or pizzeria is all they have time for. Since their clientele are often in a rush, most of these eateries do not offer seating, but rather tiny-

109

topped, tall tables for customers to stand around. Every *Stehcafe* is usually packed at lunchtime. Don't worry if this is not how you want to spend your lunch hour. Traditionally, lunch used to be the biggest meal of the day, and there are a large number of restaurants available where you are invited in to sit and take your time to enjoy your meal. Many restaurants offer a set lunch menu, which includes soup, entrée, and dessert. For those on a budget, this is the best option. If the day's special doesn't appeal to you, the menu will have all the usual traditional local dishes.

Jause

Jause is a short coffee break taken in mid-afternoon, around 3–4 pm, primarily by those who either do not eat a big dinner or who eat much later at night. It provides people with an opportunity to relax and enjoy something sweet. The cafés and *Konditorei* begin to get very crowded with retirees and students around this time of day.

Dinner

Dinner is eaten between 7 and 8 pm and is quite a substantial hot meal. This is especially true for workers who eat a quick lunch. Restaurants offer the same hearty meals served at lunch. For those who have had a substantial lunch or a particularly filling *Jause*, dinner may be ham or cold cuts, served with pickles, a salad, and one of the many delicious breads.

ETIQUETTE

If you are dining with Austrians, be sure to say *Mahlzeit* before digging in. This translates as *bon appétit*. To start eating before wishing everyone else at the table a good meal would be rude. In several restaurants dishes are served in the order in which they are prepared. Wait for others at your table to invite you to begin eating before you dig in. Also, keep in mind that Austrians eat with their knives and forks, even pizza.

WHERE SHOULD YOU EAT?

Beiseln

Beiseln are neighborhood pub-restaurants that offer low-priced, simple home-style food and beer. They are warm and cozy, and can be easily recognized by the chalkboard outside, which describes the daily menu. The pace is slow and each *Beisel* has its share of regular customers.

International Restaurants

If you want a change from Austrian fare, there is an abundance of international restaurants. Italian restaurants serve good pasta dishes and pizzas. If you like Asian food, Chinese restaurants are quite common throughout the country, but they do use MSG. In Vienna there are Japanese, Thai, Indian, and Korean restaurants, among others. There are many French restaurants to choose from as well. Central and Eastern Europe and the Balkans are well represented, and the many Turkish and Greek restaurants are particularly good. Austria is relatively free of American chain restaurants, except for fast food giant McDonald's. Middle Eastern food is also available. Another tasty option is Latin American food, including Mexican, Brazilian, Argentinian, and Chilean cuisine.

DINING OUT

Because most restaurants and *Beiseln* are family-operated, they observe a *Ruhetag* one day of the week, when the restaurant is closed so the owners and employees can "rest." Many restaurants have Sunday and holidays as their *Ruhetage*, yet this is not necessarily the norm. Some restaurants may close for a break between lunch and dinner, and you'll be pushed out the door as closing time approaches. Even if they remain open, however, you may find your options limited during non-peak hours. Susan and her mother sat down to eat lunch at 3 pm once and were forced to order the same meal so that the cook wouldn't have to dirty too many pans. Most restaurants and *Beiseln* close at around midnight, but tend to empty out well beforehand.

Once you've arrived at your chosen restaurant, seat yourself, making sure the table you select is not reserved with a card reading *reserviert.* Nonsmoking sections are uncommon, so if cigarette smoke affects you, try more spacious restaurants, dine during off-peak hours, or sit at outdoor tables in summer. The server will appear relatively soon to take your order. Water does not automatically come with your meal, so ask for *Leitungswasser* if you want tap water, or *Mineralwasser* if you want mineral water. Once served, the waitstaff tends to leave the customers alone to eat in peace: there is no checking every 5 minutes to see if you need anything. When clearing away your meal, the waiter or waitress will ask if you enjoyed your meal (*"Hat's Ihnen geschmeckt?"*), and if you've left food on your plate they'll ask you if you didn't enjoy it.

Paying

When you are ready to leave, request the bill. Restaurants that cater to the tourist market will accept credit cards, but be advised that many restaurants do not take plastic. The first time you visit, you should always have enough cash on hand to avoid an embarrassing situation. *Beiseln* and *Gasthäuser* definitely do not accept credit cards.

Normally you will be asked if it is *zusammen* (all together) or *getrennt* (separate). When paying, you may be asked to repeat everything you ordered as the waiter jots down the price for each and mentally calculates the total. Remember that you have to pay for each roll or piece of bread, so you will be asked how many were eaten.

When presented with the final bill, round the figure up, adding up to a 10 percent tip. Either give the server the total amount (bill plus tip) and say *"Das stimmt,"* or, if you don't have the exact amount, tell the server the total and wait for your change. For example, if the bill is 280 Schillings and you only have a 500-Schilling bill, say *"Dreihundert* (300)" and wait for your change. Avoid leaving a tip on the table.

Stammtisch

Austrians continue to uphold the longstanding tradition of the *Stammtisch*. This is a table reserved for regular customers. Often friends choose a night of the week for the *Stammtisch*, and they meet regularly without having to call the restaurant first or organize the evening among themselves. It provides a place and an opportunity for friends to sit down together, drink a glass of beer and chat.

Schanigärten

As the first warm breezes are felt, Austrians jump at any opportunity to be outside after a long winter indoors. Outdoor tables and chairs are brought out of storage and street cafés and *Schanigärten* emerge. *Schanigärten* can be small gardens with soft lighting or candlelight, or larger patios with large benches that are shared by a couple of restaurants. These tables fill up quickly while the indoor seats tend to remain unoccupied.

The Würstelstand

If you need to grab something quick to eat, your best option is a *Würstelstand*. They are virtually everywhere and offer some very tasty snacks. There is such a wide variety of sausages that it's easy to become confused. However, don't take the easy way out and only order a hot dog, because you will deprive yourself of the more savory offerings. A *Bratwurst* is a fried sausage. A *Burenwurst*, on the other hand, is boiled. A *Weisswurst* is a fat white sausage containing herbs. A *Debreziner* is a spicy paprika sausage, and a *Käsekrainer* has chunks of cheese inside. *Currywurst* is yet another option. If you prefer something less spicy, order a hot dog, which is just that, a hot dog stuffed into a delicious long roll; or a *Frankfurter*, also similar to a hot dog, but served on a plate with some mustard and a roll on the side. *Leberkäse* is a common item on the *Würstelstand* menu, even though it is not a sausage. It is sliced from a loaf of meat that is a mixture of liver, pork, bacon, onions, and spices, and served on a roll.

113

Würstelstände, which offer a wide array of sausages, can be found on almost any street corner.

Be sure to specify whether you want it *vom Schwein* (pork) or *vom Pferd* (horse). You may be asked if you want your order with ketchup, *süssen Senf* (sweet mustard), or *scharfen Senf* (hot mustard).

FAST FOOD

Although eating out in Austria is generally not cheap, there are several options for cheap fast food. In addition to the *Würstelständ,* you can buy pre-made cold sandwiches (usually different forms of ham sandwiches) at the bakeries *Anker* and *Ströck*. Open-face sandwiches are sold at *Der Mann, Duran,* and *Trzesniewski*. In fact, many Austrians buy open-face sandwiches from these stores to serve at home for lunch and special occasions. You can also have sandwiches made at the meat counter in a supermarket. You could try *Nordsee,* a fast food chain specializing in fish and shellfish, although the prices are not low. McDonald's, Subway, and Pizza Hut from the United States have made inroads into Austria. Be forewarned, though, that you will be charged for ketchup at McDonald's. Also, dirty trays are left behind for the staff to collect. A nice change of pace are the tasty *Döner Kebabs* (pita bread stuffed with lamb and vegetables) sold at Middle Eastern kiosks and restaurants. In winter, little stalls offer *heisse Maroni* (roasted chestnuts) and *Kartofelpuffer*. The latter are similar to hash brown potatoes and are smothered in garlic.

NONALCOHOLIC BEVERAGES

Perhaps the best way to quench your thirst is with *Apfelsaft* (apple juice) or an *Apfelsaft gespritzt* (apple juice mixed with sparkling mineral water). Soft drinks are very popular, including *Soda Zitrone*, a lemon soda, and *Almdudler*, a soft drink made with herbs that closely resembles ginger ale. The Austrians are proud of their water, which is just about the best in the world. It comes from the Alps and is so clear that it is better than bottled water.

AUSTRIAN WINES

Unlike many of their neighbors, Austrians drink a substantial amount of wine. Wine cultivation and drinking have their roots in the Celtic and Roman periods. Sixty percent of all wines are cultivated in Lower Austria, in the Wachau valley and the *Weinviertel*. The Wachau is a scenic valley of terraced vineyards climbing up the hills, alongside the Danube River between Krems and Melk. The *Weinviertel* (wine quarter), located in the northern part of Lower Austria, is the largest wine-growing region in Austria. Much of the famous *Grüner Veltliner* is produced here. One of the most popular white wines, it has won awards for the best wine grown in Vienna. The province of Burgenland, known primarily for its red wines, produces 32 percent of all wine. Styria contributes 7 percent, and the remaining one percent is grown on the hills surrounding Vienna.

Head into Lower Austria, Burgenland, or Styria if you enjoy wine tasting. You can then buy your favorite right on the spot. Most Austrian wine is consumed locally, with only about 20 percent exported. Overall, when compared with wines from other countries, the quality of Austrian wine ranges from average to very good. Most of the vintages are best when they are young, and this is the reason behind the *Heurigen*.

Heurigen

For centuries, local wine producers have served wine to their customers right where the grapes are grown. A pine branch hung on a pole outside a house in the wine villages surrounding Vienna informed passers-by that the year's wine was available. Emperor Josef II legalized the practice in 1784. Originally, these locales were only allowed to sell what had been produced on their own land, so people brought along picnics to enjoy with the wine. This continues today at certain out-of-the-way *Heurigen*. The word *Heurige*, which refers to a place where you can buy and drink new wine, comes from the Austrian term for "the current year," or *heuer*. Thus, *Heurige* also means "this year's wine." The wine becomes "old" after St. Martin's Day on November 11 and can no longer be called *Heurige*.

A refreshing way to enjoy the wine, which may seem odd at first, is to drink it *gespritzt*: carbonated mineral water is ordered separately, and mixed with the wine.

In the autumn, shortly after the grape harvest, *Most* and *Sturm* are available at *Heurigen* and jugs are sold to take home. *Most* is semi-fermented grape juice with a very low alcohol content, and *Sturm* (or storm) is fermented grape juice that is not yet wine. *Sturm* may not appear to be strong at first, but drink it in moderation because it can hit you without warning. For those who do not drink wine, nonalcoholic beverages are limited in certain *Heurigen*. True to their original purpose, some *Heurigen* serve only grape juice. Others, however, also offer apple juice, lemonade, and *Almdudler*.

You really must visit a *Heurige* if you are in Vienna, or are passing through a little wine village. Although the wine is the main reason to visit, nondrinkers can enjoy the scenery, atmosphere, and food. Most *Heurigen* have beautiful gardens where you can sit for hours and enjoy the warm summer weather. In winter, the festivities move in to warm and cozy surroundings. Several *Heurigen* have lovely views of the nearby vineyards. The atmosphere is relaxed and it is a good place for children. In fact, a few *Heurigen* have play areas in the gardens. Often, traditional Viennese songs, sung to the accompaniment of an accordion and violins, make the *Heurige* experience complete.

Many people visit the *Heurige* just to have a glass or two of wine, but if you don't sample the food, you'll be missing a real part of Austria. While wine and other drinks are ordered from the waiter, you must head to the food counter if you want to eat. Certain items, like *Wiener Schnitzel*, are not on display and must be ordered. Unlike the drinks, which are paid for at the end of the evening, you must pay immediately at the food counter. Meat is priced according to weight.

The dishes available vary with each *Heurige* but can include cooked meats, sandwich meats, cheeses, salads, and breads. Some favorites are *Kümmelbraten*, a delicious if somewhat fatty pork roast with caraway seeds. *Schweinsbraten* (roast pork), *Schinken* (ham), and *Laibchen* (meatballs) are also good. A *Knödel* (dumpling) and sauerkraut can accompany these. There are several varieties of *Auflauf* (soufflé), and a whole array of tasty salads, including *Kartoffel* or *Erdäpfelsalat* (potato salad), *Schwarzwurzelsalat* (an excellent salad made with a vegetable similar to asparagus, in a dill cream sauce), *Fisolensalat* (green bean salad), *rote Rübensalat* (beet salad), and *Krautsalat* (cabbage salad). There are several types of bread and rolls available and you may choose to top them off with *Liptauer*, a cream cheese, paprika, and chive spread. If you would like *Senf* (mustard), for which there is an extra charge, specify *süss* (sweet) or *scharf* (strong). Most *Heurigen* do not serve desserts, and others only *Strudel*. Not all *Heurigen* serve coffee or tea either.

117

Most guidebooks will direct you to Grinzing and Sievering in Vienna for your *Heurige* experience. This area, however, is flooded with tourists. If you want a more authentic experience, or just a more peaceful one, head to Neustift am Walde, Hietzing, or Nussdorf. (You can take a 40-minute tour of the vineyards north of Vienna on a quaint railway that begins and ends in Nussdorf.) *Stadtheurigen* (city *Heurigen*) can be found throughout the 1st district. If you are really interested in partaking in Austrian culture, go into Perchtoldsdorf, south of Vienna, or Stammersdorf, north of the city in the 21st district. Outside of Vienna, there are wonderful *Heurigen* in the Wachau valley, *Weinviertel*, and other wine-producing areas.

OTHER ALCOHOLIC BEVERAGES

Of the beer produced in Austria, *Gösser* is the most well known. However, it is not ranked among the best in the region. If you are a beer drinker, you might prefer the excellent *Budweiser* (the original *Budweiser* beer, not to be confused with the beer made by Anheuser-Busch in the United States), or *Pilsen* from the nearby Czech Republic. If you do want to try the local beer, be sure to specify if you want it *vom Fass* (draught) or in *eine Flasche* (in a bottle). If you want it *vom Fass*, decide between *ein kleines* (small) and *ein grosses* (large).

Austrians do drink hard liquor, and *Schnaps* is by far their favorite. *Schnaps* is incredibly strong liquor made from just about anything from fruits to herbs. The most popular are made from apples, plums, pears, and apricots. *Schnaps* are normally served after a hearty meal and should not be sipped, but downed quickly.

TOASTING

A toast is commonly made before the first drink. Most toasts are simple—a few nice words to honor a friend, family member, or special guest, or to celebrate a certain holiday. When the toast has been made, glasses are lifted and everyone clinks everyone else's glass, looking the person directly in the eye and saying, *"Prost."*

Biergartens open all across Austria with the arrival of warm spring weather.

OUTDOOR DINING

You will know spring has arrived when virtually every eatery and café sets up tables and chairs on the street. *Schanigärten* and *Biergartens* suddenly appear, and the gardens at the *Heurigen* come alive. The *Donauinsel* (Danube Island) and the *Am Kai* area along the Danube between *Schwedenplatz* and *Friedensbrücke* are lined with outdoor restaurants. The university campus at the AKH (*Allgemeines Krankenhaus*) has a number of open-air beer gardens and restaurants open until 2 am, where you can take in a cultural event while dining. Another option, in Vienna, is to spend a warm evening in front of the *Rathaus* (City Hall), watching filmed opera on a giant screen for free while eating and drinking. The *Rathaus* square is covered with stalls that offer food from over 17 countries.

CAFÉS (KAFFEEHÄUSER)

Although cafés can be found throughout Austria, they are a Viennese institution. The Viennese linger in cafés, reading, writing, thinking, and discussing, much as their ancestors did. According to popular history, the first coffeehouse was opened in Vienna shortly after the Turkish siege of 1683. Beating a hasty retreat, the Turks left behind bags of coffee beans. A Pole, Georg Franz Kolschitzky, is said to have requested the beans as a reward for his military achievements. Only he knew how to process them into coffee, and the story goes that he opened the first Viennese coffeehouse, the Sign of the Blue Bottle, near Stephansdom. Yet, evidence suggests that coffee was already being drunk in Vienna prior to this time.

Cafés played an important role in society, especially in fin-de-siècle Vienna, up until 1938. As the arts flourished, intellectual life centered around the cafés. Many of the most creative and brilliant Viennese had their *Stammcafé*, or regular coffeehouse, where they spent a good portion of their day. Here they met with others to debate the issues of the day. Among the more prominent guests at the Café Central on Herrengasse were authors Arthur Schnitzler and Hugo Hofmannsthal. Even Leon Trotsky was known to have frequented the café. Gustav Mahler regularly visited the Café Imperial. Sigmund Freud liked the Café Landtmann, and the composer Franz Lehár spent much time at Café Sperl. Artists such as Oskar Kokoschka, Gustav Klimt, and Egon Schiele, and the composer Alban Berg could all be seen at the Café Museum. Sadly, all of this ended with the annexation of Austria by Hitler, and this aspect of Viennese life never fully recovered after World War II.

Cafés tend to be a bit formal. The waiters dress in tuxedos and even the clientele take care to look nice. In fact, before or after the theater or a concert, you might see patrons in tuxedos and sequined gowns. Even though the waiters may not be the friendliest servers you'll ever encounter, they will not push you out. You can stay for hours, even if you've only ordered one cup of coffee. Newspapers and magazines are put out to help you while away the time. Other customers may play chess or cards. In the past, cafés only offered a small selection of pastries. Today, however, many cafés not only offer pastries, but also alcohol, savory snacks, and sometimes even a full menu.

KONDITOREI

If you like pastries, visit one of the countless *Konditorei*. Of these, *Demmel* is the most famous and clearly ranks among the best. Other elegant *Konditorei* can also be found within the 1st district, primarily on Kärntner Strasse, Graben, and Neuer Markt. There is also a whole other class of *Konditorei*. While the quality of their pastries is still very good, their lower prices reflect the cramped, stark, utilitarian surroundings. You won't find any cozy plush furniture here, and in fact, most have only a standing section. The most common *Konditorei* is the *Aida* chain. *Konditorei* are easily recognized by the elaborate marzipan figurines and other sweets in the windows.

COFFEES

Ordering a cup of coffee in Vienna is not as easy as it may seem, as there are several types to be had. Because coffee is made with Italian espresso machines, it can be very strong. *Mokka* is black coffee, a *kleiner* (small) or *grosser* (large) *Brauner* is coffee with milk, and café latte is espresso with lots of steamed milk. Other choices are:

* *Melange*, coffee mixed with steamed milk
* *Kapuziner* or cappuccino, served with whipped cream
* *Einspänner*, black coffee topped with a heaped serving of whipped cream and served in a tall glass
* *Fiaker*, black coffee with rum or brandy served in a glass
* *Kaffee Johann Strauss*, a large black coffee served with whipped cream and apricot liqueur
* *Wiener Eiskaffee*, cold coffee poured over vanilla ice cream topped with whipped cream
* *Türkischer*, very strong Turkish coffee

In cafés coffee is always served on a silver tray with a glass of water.

You can enjoy a café even if you don't drink coffee. If you want a cup of tea, ask for *ein schwarzen Tee* and specify if you want it with milk or lemon. You could also try *Früchtetee* (fruit tea) or *Grüner Tee*

121

(green tea). There is also a wide array of herbal teas such as *Fenchel* (fennel), *Kamille* (camomile), and *Pfefferminz* (peppermint). For those with a sweet tooth, hot chocolate is always a good choice.

SUPERMARKETS

There is no shortage of supermarkets. Traditionally, Austrians purchase groceries in small quantities daily, so every neighborhood has at least one small store. This turns out to be very convenient because the opening hours are limited. Supermarkets close between 6 pm and 7:30 pm on weekdays, and at 5 pm on Saturdays. They are closed on Sundays. A couple of *Billa* supermarkets are open longer hours, and on Sundays. This is permitted because they are located at the *Wien Nord* train station and the Vienna International Airport. Technically, they are only allowed to sell food to be eaten on the road, so you may find certain sections closed off. The *Billa* at *Bahnhof Wien Nord* is open on Saturdays from 7 am till 7:30 pm, and on Sundays from 8 am until 7:30 pm. The *Billa* at the airport is open daily from 7:30 am until 10 pm. If you are in a hurry, you can find staple goods in convenience stores of some large gas stations.

Grocery stores in Austria, and especially in Vienna, usually carry a wide range of products. If you are looking for something particular, there are a few specialty stores in Vienna. Bobby's near the *Naschmarkt* has a good selection of products from Britain. Nearby are stores that carry Italian foods and Asian goods, like Piccini and the Asia Shop, respectively. Europa Delikatessen, Neli Malkov, and Rebenwurzel & Co. in the 2nd district sell kosher products.

Some Austrian shopping habits you should be aware of are described in the previous chapter (see "Food," pages 92–94).

NASCHMARKT

In Vienna, you can buy fresh produce at the *Naschmarkt* in the 6th district. This is a huge outdoor market made up of many different stalls selling an incredible variety of items. The produce here is usually cheaper and fresher, although Susan once returned home with a bagful of rotten tomatoes from an unscrupulous vendor. Generally, you place your order by weight or pieces, and the vendors select and bag the items. If you prefer to pick out your own produce, demand that you be able to do so. Once again, you should bring a heavy canvas bag to carry everything home in. In addition to the usual fruit, vegetables, and fresh meat and seafood, the *Naschmarkt* is the place to go for special items such as sweet potatoes, tropical fruit, exotic spices, cheeses, nuts, olives, and Halal meat (ritually cut and blessed by an Islamic cleric). There are also stalls selling flowers and clothing.

The *Naschmarkt* is not merely a grocery market. Many stalls sell prepared snacks and sandwiches. In fact, this is one version of how the market got its name. The word *naschen* means to "nibble", and it is said that the name evolved into *Naschmarkt* because everyone walks around nibbling on something. Another story is that the name is derived from shouts of "*An aschen*" or "*Eine Asche*" meaning "ashes," which were sold in the market as detergent. Yet another version states that in very old German, the word *Asch* used to mean milk pail, and the name comes from the fresh milk sold at the market.

There are also indoor markets on the Landstrasse Hauptstrasse near the *Wien Mitte* train station in the 3rd district, at the Sonnbergplatz in the 19th district, at the Nussdorfer Halle in the 9th district, and at the Karmelitermarkt in the 2nd district. A free shuttle bus runs between Rotenturmstrasse in the city center and the latter.

HOLIDAY MEALS

Fasching and Lent
Fasching begins on November 11 and continues until Ash Wednesday. *Fasching* is a time to eat, drink, and be merry before Lent arrives on Ash Wednesday. It is a festive season when deep-fried pastries and *Krapfen* (donuts filled with apricot jam or vanilla cream) are especially common.

123

For Roman Catholics, Lent is a time of sacrifice and fasting as they prepare for Easter. In fact, the German word for Lent is *Fastenzeit*, or "a time of fasting." Ash Wednesday begins the Lenten season when Catholics are not allowed to eat meat. In keeping with the rules, but somewhat contrary to the spirit of the order, many Austrians begin Lent by enjoying *Heringsschmaus*, a huge herring feast.

Easter

The days preceding Easter Sunday have religious significance. On *Gründonnerstag*, Maundy Thursday, some people eat spinach and green colored eggs. *Grün* stems from an old German word for "weeping," but also means green, hence the green food. On Good Friday, a holy day, many people fast. On Easter, a day of celebration, Austrians indulge in food and sweets.

Colored hardboiled eggs representing life and fertility are identified with Easter, but their use predates Easter to pagan festivals honoring spring. *Osterstriezel* (braided white bread) and *Pinze* (sweet white bread) are also eaten at breakfast. Most Austrians feast on an Easter dinner of ham, *Schinken im Brotteig* (ham baked in dough), or turkey. Cakes, chocolates, and marzipan are shaped into bunnies, lambs, chicks, and eggs.

Spargelzeit

You know spring has arrived when *Spargel* (asparagus) makes its appearance. During asparagus season, the delicate vegetable is featured in special dishes on many menus, and is promoted by every supermarket. It comes in both the white and green varieties.

Pilzwochen

Just as asparagus signals the arrival of spring, *Pilzwochen* lets us know that autumn is here. During "mushroom weeks," restaurants serve special dishes containing several varieties of fresh mushrooms. You will also see a wide variety on sale.

Fresh green and white asparagus appear in various dishes during Spargelzeit.

Martinigansl

St. Martin's Day, November 11, is celebrated with a heavy but delicious meal of *Martinigansl* or St. Martin's Goose. To many Austrians, St. Martin is an important saint. Born in the 4th century, he was a humble man who became a monk. According to legend, when he found out that he was to be named bishop, he hid to avoid taking the position. A honking goose gave him away, and now the bird is sacrificed in honor of St. Martin.

The goose is served with red cabbage (which helps with digestion), dumplings, and a hearty red wine or a full-bodied beer. If you are invited to someone's house at this time, expect *Martinigansl* to be served. This special meal is also available in many restaurants.

Game

Austrians have always enjoyed hunting, as evidenced by the decor of many eating establishments. During hunting season in autumn, wild game is often found on menus. You can choose from *Hirsch* (venison),

Ente (duck), *Fasan* (pheasant), *Hase* (hare), *Kaninchen* (rabbit), and *Wildschwein* or *Eber* (wild boar). If you would like to prepare some at home, wild game can be bought at stands in the *Naschmarkt* and the *Landstrasser Markt*.

Christmas

Traditionally Austrians eat carp on Christmas Eve. These fish can live to a ripe old age, and it was once believed that if you ate carp you could also live a long life. Some Austrians have broken away from this tradition and prefer to eat goose, chicken, or turkey for Christmas.

Like Easter, most Christmas food is sweet. *Stollen* (sweet bread) and *Kletzenbrot* (Christmas fruit bread) proliferate. There are several varieties of Christmas cookies. Some of the better-known are *Husarenkrapferl* (Husar Rounds), cookies flavored with almonds and a dab of apricot jam in the center; *Vanillekipferl* (vanilla crescents); *Kokosbusserl* (coconut kisses); *Zimtsterne* (cinnamon stars), and *Ischler Nussbusserln* (nut kisses). *Lebkuchen*, spice cookies flavored with cinnamon, cloves, and honey, are also a favorite. These cookies date back to the Middle Ages when sugar was difficult to come by. The *Christkindl* markets are also full of tempting sweets such as *Negerküsse* (chocolate-dipped marshmallow confections), red candy apples, and cotton candy.

New Year's Eve/Silvester

As in many other countries, the New Year is rung in with *Sekt* (sparkling wine). Because many people celebrate midnight outside in freezing temperatures, *Glühwein*, a hot spiced wine sold at outdoor markets throughout the winter season, and *Punsch* are very popular. Little marzipan pigs, mushrooms, clovers, and chimneysweeps are given to friends and family as good luck charms for the coming year; they also decorate pastries and cakes. Superstition has it that lobster and crayfish are not to be eaten, because they walk backwards, making them counter to the New Year spirit of looking to the future.

— Chapter Six —

LANGUAGE

The German language can be mind-boggling. German, surprisingly enough, is a relative of English. In fact, German, English, and Dutch are known as West German languages. High German, which is used today, comes from a Saxon dialect. Other German speakers often regard the version spoken in Austria as singsongy.

Once your ear has become used to the language and you have taken a few German lessons, things get easier. Fine, you think. I'll be living in Vienna, the cosmopolitan capital city of Austria where they only speak the formal German (*Hoch Deutsch*). Well, think again. Vienna probably has more dialects within its districts than any other

Austrian city, as it has always been home to a variety of ethnic groups, primarily from neighboring countries. The language is a cache of terms from Czech, Hungarian, Italian, Yiddish, and even medieval Teutonic. For example, the word *Beisel*, which refers to a bar, is derived from the Hebrew *bayith*, meaning house. In fact, Viennese theater and literature are where the Viennese dialect shines through. Many operettas by Viennese composers such as Strauss and Lehár also make use of the dialect spoken by the common man. It takes a special ear and frame of mind to understand what is being said.

Here is an example of a *Wiener Deutsch*, or Viennese German, sentence, broken up into phrases. The proper German equivalents are given in the next column. The English translation follows. See if you can make it out:

Viennese German
Kuaz und Guad von Herbert Pirker
Denkmoeschuz-wikl
Min schenbrunna bod
Haums wos beinaund
De aan woens oreissn
De aundan woens eahoetn
Brenna wü kana
S denkmoeaumd
Benimmd si
Wia wauns des soezaumd waa
Und wauns so weidaged
Kennan
Wuaschd ob des bod
Offn is oda zua
Olle midaund
Bodn ge

If you thought German was difficult, wait until you hear the Viennese dialect. This sign translates as "Weil keine brennt gerne zu viel," or "Because no one likes to get too burnt."

Proper German
Kurz und Gut von Herbert Pirker
DenkmalSchutz-Wickel
Mit Schönbrunner Bad
Haben's etwas bei einander
Die einen wollen es abreisen
Die anderen wollen es erhalten
Brennen will keiner
Das Denkmalamt
Bennimt sich
Wie wenn es das Salzamt wäre
Und wenn es so weiter geht
Können
Wurst ob das bad
Offen ist oder zu
Alle mit einander
baden gehen

129

Hier standen im 15. Jahrhundert das Leinwandhaus, die Verkaufsstelle und Börse der Leinwandhändler und das Zunfthaus der Schuster, das Schubhaus, begrenzt vom Linnengässchen und der Schranne. Beide Zunfthäuser wurden im 16.u.17. Jahrhundert als Schuldenarrest und Richtstätte verwendet. 1861 erstand ein neues Gebäude das 1877 von der Ersten österreichischen Spar-Casse erworben wurde. Dieses fiel 1945 Bomben und Feuer zum Opfer und wurde in den Jahren 1949/50 durch die ERSTE ÖSTERREICHISCHE SPAR-CASSE aufgebaut, wobei die Camesinagasse, früher Linnengässchen, in die Baufläche einbezogen wurde.

A little knowledge of German will help you find your way around a number of cultural venues where no translations are offered.

English Translation
"Short and Good" from Herbert Pirker
Monument Trouble

There is statue protection trouble at the Schönbrunner pool. They have a difficult situation. One wants to tear it down, the other wants to keep it up. No one wants to pay. The Statue office behaves itself as the Salt office would. And if it goes too far, then it doesn't matter if the pool is open or closed, as we will all be in trouble.

THE INFORMAL AND FORMAL "YOU"

German is very formal. While the English language does not distinguish between a formal and an informal "you," in German, such formality is very much in use. *Du* is the informal "you," and *Sie* the formal "you." If, for example, you were talking to an adult whom you had just met, you would use the *Sie* form of "you." For example:

*Wo wohnen **Sie**?* (Where do you live?)

If I knew the person well, and they asked me to please use "per Du" then I would say the following instead:

*Wo wohnst **Du**?* (Where do you live?)

If you are speaking to a child or to someone you have become friendly with, use the *Du* form. Some of the older folk always expect the courtesy of *Sie*, even from a long-time acquaintance. The formal *Sie* would also be used with shopkeepers, your boss, and the stranger on the street.

SENTENCE CONSTRUCTION

Sentence construction is one of the most difficult aspects of learning German. The reason that it is hard to master is that in German, the verb often ends a sentence, whereas in the English translation it would come in the center. For example:

*Ich **muss** in die Schule **gehen**.* (I must go to school.)
*Ich **hole** dich um 4 Uhr **ab**.* (I will pick you up at 4 o'clock.)

Thus, one is forced to listen intently to what is said in order to understand the meaning of a long drawn-out sentence. On the other hand, it is a good means of teaching children to listen. The problem for the student of the German language is that, when speaking, one cannot translate from one's own language, but instead must think in a whole different way. It is an experience similar in many ways to playing the piano for the first time.

131

THE MANY DIFFERENT CASES

The declension of the cases of the German language is the cause of many mistakes. The English language does not change with the case being used, but German does. There are four cases: nominative, accusative, genitive, and dative. In each case the pronoun, adjective, and noun change. For example:

Nominative	*Mein guter Freund*	my good friend
Accusative	*Meinen guten Freund*	my good friend
Genitive	*Meines Guten Freundes*	of my good friend
Dative	*Meinem guten Freund*	to my good friend

CAPITALIZING NOUNS

One simple and seemingly easy rule is that all nouns are capitalized. This would make any elementary student very happy indeed. However, confusion sometimes arises when you are not sure whether the noun is actually a person or a thing. For example:

Die Rose ist eine Blume. (The rose is a flower.)

GENDER

Nouns can be feminine, as in *Die Zeitung* (the newspaper); masculine, as in *Der Mann* (the man); or neutral, as in *Das Restaurant* (the restaurant). There is no rhyme or reason for which noun gets which gender, but there are patterns. Take this as a challenge for the memory.

COMPOUND WORDS

Compound words are mesmerizing. Several words are "scrunched" into one. Some examples are:

Kinderbewahrungsanstalten (childcare)
Donaudampfschifffahrtsgesellschaftskapitän (Captain of the
    Danube Steamship Company)
Unabhängigkeitserklärungen (Declaration of Independence)
Wiederherstellungsbestrebungen (Endeavor to reconstruct)

GERMAN IS PHONETIC

The loveliest part of the German language is that it is phonetic. All vowels and consonants are pronounced, and the tricky ones lie only with a few sounds:

reich (rich), like *Loch* in Loch Ness but pronounced very softly
Schüssel (bowl) has the "sh" sound, as in **sh**ame
zahlen (to pay), pronounced "ts"
Mutter (mother), same vowel sound as in b**oo**k
Vogel (bird), pronounced with a hard "f," as in **f**ood
stehen (stand), pronounced as if there was a "ch" between **s** and **t**
stoß (push, knock) ends with a sharp "s." The German language is
    slowly evolving to replace the **ß** with a double s, or "ss".
Quelle (source), pronounced **kv**
Julia (proper name), pronounced **y** as in **y**ule
wandern (to hike), pronounced **v** as in **v**an

Pay special attention to *umlaute*, fondly known as the "rascalion upper double dots." If pronounced badly, the word is not understood. *Süd* (south) is like the French "u" as in s**u**r; *Männer* (men) uses the same vowel sound as in f**ai**r; and *schön* (pretty) is like the "o" in s**o**me. If you are typing a letter and do not have *umlaute* on your keyboard, type an **e** after the vowel; for example, instead of *schön*, write *schoen*. Remember, the secret is to soften those vowel sounds.

133

ANIMAL NAMES AND THEIR CALL

One of the most interesting aspects of the language is that animals are named according to the sound they make: *Kuck-kuck* is cuckoo bird, *Pfau* is peacock, *Uhu* is owl, *Kuh* is cow, *Bär* is bear, and *Krähen* or *KraKra* is crow.

NUMBERS

Reading or writing numbers can be an extremely trying endeavor. Either way, one must think backwards after the number 20. For example, 21 is read as "one and twenty" or *einundzwanzig*. When writing a number, it is always good practice to leave plenty of space and start writing the number as it is read off.

The next challenge is to tell the time. If it is 8:30, the time is read as *halb neun* and sometimes written as $^1/_2$ 9. If it is 8:15, it will be read as *viertel neun* and sometimes written as $^1/_4$ 9. Take note that Austrians may also write or say the time using the 24-hour clock.

A COMMENT FROM MARK TWAIN

Mark Twain, the famous American writer and satirist, felt very strongly about the German language. This is what he wrote:

"Surely there is not another language that is so slipshod and systemless, and so slippery and elusive to the grasp. One is washed about in it, hither and thither, in the most helpless way; and when at last he thinks he has captured a rule which offers firm ground to take a rest on amid the general rage and turmoil of the ten parts of speech, he turns over the page and reads, 'Let the pupil make careful note of the following *exceptions.*' ... There are ten parts of speech, and they are all troublesome. An average sentence, in a German newspaper, is a sublime and impressive curiosity; it occupies a quarter of a column; it contains all the ten parts of speech—not in regular order, but mixed; it is built mainly of compound words constructed by the writer on the spot, and not to be found in any dictionary—six or seven words compacted into one, without joint or seam—that is, without hyphens; it treats of fourteen or fifteen different subjects, each enclosed in a parenthesis of its own, with here and there extra parentheses, making pens with pens; finally, all the parentheses and reparentheses are massed together between a couple of king-parentheses, one of which is placed in the first line of the majestic sentence and the other in the middle of the last line of it—*after which comes the* VERB, and you find out for the first time what the man has been talking about; and after the verb—merely by way of ornament, as far as I can make out—the writer shovels in '*haben sind gewesen gehabt haben geworden sein,*' or words to that effect, and the monument is finished. I suppose that this closing hurrah is in the nature of the flourish to a man's signature—not necessary, but pretty. German books are easy enough to read when you hold them before the looking-glass or stand on your head—so as to reverse the construction—but I think that to learn to read and understand a German newspaper is a thing which must always remain an impossibility to a foreigner.

"My philological studies have satisfied me that a gifted person ought to learn English (barring spelling and pronouncing) in thirty hours, French in thirty days, and German in thirty years. It seems manifest, then, that the latter tongue ought to be trimmed down and repaired. If it is to remain as it is, it ought to be gently and reverently set aside among the dead languages, for only the dead have time to learn it."

—Mark Twain, "The Awful German Language"
from *A Tramp Abroad*, 1880

— Chapter Seven —

SOCIAL AND BUSINESS CUSTOMS

SOCIAL CUSTOMS

Austria is built on "the right way" of doing things. In the cities, customs haven't changed much since the time of the Habsburgs. The formalities are overwhelming at first. After a while, some become second nature and can be charming.

Greeting One Another

The greeting is essential in many social situations. When walking into a public area, whether a boutique, coffee shop, or doctor's office, an obligatory *"Grüss Gott"* (hello) is said. In some of the nicer boutiques, a woman may be greeted as *"Gnädige Frau,"* an old-fashioned term meaning "most gracious woman." When leaving, one would say *"auf Wiedersehen"* or *"Wiederschaun"* (goodbye). This greeting does not apply when out of confined spaces, unless you pass someone in your apartment building.

You will notice that when walking or jogging about, Austrians will not go out of their way to greet you. This can be rather puzzling as they do it automatically in the shops. It is also understood that a younger person should greet a mature person, and not the other way around. This can change dramatically in villages or smaller cities around Austria, which tend to be friendlier and less inhibited.

Shaking Hands

Shaking hands is another important gesture for first meetings. Generally, the woman offers her hand to the man, and the older person to the younger. Handshakes are firm, with direct eye contact, and you usually say your last name without prefacing it with a greeting.

At a party or a dinner at a friend's house, wait until the host introduces you before you go around introducing yourself. The host will generally introduce you by your last name. While being introduced, you shake each person's hand accordingly. At large parties, the introduction seems to take forever. However, Julie finds it to be a wonderful way to break the ice.

Kissing Each Other's Cheek

Once you have become close to someone, and are on a first name basis, you may kiss each other's cheek in greeting. If you are a woman, you have the privilege of kissing both women and men on each cheek: first right, then left. A man would only shake the hand of another man. If unsure what to do, go for the handshake and wait until the Austrian makes the next move.

Küss die Hand

A very Austrian male greeting is the one called *Küss die Hand*. It means to kiss the back of the hand, but the man never actually kisses the hand, merely the air above it. The custom is old-fashioned and very formal. You could envision Emperor Franz Josef doing it with his many women friends.

The greeting is used at formal events such as balls, weddings, special parties, and among the supposedly defunct aristocracy. The male will normally be older and from an old Austrian family, or a younger man with savoir-faire who wants to make a good impression. We wouldn't suggest this practice to any non-Austrian.

Body language isn't excessive after kissing or shaking hands. Hugging is not done except with close family members or with a friend that you haven't seen in a long time. Gesticulating to put a point across is rarely done. Simply put, the Austrian way is reserved and calm unless driving on the Autobahn (freeway)!

Manners

Manners on Public Transportation

The public transportation system is a good example of Austrian civility. Before getting on the train, tram, or bus, everyone waits for the people on board to alight. There is also special seating near the exit doors for the elderly, pregnant women, children, and the handicapped. Lively discussions are rarely carried on between strangers, although these do take place, more often in the smaller cities than in the larger ones. No one goes out of his or her way to make small talk, even about the weather.

Children are also well controlled on public transportation, and do not chatter, jump, or run around. Our inference is that older ladies can stare so creepily at children who have made any untoward noise that they are dumbstruck forevermore.

Furthermore, even though eating and drinking are allowed on public transportation, one seldom sees passengers taking the privilege. Drinking coffee on the go is never done as coffee drinking is seen as something one does to relax.

Table Manners

Table manners are similar throughout Europe. When invited to someone's home for a meal, start eating only after the host has begun. It is customary to say *"Guten Appetit"* or *"Mahlzeit,"* which means "have a good meal," beforehand. The former is for more formal situations and the latter is used among friends and family. The napkin then goes on the lap, the fork in the left hand, and the knife in the right. The hands are above the table at all times. Elbows are close to the body and never put on the table. While pausing to drink or talk during a meal, put your silverware on either side of the plate facing downward. Close your mouth when chewing and, please, no slurping while eating soup. Only take what you can eat. When the meal is finished, the knife and fork are put together on the right side of the plate.

Telephone Manners

Austrians address each other in a certain way on the phone. When making a call or answering the telephone, they state their family name first to immediately inform the other party of their identity.

Smoking

Austrians love to smoke. As a consequence, cigarettes are ubiquitous. The sad truth is that cigarette smoking is on the rise among women and teenagers. There is no lobby against smoking, and no posters or commercials educate the public on the health risks involved. Austria Tabak, the tobacco state monopoly, recently celebrated its most profitable financial year.

It is difficult to find restaurants that are either well ventilated or which serve dinner early. Most bars, jazz centers, and dancing areas are so filled with cigarette smoke that it is impossible to breathe. Windows are closed in winter, and air-conditioning is nonexistent in the summer. In addition, your clothes take on a horrible stale smell.

There is hope. Smoking is not permitted on public transportation, in underground stations, government offices, elevators, and non-

smoking areas of restaurants, although these are right next to the smoking areas. Things are changing ever so slightly, and not enough to make a difference.

Tipping

Tipping is normal in restaurants and bars, and for taxi drivers and porters. There are many others who also look forward to a tip.

Blue-collar workers who do something special often get a tip. For example, the repairman who fixes your heating would get ATS 50; the postman who delivers a package up three flights of stairs ATS 20; and a mover, ATS 100 per day. The tips aren't mandatory, and are appreciated all the more for it.

During the Christmas season, it's also nice to remember the people who often provide services to you. Money, alcohol, or gifts are graciously accepted; the first is the most welcome. The people you shouldn't forget are your cleaning lady, the trash collectors (if you live in a house), the postman, the building superintendent (*Hausbesorger*, if you live in an apartment), and your hairdresser.

Noise

Noise levels are kept at a minimum. In fact, while driving, it is against the law to use the horn except in extreme emergencies.

In public dining or drinking areas, it is common courtesy not to talk above a certain pitch, as it would disturb other customers. There are also signs up in outdoor eating areas that warn the public to keep their voices down, in order not to disturb others. Julie and her friends have occasionally been told by maîtres d' to please keep the noise down, much to their embarrassment.

The children rarely make noise in public. The only places you notice them are at playgrounds or amusement parks. They, too, have been conditioned not to disturb others.

At home, in your house or apartment, noise is also kept at a minimum. You never hear music blaring out of any home, and there are, in fact, apartment rules prohibiting it. Private parties are usually toned down past 10 pm. Taking care of the lawn, working on the car, and the like, are also never done on Sunday, as it is considered the day of rest.

What is noisy to one is not to another. A rule of thumb is to keep your ears open, and try to blend in.

The Dress Code

The dress code varies from one occasion to the next, but the Austrian is conformist, and will never wear something ostentatious.

When attending a theater or concert performance, one always dresses up in formal wear (long gowns are usually only worn for balls but they can be worn for the opera as well). Julie has known young people who were not allowed into the Opera House for a performance because they were wearing jeans.

Dinner at a restaurant requires semiformal wear: no jeans, beach sandals, or shorts. It is extremely embarrassing when you are thrown out for improper attire. However, in the summer, the *Schanigärten* and *Heurigen* do not care what you wear.

Going for walks in the country sometimes means dressing in *Trachten* or traditional Austrian clothing (many stores carry a modern, affordable version): *Lederhosen* for men (usually older men) and boys; short-walking *Loden* jackets (buttons can be made out of bone or plastic) for men, women, and children; checkered or plain white shirts for men, women (sometimes with frilled collar and cuff), and children. Walkers often wear pants of linen or denim, with flowers stitched on the pockets for women; traditional *Dirndl*, or dresses, for women and girls; scarves with *Edelweiss* (mountain flower) for women and children; sturdy shoes for men and children with *Edelweiss* decoration, and similarly decorated high-heeled versions for women; and green or grey felt hats worn with a *Gamsbart* (like a shaving brush). Even if one doesn't get "into" the Austrian style of dressing, one should still dress quite nicely, meaning no jeans, T-shirts, or tennis shoes.

An Invitation to Lunch or Dinner

If you are invited to an Austrian home, be punctual, not 10 or 15 minutes late! Always bring a small gift of flowers for the hostess and a bottle of wine for the host. While these are standard, chocolates and special gifts are also appreciated.

After you enter the home, offer to take off your shoes unless told otherwise. Most homes have a myriad of slippers to be doled out, if necessary. Julie often brings her own as she can be sure they will fit, and perhaps even match her outfit. Men should stand the first time a woman enters or exits a room, but not each time thereafter.

If you are at someone's house for dinner, aperitifs are usually served beforehand. Campari soda seems to be the classic drink, but sparkling wine on its own or mixed with fruit juice is also popular. Appetizers will sometimes be served, but they are an exception.

Before beginning to eat, a toast of *"Prost, zum Wohl"* is said by the host or hostess. The company then toasts one another, looking directly at each other, clinking glasses, and saying *"Prost."*

142

Sunday dinner is a time for Austrian families to get together and share the week's gossip.

It's always nice to call the day after the event. The host will welcome it. Some people write thank-you notes as a gesture of gratitude.

Obscene Gestures

Austria isn't a country that uses its hands to express anger. However, put an Austrian behind a wheel, and, well, things are slightly different. Here you might see hands or fingers doing strange things. The standard middle finger is used when someone is cut off, but pointing to the head with the middle finger repeatedly is also common. The latter means that you are crazy or that you have *"einen Vogel im Kopf"* (a bird in your head).

143

BUSINESS CUSTOMS

The average office is formal in the way employees interact with one another and with clients. There is an emphasis on doing the "right thing." Of course, to some non-Austrians this can mean an atmosphere that is rather uptight. The greatest difference for many foreigners, however, is that what you know doesn't count as much as who you know.

Etiquette

Etiquette is standard in a business setting. Shaking a client's or a colleague's hand is customary and a good way to begin a relationship or maintain one. Punctuality is central to the process of any business meeting, and is a principle adhered to by employees. Exchanging business cards is also customary and a smart way to make contacts.

At work, the average businessman or businesswoman wears a classic suit to work, civil servants dress down, and blue-collar workers wear uniforms. For instance, garbage collectors wear orange and construction workers wear blue.

Colleagues

The people you work with are all referred to as colleagues (*Kollege/ Kollegin*), meaning people you will only relate to in a business or formal setting. It is understood that colleagues are not people you mix with on a social basis. There is a tendency to keep work and social time separate. The company doesn't put pressure on its employees to get together for social events.

Titles

There is a predisposition for the use of titles, handed down from the Habsburgs. Although the law has banned the use of noble titles, the list of professional titles is endless. The titles serve the dual purpose of advancing your status and of flattering people who will, hopefully, make a difference in your professional life.

Julie Krejci

The strict use of titles affects how Austrians perceive and relate to one another.

In addressing one another, one's boss is either Mr. (*Herr*) or Ms. (*Frau*), followed by the family name. The boss is always addressed with the formal "you" (*per Sie*). If someone were your elder, the same formality would be applicable. For your colleagues, begin with the formal "you" (*per Sie*) and address them by their last names, then, after a while, you can use the informal you (*per Du*) and call them by their first names.

In academia, *Herr Professor* or *Frau Professor* is used to address a teacher. *Frau Professor* could also be the wife of a professor, but the same would not apply to a man married to a *Frau Professor*. The title *Doktor* is held by a Ph.D., a master's degree begets you a *Herr* or a *Frau Magister*, and for an engineer (who, like *Herr Magister*, also has had six years of university training), a *Diplom-Ingenieur*.

145

Service? Was ist das?

Service is still a foreign word to many government offices, stores, restaurants, and coffee shops. In many government offices, the clerk decides when to come to your aid. If you push, the clerk will pull back.

In stores, and especially in boutiques, you are often judged by your outward appearance: hair, clothing, and shoes. Of course, it helps to have shopped there before or to know someone with a title who has sent you to "this special boutique." In larger stores, the outlook is different, but the customer is still rarely king. Try to take something back and the store employee might come up with the line that "if you can't handle the product, it's your own fault."

Restaurants and coffee shops can be mind-boggling. Getting a waiter can seem like waiting for the Red Sea to part. Even when you have the waiter's attention, they might say "just a moment." Once you are served, it is best to pay the waiter right away in order not to have to go through the same trial again.

Attitude towards Business

Austrians are not known to pursue their career aggressively. However, they are very aggressive against equal or lower ranks. They want to maintain and protect their job and salary (which they never speak about to one another) from younger, aspiring colleagues. One could equate it to a cat-and-mouse game.

Wheeling and Dealing

Austrians are thought of as businesspeople who don't like to have things in black and white, but who rather enjoy the idea of bargaining and trying different ways to get what they want. There is a saying, *"In Wien beginnt der Balkan ...,"* literally "the Balkans begin in Vienna." One could say that the old-fashioned marketplace is still at work.

The Civil Servant on the Job

Jokes are made about the clerk or official (*Beamten*). It is said that in government offices, the traffic of clerks arriving late and leaving early can be as bad as a car jam on a busy highway. Lunchtime can be, well, any time. Sick leave seems to be every other day, although after one day you need a doctor's note (still, there is no restriction on the amount of sick leave you can have). Then there are the holidays and vacations. The holidays correspond, generally, to the Catholic holidays, and vacation time depends on your status (up to eight weeks a year).

The bureaucracy is so great that it requires an astronomical workforce (25 percent of Austria's workforce) to keep it running. Employment as a clerk doesn't require much education, and many clerks are hired for social reasons, which propagates an abuse of privileges. Many clerks aspire to become tenured or to join the permanent (*pragmatisiert*) staff, as it means having job security.

Women in the Workforce

Women in Austria are at work. Their education is as good as men's, enabling them to land professional positions. Salaries are still lower than for men, but improving. The hardest time for an office is when a female employee has a baby. Besides granting maternity leave of 18 months (longer if the woman is a high-ranking civil servant), the firm must give an allowance, and guarantee the employee's job.

The women make up 25 percent of staff in parliament, and about 35 to 40 percent in private business. In total, they represent half of the workforce.

The Private Businessperson

The average businessperson is content to get the job done. It is very rarely that one puts in overtime, or works on the weekend to do more than expected. In general, management doesn't create enough incentive to encourage a faster pace of work, or to bring out the full creative potential of its workforce.

Julie Krejci

Austria has been revolutionized by the handy (cell phone), yet maintains its old-world charm.

Changing Jobs

There is not much desire to move from job to job. Most Austrians stay with the same company because they get comfortable and become used to the status quo. Perhaps this attitude has to do with their way of handling problems: many will ignore it or complain about it and go on. Surprisingly enough, it would be easy for most Austrians to gain new employment as Austria's social security system is so comprehensive that changing jobs would not have any effect on one's vacation pay or retirement. The system does, however, hit those who start their own business or go freelance. Salaried earners are worshiped by the system, and anyone daring to leave the social system is punished.

Starting Your Own Business

Leaving the social system requires strength of character, a great business IQ, and quite a bit of capital. The business that you begin cannot be a gamble. There is little help for those who fail, and if loans are taken out to help your business survive, and then you fail, your life will never be the same. The result is that Austria is last on the entrepreneurial totem pole in Europe.

Success is a Bad Word

You could be one of the most hardworking people in your office or you could have created something new and different, but the skeptical Austrian will just shake his head and wonder who helped you out, or tell you in no uncertain terms that there are dozens of people just like you. Lack of opportunity, few jobs at the top, and a highly educated population breed cynicism in the majority.

This attitude gives rise to contempt for new inventions too. It is called *österreichisches Erfinderschicksal*, or the Austrian's fate for being ignored when he comes up with anything new. The bureaucracy will find various reasons to degrade the invention: we have never done that before; we have always done it another way; or, if we accept

149

yours, anyone could come along and try and convince us of their ideas. Thus, modernization takes a backseat to tradition.

Titles and status take on more meaning than they should, and creative, hardworking people, even perhaps a few geniuses here and there, are squelched before they even begin.

Human Factors in the Working Environment

A lot of thought is put into trying to make employees happy in their working environment. There is an awareness of the human factors such as natural lighting, spacious room (no cubicles), and plenty of ventilation. Bathrooms in offices are enclosed and provide much-needed privacy.

Working with the Austrians

Most expatriates who work in managerial positions do get along well with their Austrian subordinates. There are differences in work ethics, but the boss is treated with respect.

For an expatriate with an Austrian employer, the offices are comfortable to work in. The formality, however, can be stifling. There isn't much laughing or joking around. Most of the employees are *Kollege/Kollegin*, or colleagues, to one another, thus setting up an automatic barrier to any kind of friendship or social interaction outside the office.

The flip side of the stuffiness is that it serves to protect one's private sphere and keeps working relationships uncomplicated and free of silliness, wounding gossip, and ugly bickering. The time it takes to get to know other Austrians is valuable, as it allows a slow, peaceful, and respectful development of the relationship. A friend of Julie's who is now a professor at the Music School in Vienna appreciated the transition between using the formal *"per Sie"* with professors of hers while she was studying, to the informal *"per Du"* with the same teachers after she herself was accepted as an equal doing the same work.

UNIVERSITY STUDENT CUSTOMS

University education is free for the Austrian. The only costs are the books and rent, if living away from home. If you are a foreigner, you can also study but you must have the special diploma called the *Matura,* and you will also have to pay a minimal amount for your classes. One great advantage of the free education system is that an Austrian can be a student until the end of his or her life. Most students finish their studies at about the age of 24, depending on their discipline. But nothing prevents them from resuming their studies after an interval.

One must be self-motivated as the system is impersonal, with classes having up to 100 students. Attendance is usually once a week for each class, but is not mandatory. The only thing that you must do is to take a written or oral exam, which is given either once a semester or once a year. The oral exam is in front of the whole class, which can be rather nerve-wracking. If you are athletically inclined, there is no outlet for your abilities: a university education is structured for the intellectual.

The idea of a university campus is nonexistent in Austria. In the case of the University of Vienna, for example, the main building is in the 1st district, while a myriad other academic buildings are located in nearby districts.

Austrian students do not belong to fraternities or sororities like in the United States. The push to drink to excess or to perform odd rituals to be accepted into a group is nonexistent. Undergraduates don't feel the need to conform or prove themselves. Privacy is also important to them.

The dress code is reserved. Dark colors reign supreme. Baseball caps, shorts, sweatshirts, and pants are not the norm.

Chapter Eight

THE ARTS:
BAROQUE TO JUGENDSTIL

A friend of Julie's was coming to live in Vienna. A key item on his "to do list" was to learn to play the piano. "Why piano?" she asked. "It only makes sense to learn to play an instrument and play beautiful classical music in the city that made it so famous," he said.

Vienna is known the world over for its music, opera, and composers such as Mozart, Haydn, Beethoven, Schubert, Strauss, Mahler, Bruckner, and Schönberg. Vienna's architecture, fine arts, and applied arts are also well known and much admired. The city's accomplishments in the arts is attributed to Austria's history under Habsburg rule. The Habsburgs developed into a dynamic and effervescent force throughout Europe that directly influenced the social, political, and artistic development of their empire. Consequently, new and different artistic styles were created: Baroque with its exuberant forms, Biedermeier with its cozy snugness, Historicism with its cornucopia of artistic influences from centuries gone by, and Jugendstil with its sinuous ornamentation.

HISTORY OF LITERATURE AND DRAMA

Austria's literary history extends back to the 12th century, going by a collection of poetry found in an abbey in Styria. Courtly poetry also surfaced in the 12th and 13th centuries.

Emperor Maximilian I (1459–1519) was himself a poet who supported the theater and dramatic arts. Operas, which often involved the whole court, gave rise to popular religious drama.

During the Baroque period, Austria became the center of dramatic art, and its influence is still felt in today's theaters.

BAROQUE ERA (1685–1780)

Buildings on a grand scale, sumptuously decorated palaces, marbled and gilded churches, and monumental curvaceous statues are all depictions of the 17th and 18th century Baroque art style. The three Baroque monarchs—Karl VI, his daughter Maria Theresa, and her son Josef II—each played a part in forming the era. The monarchy held absolute power, Catholicism reigned supreme after the defeat of Protestantism, the threat of a Turkish invasion was gone, and the wealth of the empire shone through in all forms of art at that time.

Architecture

Without a doubt, the Baroque era left its most profound mark on architecture. Artists knew of the wealth of the empire, and its frenzy to build was a means to showcase the strength of the Church and State. They came from far and wide to exhibit their talents. The most famous architect was Johann Bernhard Fischer von Erlach. Some say he was

153

Susan Roraff

When walking through the streets of Vienna, be sure to look up so as not to miss the beautiful details, such as this caryatid, that adorn many buildings.

Johann Fischer von Erlach, the most distinguished Baroque architect, designed many parts of the Hofburg, like the Michaelertor, and several smaller palaces in Vienna.

the true inventor of Austrian Baroque, adapting it from the Italian style, which others before him had merely copied. He designed the *Karlskirche* (St. Charles Church), National Library, State Chancellery, Royal Stables, and palaces for the nobility. He died in 1723 and his son Joseph Emmanuel completed many of his projects.

Johann Lukas von Hildebrand designed the Belvedere and the winter palace for Prince Eugene of Savoy, palaces for the nobility, and the Federal Chancellery, *Peterskirche* (St. Peter's Church), and the *Piaristenkirche* (Piaristen Church) for the court. He also designed the Mirabell Palace in Salzburg. Joseph Prandtauer can also be grouped with these two architects, but because he spent most of his time working on the glorious Abbey at Melk, he was not as prolific.

During this period, sadly, many Gothic churches and monasteries were also redone in the Baroque style. The *Minoriten* Church in Vienna suffered this fate, but thankfully was returned to its original Gothic style in 1784. *Maria am Gestade*, also in Vienna, is one of the few beautiful Gothic churches in Austria which escaped the renovations. When Maria Theresa married Franz Stephan from Lorraine, a number of advisors followed him back from France. Thus, the city was slightly influenced by the French style, especially in its architecture. The best example of this style is the imperial summer residence, Schönbrunn Palace, commissioned by Maria Theresa.

Painting

The effervescent frescoes of Johann Michael Rottmayr are found at the monastery in Melk, and again at *Karlskirche* and *Peterskirche*. Daniel Gran's ceiling frescoes at the *Annakirche*, and the Prunksall at the National Library are magnificent in their color and detail.

Music

Haydn, Franz Joseph (1732–1809)

Haydn is known the world over for laying the foundation of the classical style. After leaving his home in Rohrau, Burgenland, he started his career in Vienna as a choirboy at St. Stephen's Cathedral. Besides spending 29 years of his life working for the Esterházy royal family in Eisenstadt, Burgenland, he was known throughout Europe, and even in North America. London, especially, loved him. He wrote to a friend after arriving in London, "My arrival caused a great sensation throughout the whole city and I was mentioned in all the newspapers for three successive weeks."

Haydn was a slow worker but a consummate artist, who worked tirelessly in many different realms of musical composition. He was often affectionately called "Papa Haydn," as he was a fair conductor compared to his dictatorial contemporaries. His masses included the *Missa in honorem Beata Maria Virgine, Nelson Mass,* and *Maria Theresa,* and his most famous oratarios were *The Seasons* and *The Creation.* He loved opera and composed and directed about 20 of them, generally Italian comedies and classical tragedies, among them *Lo Speziale, Il Mondo della Luna, La Vera Constanza,* and *Armida.* Haydn lost interest in composing operas after recognizing Mozart's superiority in this field. Of his 100 symphonies, the most popular are *La Passione, Trauer, Farewell, Toy Symphony, The Surprise,* and the *Paris Symphonies.* He also wrote numerous concertos, marionette operas, string quartets, piano trios, keyboard sonatas, songs, and 377 arrangements of Scottish and Welsh airs.

Haydn knew both Mozart and Beethoven well. He loved Mozart like a son and commented after the production of *Don Giovanni,* "Mozart is the greatest composer the world possesses at this time." Of Beethoven he said, "(he) will eventually attain the position of one of the greatest composers in Europe, and I shall be proud to call myself his teacher." To Mozart, Haydn became a surrogate father, and to Beethoven, a mere teacher whom the latter would later criticize.

Mozart, Wolfgang Amadeus (1756–91)
Mozart played before Empress Maria Theresa as a child and before her son, Josef II, a few years later. The Viennese nobility soon courted him, and Emperor Josef II commissioned a dramatic musical or

157

Singspiel entitled *The Abduction from the Seraglio* or *Il ratto dal seraglio*. The piece pleased both the king and his court, and Mozart went on to compose other operas.

The operas that he wrote after his first success were *The Marriage of Figaro (1786), Don Giovanni (1787),* and the *Magic Flute (1791).* These operas were more popular with the common man. Part of the reason that Mozart failed to win the court's approval was that he decided to work on his own as a freethinking, "freelance" composer, instead of under the patronage of the court. This defiant and independent attitude caused him financial difficulties and the loss of his popularity among the aristocracy.

The sad truth is that Mozart was a musical genius unrecognized in his day. He was a mastermind as a composer, and a keyboard virtuoso who wrote popular music with astounding alacrity and ease. His works often combined both Classical elements in their perfection of formal balance, and Romantic elements in the intensity of their expression. His symphonies contained the contrapuntal, combining two or more parts which were melodically and rhythmically independent. He also wrote chamber music, piano sonatas, and church music, including the *Requiem.*

If Mozart ever reflected on his life, he must have thought it an incredible disappointment and fraught with hardship. Acclaimed a child prodigy at 6, by 11, he had written three symphonies; but by his early 30s, he was widely condemned, and mired in poverty and ruin. He was never able to afford an adequate living, and he and his wife, Constanze, were hopeless in administering financial and household affairs. He died lonely and exhausted, and was buried as a pauper in a mass grave at St. Marx in Vienna's 3rd district. His bones were never recovered, but there is a memorial stone bearing his name. The rest of Europe has mourned his loss more than Vienna ever did at the time.

Beethoven, Ludwig van (1770–1827)
Beethoven was a student of Joseph Haydn and Mozart. From a young age Beethoven was extremely arrogant, self-confident, and aware of

his own genius. Like Mozart, he lived off his compositions under the sponsorship of many aristocratic patrons. His music was brand new and popular. Although he lacked social graces and had a profound contempt for many of his fellow men, he was able to act professionally when necessary. The onset of his deafness redefined him, and his compositions became more spiritual. For all his social defects, J.W. Sullivan writes about Beethoven's spiritual development, "he was a composer unique not only for his depth, importance, and number of his inner states but also the power to realize them and give them expression." He was one of the first composers to be appreciated during his lifetime. Twenty thousand people, or about 10 percent of Vienna's population at that time, attended his funeral. It was a lavish *Schöne Leich'* (pageant): eight singers of the Court Opera carried his coffin, famous musicians were pallbearers, and Franz Grillparzer, Schubert, Czerny, and other well known figures held torches.

Beethoven was responsible for the opera *Fidelio*; 32 piano sonatas including the *Apassionata*; 16 string quartets; the *Mass in D* or *Missa Solemnis*; a violin concerto and a piano concerto; and nine symphonies, of which the following are best known: the *Eroica* (Third), *Victory* (Fifth), *Pastoral* (Sixth), and the *Choral* (Ninth).

BIEDERMEIER ERA (1780–1848)

The simple, smaller, purposeful buildings of the Biedermeier soon replaced the large, ostentatious buildings of the Baroque period. *Bieder* translates to "respectable," and *Meier* was a common surname that symbolized the perfect citizen. At this time, democratic sentiments were on the rise after the American and French revolutions, but the economic situation was bleak as the state finances were being drained by the Austrian military's unsuccessful campaigns. State Chancellor Metternich created a secret police, began a policy of censorship, and caused the loss of many civil rights.

The people withdrew to their private interests. At home, it was commonplace for music to be performed, literature to be read, and

Baden, south of Vienna, is the center of Biedermeier style: simple, two-story buildings marked by straight lines.

games to be played in private salons among friends and family. Musical evenings, known as *Schubertiades*, where Schubert's *Lieder* (songs) were played, were popular. Theaters, concert halls, and other venues were becoming more accessible to the middle class.

The salons were decorated in a pleasant yet simple style. There were fine paintings decorating the walls, comfortable lightwood furniture to lounge on, charming clocks on the mantelpiece, and delicate china and silverware adorning the dinner table. Biedermeier decor is still popular in many homes today.

Painting

Paintings of the Biedermeier period reflected the need to capture a realistic image of nature. Known as Austrian Realism, the style focused on forests, lakes, mountains, and idyllic rural landscapes. The movement was toward the impressionistic idea of capturing a single

160

moment in time. Ferdinand Georg Waldmüller, Friedrich Gauermann, Friedrich von Amerling, Rudolf von Alt, Moritz von Schwind, and Peter Fendi all contributed to finding this realism in art.

Music

Franz Seraph Peter Schubert (1797–1828) was thought to be the epitome of a Biedermeier artist. Although he never attained the recognition of virtuoso performers like Mozart and Beethoven, his music was lyrical and melodic, and his 600 *Lieder* were in the spirit of early Romantic poetry. For one who died so young, he composed numerous symphonies, masses, quartets, and sonatas.

Playwrights and Poets

The playwright **Johann Nestroy** (1801–62), who wrote *Freedom in Krähwinkel,* is famous for shattering the Biedermeier idyll with unforgiving skepticism. In his 80 farces and parodies of dramatic works, he became the king of psychological insights, and a mirror for society in his portrayal of his fellow citizens. His best known dramatic devices were language twists, name invention, and Viennese dialect.

Ferdinand Raimund (1790–1836), author of *The King of the Alps and the Misanthrope,* is also representative of the golden age of the Viennese popular comedy and Viennese dialect theater.

Franz Grillparzer (1791–1872) was Austria's foremost poet and dramatist. His work, described as being ahead of its time, is a mixture of Austrian and Spanish Baroque drama and artistic devices borrowed from Vienna's popular theater traditions and from classical drama.

HISTORICISM (1848–97)

Great social change followed the oppressive police state of Chancellor Metternich. Its culmination was the popular revolution of 1848, which demanded reforms guaranteeing free speech, free press, and free universities. Emperor Franz Josef took over the empire at the tender age of 18. In a few short years, Austria had suffered debilitating war defeats, lost much of its empire, and had major domestic worries. The country was ready for change and renaissance.

Building the Ringstrasse

Among Franz Josef's missions was to beautify his residence at the Hofburg, create a connection linking the outer districts with the inner city, and enlarge the city center. He ordered the removal of the medieval wall, which consisted of gates and fortifications around what is now the 1st district, and in its stead built a street, Ringstrasse. Unparalleled in grandeur, the Ringstrasse was lined on both sides with beautiful palaces for the aristocracy, government buildings, parks, museums, and theaters. Renowned architects came from all over Europe to compete for the honor to build on the Ringstrasse.

Architecture

Architecturally, Historicism was a mixture of past styles: Ancient Greek and Roman, Romanticism, Gothic, Renaissance, and Baroque. The buildings on the Ringstrasse reflect the style. The *Staatsoper* (State Opera House) was the first building to come up, designed by August von Siccardsburg and Eduard van der Nüll in 1861–69, in the French Renaissance style. The *Rathaus* (City Hall) was designed by Friedrich Schmidt in a Flemish Gothic style in 1872–83. Carl Hasenauer designed the *Kunsthistorisches* (Art History) Museum and the *Natur-historisches* (Natural History) Museum with Italian Renaissance style features in 1866. (Gottfried Semper later redesigned the facades.) Heinrich Ferstel redesigned the *Universität* (University) in the Italian Renaissance style in 1873–83. The *Burgtheater* (National Theater) was designed by Semper (exterior) and Hasenauer (interior) in the Italian Renaissance style in 1874–88. The *Parlament* (Parliament) was designed by Theophil Hansen, a Dane from Athens, who chose the Hellenic style for the home of the imperial council and to honor the birthplace of democracy. Hansen also designed the *Börse* (Stock Exchange) in the Italian Renaissance style in 1874–77.

Music

Johann Strauss the Elder (1804–49)

Although also popular during the Biedermeier period, Strauss sought a different, livelier music than Schubert's. He started and conducted his own orchestra. With its rhythmic and tuneful melodies, his music appealed to people of all social classes. Along with Josef Lanner, an associate and rival, he popularized the three-quarter-time waltz. His most famous tune is the *Radetsky March*, which is always played on New Year's Eve at the *Musikverein* (concert hall of the Society of the Friends of Music).

Johann Strauss junior (1825–99)

is known the world over for his engaging waltzes, polkas, and operettas. He took over his father's orchestra after his death, and traveled far and wide with it. His life, however, was unlike his music. He married three times and had a rather dark and driven demeanor.

His most memorable waltzes are *The Blue Danube* and *Tales of the Vienna Woods*. He also composed operettas such as *die Fledermaus* (The Bat) and *The Gypsy Baron*. When Julie took a tour around Vienna, the guide called Strauss one of the first modern pop stars. He inspired the masses to forget their troubles, be happy, and dance!

Johannes Brahms (1833–97)

Brahms brought new life to the art song. He followed the classical approach like Mozart and Beethoven, concentrating on absolute music as opposed to composing program music or opera. Although considered a traditionalist, Brahms is said to have invented the use of variations, from classical to modern compositions, in his music.

Anton Bruckner (1824–96)

Bruckner had served as an organist at the cathedral in Linz, and came to Vienna at the age of 44. Bruckner's main goal in life was to write for God. In fact, many people referred to him as "God's musician."

163

He spent much time revising his powerful symphonies and masses, which encompassed great blocks of sound. He was best known, however, for his improvisation abilities on the organ. Mahler was a great fan of his and would often conduct his work.

Gustav Mahler (1860–1911)
In his music, Mahler captured the stormy changes within society and the monarchy toward the end of the 19th century. He was interested in a new path for modern music and experimented in polyphony—the immense use of sound—and employed a wide variety of percussion instruments. As a conductor, he brought discipline to the singers, musicians, and audiences. He also improved the position of the orchestra pit so that the musicians' lights would not bother the audience. After ten years at the Vienna Opera House he left for the United States, tired of gossip about rivals wanting to get him out because of their anti-Semitism or their opposition to his modernism. His talents were well received in New York City where he became the New York Philharmonic's conductor until he died.

Mahler composed nine symphonies in the Romantic style, including the *Resurrection Symphony* and *Symphony of a Thousand*.

JUGENDSTIL AND THE SECESSION (1897–1918)
Jugendstil is a variation on art nouveau. The name is derived from the periodical *Jugend*, which debuted in Munich in 1896. It was a flattened, stylized form of the abstract where designs were exuberant and jubilant, with decoration and ornamentation outlining the figures. The smallest element of graphic detail was as important as the ground plan to establish a flow and movement in the whole piece.

Secession
Secession, or *Secessionstil*, and Secessionism are often erroneously associated with Jugendstil. Secession was not an art form, but the

ideology or school of thought behind Jugendstil. Members of the Secession had belonged to the old school *Künstlerhaus*. Wanting to establish a modern approach to exhibitions, with less focus on commercialization and more attention on a purified view of art, they drew the term Secession from the Roman *Secessio plebis*, whereby the plebs withdrew from the patricians due to the latter's misrule.

The men who first joined to form the Secession were Otto Wagner, Gustav Klimt, Josef Maria Olbrich, Kolo Moser, Carl Moll, and Rudolf von Alt. Their motto was "To each Age its Art, to Art its Freedom." They had a museum built, designed by Olbrich, and called it the Secession. Its golden laurel dome became known as the "cabbagehead." Inside the museum sat a statue of Beethoven, a symbol of misunderstood artists. During that time they also published a magazine, *Ver Sacrum*, which publicized Jugendstil art and provided a mouthpiece for their artistic and political demands.

Architecture

Otto Wagner (1841–1918)
Wagner was one of the foremost leaders of the Secession, but he also became known as the father of modern Viennese architecture and the educator of an entire generation. Wagner believed that new styles in art and architecture usually followed great social change. However, the social changes of the end of the 19th century happened so fast that the development of art could hardly match them. Instead, artists were copying styles of days gone by, in a movement called Historicism. He condemned the style and pushed instead for something that fitted modern man's need, something utilitarian. In his book *Moderne Architektur*, he says, "Modern forms must correspond to new materials, contemporary needs, if they are to be found suitable for mankind today. They must embody our own development, our democracy, our self-confidence, our idealism. They must take into account the colossal technical and scientific advances of our age, as well as the practical requirements of society."

Wagner worked assiduously to achieve his goal. He ended up designing the entire railway system (all 36 stations), which connected the inner city to the suburbs. He was also responsible for major city and traffic planning, especially the regulation of the Danube Canal and the Wien River. He designed the Postal Savings Bank, where space was used economically for 2,000 workers. The *Steinhof*, or the Golden City on the hill, is a church that Wagner designed with function in mind as it was to be used for the mentally handicapped. The *Majolica House*, its exterior decorated with colored ceramic, faces the *Naschmarkt*; it was built to fulfill sanitary requirements, with materials that made it easy to maintain.

Adolf Loos (1870–1933)
Loos also wanted to modernize the Viennese. He preferred clear-cut lines to ornamentation. Defending the aesthetic principle that usefulness is elegance and ornamentation is a form of ostentation, he paid more attention to the interior of buildings. He believed that designs should only reflect the feel of a place: a bar should be comfortable, a prison should show strength, and a bank should have the look of safety. His buildings were space-saving, economical, useful, and had a comfortable style. His thrift influenced him to use sunlight to illuminate interiors. Many of the apartments he designed offer highly original solutions to severe spatial problems, using materials thoughtfully, and with as little expense as possible. The stores he designed used brass, linoleum, marble, and glass to form interiors that have been described as having "geometric elegance and clinical precision." His most famous works in Vienna are the American Bar, Cafe Museum, and the House on Michaelerplatz (now a bank).

Painting

Gustav Klimt (1862–1918)
Klimt was revered by his Secessionist friends as one of the best painters of his time. He was so popular that he was elected the

president of the Secession. Like many of his contemporaries, he initially painted in the Historicist style. His greatest desire was to be part of the great building frenzy on the Ringstrasse. He worked on ceiling paintings at the *Burgtheater* (National Theater) and was also commissioned to decorate the *Kunsthistorisches* (Art History) Museum. Soon thereafter, changes in his style occurred and are best viewed in his painting *Schubert am Klavier*. Here he departs from the naturalist rendering of space and light, into more muted, impressionistic characters. Even then, Klimt's style did not yet portray the inner turmoil he was feeling. Through the use of the female figure, he was able to portray the future and femininity, which was his answer to the tension between patriarchal culture and chaos.

In *Der Küss* (The Kiss), his most famous work, he used the same decorative elements of geometric shapes and flowers on gold background as in his *Beethovenfrieze*; he avoids any sense of depth, putting the emphasis on ornamental structure, and rendering the body abstractly. The meaning, therefore, is seen in form and material rather than content. *Der Küss* is the model for the Jugendstil philosophy; the lovers are shown as "universal, cosmogonal, and in tune with nature."

Egon Schiele (1890–1918)

Schiele's work was initially influenced by Klimt and Jugendstil. He paid Klimt an unconcealed homage in both the *Watersprites* and *Zug der Toten* (Procession of the Dead). The themes that chiefly concerned him were love, life, and death. Schiele was often accused of drawing pornography, and in fact did live at one time off his more explicit drawings. He also went to jail for 24 days for supposedly seducing a minor. Like Klimt, he used nudity as a source of inspiration. Unlike Klimt, his nudes, and people in general, expressed ugliness, misery, and pain. Toward the end of his life, he married and his work changed. Gone were the emaciated nudes; in their stead, feelings of belonging and security were expressed, as in the painting *The Family*.

Oskar Kokoschka (1886–1980)

Kokoschka's talent was obvious to his teachers from the beginning. As a student, his work was so admired that he ran some of the preparatory classes in his school. His artistic life thereafter was cause for much verbal abuse by his critics, although his work was much appreciated by artists such as Loos, who became one of his dearest friends and supporters.

Kokoschka's paintings today rank among the masterpieces of early Expressionist painting. He pushed for a constant search for inner meaning and, like Freud, for the important role which nightmare, dream, and fantasy played in one's life. He was always probing the inner essence of the personalities he drew.

Apart from painting, Kokoschka was a talented writer. He wrote a children's poetic fairytale, *Die Träumenden Knaben* (The Dreaming Boys), illustrating it with beautiful color lithographs. He was also deeply interested in every aspect of book production, and lectured on the subject. His literary achievements included *Sphinx und Stromann* and *Mörder Hoffnung*, two dramas in the Expressionist style.

Applied Arts

Josef Hoffman (1870–1956)

Hoffman was a gifted architect and designer who believed in the simplification of forms. He is known throughout Vienna for designing both the interior and exterior of numerous buildings. Along with Moser, he headed the *Wiener Werkstätte* (Vienna Workshop).

Koloman Moser (1868–1918)

Moser was the most universal artist of his time. He worked with all kinds of materials in many different mediums: painting, graphics, commercial and industrial design, glass painting, furniture, and state and costume design. Moser is responsible for the transition in Jugendstil art from the use of flowers to geometric forms as decorative elements.

Wiener Werkstätte (1903)

The aim of the *Wiener Werkstätte* (WW) was to have contemporary art for contemporary society, and its slogan was "quality before quantity."

Designers Josef Hoffman, Koloman Moser, and a wealthy young businessman, Fritz Wärndorfer, led the workshop. Their aim was to design exclusively by hand without the use of machinery, out of pure materials such as ceramic, glass, leather, enamel, and metal. The Biedermeier era motivated them, as its focus was on the home; therefore it was a means to manufacture products for domestic purposes with style and function. Their inspiration, however, came from Scottish designers Charles Rennie Mackintosh and his wife Margaret MacDonald.

The main aims of the group were to establish contact between the public, designers, and craftsmen to create simple and elegant articles for household use, and objects with a purpose and need; to gain recognition for the value of work or ideas; and to unify art, architecture, and design. However, the high cost of WW designs placed them out of reach of all but the wealthiest patrons.

Music

Arnold Schönberg (1874–1951), Alban Berg (1865–1934), and Anton von Webern (1883–1945) represented the *Wiener Schule* (Vienna School). They made use of atonality and invented the 12-tone technique. Schönberg's compositions reflected the mystery of stillness and the curiosity of the subject in his own instinctual being.

The music of the *Wiener Schule* has been described as an "emancipation of dissonance" that destroys harmonic order and cadence, and allows for clusters of tones and enlarged rhythms and themes. Different and new, the music was shocking to the Viennese, such that at a performance of it at the *Musikverein,* fighting erupted on the floor.

Literature

The Secession also opened doors for new expression in literature. **Arthur Schnitzler** (1862–1931) was one of the most popular and frequently performed playwrights in the German-speaking countries. His psychologically subtle works, such as *Liebelei* and *Anatol Cycle*, depict the angst and hedonism of an affluent sector of Viennese society. *Der Weg ins Freie* (The Road to Freedom) is a vivid portrayal of Viennese society and various Viennese Jews at the beginning of the 20th century. This book is ironic and prophetic; some of the best academicians were living in Vienna during the infancy of anti-Semitism.

Hugo von Hoffmannsthal (1874–1929) was a poet and a librettist. He was a good friend of Schnitzler's, who thought him a true genius. His librettos were mainly written for the composer Richard Strauss, and include *Ariadne auf Naxos*, *Elektra*, and, his most famous, *Der Rosenkavalier*, in which he glorified the Viennese Baroque. In his book, *Brief des Lord Chandos*, he explores the duality of the relationship between the individual and the world, and social and moral chaos. Hoffmannsthal also wrote *Jedermann*, a revival of the medieval mystery play which is so popular that it is performed every year at the Salzburg Festival.

Stefan Zweig (1881–1942), like Schnitzler, was interested in the subconscious world and wrote *Die Welt von Gestern* (Yesterday's World), the evocation of a Europe that no longer existed. He also wrote the biographies of Marie Antoinette, Mary Stuart, Fouche, and other historical figures.

Karl Kraus (1874–1936) provided more reflections of the times in the critical periodical *Die Fackel* (The Torch), which urged truth and simplicity. Later he wrote about the period between the wars in the revealing play *Die Letzten Tage der Menschheit* (The Last Days of Mankind), whose style brought about many changes in theater.

— Chapter Nine —

WALTZING THROUGH
YOUR FREE TIME

The best way to enjoy your stay in Austria is to take advantage of your free time, and hopefully you will have plenty because there is so much to do. It's well known that Austria is a classical music lover's paradise, but if you're not a big fan, there are many other activities to keep you occupied. You can while away entire afternoons in a café, explore a museum, race down the slopes at a world-class ski resort, or spend a quiet weekend at a farmhouse in the country.

CLASSICAL MUSIC
If you love classical music you probably could not be in a better place.

Even if you are not a great enthusiast, the quality of the performances staged in Austria might just turn you into one. Vienna is regarded as a top musical city, boasting a proud history that includes Franz Joseph Haydn, Wolfgang Amadeus Mozart, Ludwig van Beethoven, Franz Schubert, Johannes Brahms, Anton Bruckner, the Strauss dynasty, Josef Lanner, Gustav Mahler, and Arnold Schönberg. Although we begin with Vienna, it is not the only city in Austria where you can find a wide variety of exceptional musical performances.

Musikverein

The *Musikverein*, the concert hall where the Viennese Philharmonic Orchestra and other internationally renowned orchestras, conductors, and soloists perform, is a pure delight. It was built in the late 1860s and is most famous for the annual New Year's Day concert, broadcast live around the world. If you can't attend that concert (you have to book more than a year in advance), you have hundreds of others to choose from. You must attend a concert in the lavishly decorated *Grosser Saal* (Main Hall). The acoustics are impeccable, which means that even the seats behind the orchestra are well worth the price. Depending upon the program, tickets may be difficult to obtain. You might want to consider becoming a member or purchasing a subscription. For those of you on a tight budget, *Stehplätze* provide an opportunity to hear the greatest symphonies in the world for very little money. These cheap tickets are sold shortly before the performance, but you should arrive early because a long line can form. Then you will be allowed entry into a standing room area at the back of the hall. Once the show begins and you become lost in the music, you won't even notice that you are standing as the hours slip by.

Konzerthaus

The *Konzerthaus* is another beautiful place to enjoy first-class musical performances. This is home to the Vienna Symphony Orchestra, but other world-class artists, not necessarily classical ones, also take

although some may be in their original language with electronic German subtitles. The *Volksoper* also provides about 100 *Stehplätze*.

Vienna Boys' Choir and Church Music

Perhaps Vienna's best known symbol is the Vienna Boys' Choir. Founded by Emperor Maximilian I in 1498, it has continued to this day with only a small break between 1918 and 1924. Choir members perform mass at the *Burgkapelle* in the Hofburg every Sunday from mid-September to June. They are a pure joy to hear, but if you'd rather not be surrounded by tourists, there are a number of other churches where you can attend mass and hear beautiful music.

The *Augustinerkirche* (part of the Hofburg), the *Universitätskirche*, St. Michael's, and *Stephansdom*, all in the old center, feature a mass on Sundays and holy days with either an orchestra, quartet, and/or choir. The first three churches may also be crowded at the height of the tourist season, but many Viennese do attend these masses, giving a sense of normalcy. The *Stephansdom*, however, tends to be overrun by tourists, even though attempts are made at keeping pure sightseers in the back. Susan once attended Sunday mass here and was shocked to witness a woman near her being photographed receiving communion. Churches are not well heated in winter so be sure to dress warmly.

MUSIC FESTIVALS

Viennese Festivals

Ever proud of their rich classical music history, many Austrian cities host at least one full-scale music festival, often in honor of a specific composer. The Viennese celebrate the *Wiener Festwochen* in May and June with special musical and theatrical performances and art exhibitions. This is considered the main festival in Vienna, yet there are numerous other festivals held in the capital throughout the year. The Vienna Spring Festival in March and April features works from the Baroque period to the 20th century. The *OsterKlang* Festival is celebrated at Easter and highlights the Viennese Philharmonic Orchestra and other world-renowned orchestras. The Festival of Early Music, or *Resonanzen* Festival, in January at the *Konzerthaus* celebrates religious and secular music from the 14th to 17th centuries.

At the other end of the spectrum is the *Wien Modern* Festival, which highlights contemporary music. Concerts are held at different venues throughout Vienna in October and November. *KlangBogen-Wien* is held in July and August to offset the absence of the Viennese Philharmonic and the opera companies from the music scene. This festival highlights modern music theater, operetta, and concerts.

Salzburg Festivals

Salzburg is well known for its summer *Salzburger Festspiele*. The festival was established in 1920 and features works by Mozart, the city's most famous son. It started with the original production of *Jedermann* (Everyman) by Hugo von Hofmannsthal. The festival opens every year with a performance of this play in the Cathedral plaza, but it has grown to include several different plays and operas, and many concerts.

Although Mozart is the main focus, there are new works by young composers. At first only the Viennese Philharmonic performed at the festival, but since 1931 highly distinguished international orchestras and conductors have played in Salzburg. Performances take place throughout the city at the *Mozarteum* (the musical academy), the *Festspielhaus* (Festival Hall), the *Landestheater* and Mirabell Palace. Tickets can be pricey and may be difficult to obtain (in 1999, over 230,000 people attended). If you can't make it, the city has other, less crowded festivals for you to enjoy.

Mozart Week is celebrated every January. The Easter Festival has added to this beautiful holiday since 1967. In June, the *Pfingsten* (Whitsun) Festival is devoted to Baroque music and focuses on the works of Händel and Bach. Musical events take place throughout the summer at Hellbrunn Palace and Hohensalzburg Fortress, and in several of the city's gardens and courtyards. Salzburg's Cultural Days have offered ballet, music, and opera since 1972. During Advent (the four weeks before Christmas), singing performances get you into the Christmas spirit. Many flock to the small town of Oberndorf, north of Salzburg, to hear *Silent Night* where it was written and first performed. Finally, the Marionette Theater is a wonderful way to interest children in opera. Bad Ischl in the Salzkammergut, not far from Salzburg, hosts the Operetta Festival every July and August.

Linz

Linz, just two hours west of Vienna, was home to Anton Bruckner, who was often called "God's musician." He was organist at the Linz Cathedral for 14 years and his presence can still be felt in the city. A modern concert hall built on the banks of the Danube was named *Brucknerhaus* in his honor. Every fall Linz celebrates *Brucknerfest*, which highlights many of Bruckner's hymnal symphonies, as well as those of other great composers. Performances throughout the regular season range from classical to folk, jazz, and world music, and there is also a program for children.

Linz is also the site of the *Klangwolke* Festival, a mixture of art and technology; and the *Pflasterspektakel*, a street artists' festival in the pedestrian zone.

Lower Austria

Franz Schubert spent the summers from 1820 to 1828 in the town of Atzenbrugg (halfway between Tulln and St. Pölten). So every May and June the town celebrates the *Schubertiade* Music Festival.

Grafenegg Castle near Krems presents concerts from May through October. Every other year it hosts the Romantic Music Week. Christmas season brings "Grafenegg Advent" in early December. In the summer you can see operetta at the Open-air Theater in Baden, and plays at Perchtoldsdorf and Neulengbach. St. Pölten and Krems are the main venues for the Danube Festival. The town of Melk, best known for its majestic abbey, is home to the Summer Theater Festival.

Burgenland

Burgenland honors Haydn, the chief conductor of the Esterházy dynasty's private orchestra from 1761 until 1790. His time was split between the two Esterházy palaces, in Eisenstadt, the capital of Burgenland, and in Esterhaza, in present-day Hungary. The *Haydnsaal* at the Eisenstadt palace offers concerts and matinee chamber music from September until July. It's definitely worth a visit, especially since Haydn himself conducted many of his own works there. A highlight of the musical season is Haydn Days, a festival that features his works as well as those of other composers.

The Mörbisch Lake Festival is held outdoors in the small town of Mörbisch on the large Neusiedler Lake. Operettas are performed here in the summer warmth. Nearby, the Opera Festival St. Margarethen is held in July and August in the town of the same name, in a quarry, with the stage set deep between the rocks. Lockenhaus Castle, near the Hungarian border, hosts a chamber music festival every summer.

Bregenz

Bregenz, the capital of Vorarlberg, is world-famous for its annual festival. The city lies on the shores of the *Bodensee* (Lake Constance), and every July and August an elaborate floating stage is built. The audience, safe on dry land, enjoys lavish productions of operas and operettas, musicals and ballets.

Innsbruck

Innsbruck hosts an Early Music Festival in August that highlights Baroque music. Performances are primarily held at Ambras Palace. Year-round musical events are performed at the *Kongresshaus* (Convention Center), *Stadtsäale*, and *Konservatorium* (music school).

Styria and Carinthia

Every June since 1985, Graz, Styria's beautiful capital which is a United Nations Cultural Heritage Site, has celebrated *Styriarte*, a festival highlighting classical music. The Styrian Autumn Festival, Austria's largest avant-garde festival, is celebrated in Graz and the surrounding towns. But you don't have to wait for a festival. You can attend one of the many performances at Graz Opera House.

The Carinthian Summer Festival has been held in Ossiach and Villach since 1969. Mostly religious pieces are performed.

CLASSICAL MUSIC FOR THE NOVICE

Programs designed for tourists delight audiences with well known classical pieces by performers in period costume. They are lighthearted and entertaining, while they maintain the high quality found in the somewhat more serious regular season performances. If you want an easy introduction to classical music, these performances are for you. Keep in mind, however, that some of these shows are held only during the height of the tourist season.

Mozart's best loved works are magically presented at the *Musik-verein* about three times weekly during the summer. Works of Mozart and Strauss are performed at the Orangerie at Schönbrunn Palace, complete with professional dancers. Schönborn Palace on Renngasse in the 1st district offers a similar program by the *Wiener Residenzor-chester*, while the *Wiener Konzertquintett* performs the works of Beethoven, Bach, Vivaldi, Haydn, and Mozart. The Hofburg and the Liechtenstein Palace (1st district) are also venues for classical music.

Marionette Theaters

For something different, you might want to attend one of the marionette theaters where operas, ballets, and other stories are performed by marionettes. In Vienna, you can see such a show at Schönbrunn Palace, which was quite famous during Maria Theresa's reign. Salzburg also has its own very popular Marionette Theater.

179

CONTEMPORARY MUSIC

Jazz

If you've tried but just can't appreciate classical music, don't worry. Austria has plenty of other musical performances to enjoy. Jazz is a big favorite and Austrians such as Joe Zawinul, Karl Ratzer, Hans Koller, and Friedrich Gulda have made significant contributions to the international jazz scene. It shouldn't be difficult to find jazz performances in your area. In Vienna, Jazzland in the 1st district is the best known club. Another popular club, Porgy and Bess, will reopen soon. Several other places alternate live jazz with other kinds of music. In May, the *Konzerthaus* presents the International Spring Jazz Music Festival, and in June and July, *Jazzfest Wien* is held in clubs and open-air venues, as well as at the *Staatsoper* and concert halls.

The ORF's (Austrian Broadcasting Corporation) Radio Café on Argentinierstrasse has live performances that range from jazz and folk to literary readings. Because it is associated with FM4, which has many English-language on-air programs, a significant number of performances are in English. Nonetheless, do check before going.

Folk Music

If you want to truly immerse yourself in Austrian culture, folk music is for you. One trip to the music store with the endless rows of folk CDs will tell you that there are many popular Austrian folk groups. One way to familiarize yourself with their music is to watch one of the several folk music shows and contests televised throughout the country. Always in traditional dress, folk groups sing upbeat songs. Some groups have mixed these songs with elements of rock and blues. Favorites are Peter Alexander, Die Knödel, the Broadlahn, Hubert von Goisern und die Original Alpinkatzen, and Attwenger.

Schrammelmusik

Heurigen, best known for their wine and hearty food, are the natural setting for *Schrammelmusik*—well loved traditional Viennese songs accompanied by accordion, violin, and many of the guests. The very first ensemble to play such music was formed by Johann and Josef Schrammel in the late 19th century. Many of these songs tend to deal with death and other life tragedies, and are somewhat morbid.

Pop Music

You will notice that much of the contemporary music played on the radio is in English. Many international popular music acts include Vienna in their world tour schedules, and some big names also play in Salzburg, Innsbruck, Graz, and Linz. In Vienna, many play at the *Stadthalle*, *Kurhalle Oberlaa*, Austria Center, and Libro Music Hall.

This does not suggest that Austria doesn't have its own pop music industry. Though small, it has produced internationally famous stars. Austrians are extremely proud of Falco, who had a Number 1 hit on the U.S. charts in 1986 with "Amadeus." He also scored hits with "Der Kommissar" and "Vienna Calling." In 1998, at age 39, he was killed in a car accident while on vacation in the Dominican Republic. Yet he remains a part of the Austrian music scene with over a dozen CDs and videos to his name, and is honored in musical tributes. There is even a cyber musical about him.

Udo Jürgens has also been a big name in German-language pop music for many years. Hansi Hinterseer is a pop singer whose first album went gold in Austria in just six months. Like other Austropop artists, he sings simple, romantic, cheerful songs. Other popular Austropop singers are Georg Danzer, Wolfgang Ambros, Rainhard Fendrich, and Stefanie Werger.

Street Performers

Kärntner Strasse and Graben, the two main pedestrian zones in Vienna's old city center, are full of street performers. Anything goes,

181

from breakdancing to comedy acts and mimes, from untalented singers to highly enjoyable quartets. There is an international flavor also, with Italian opera singers and South American folk groups joining the fray. Winter or summer, these performers are out there putting on an entertaining show for spare change.

NIGHTLIFE

Many people in Vienna, particularly the young and hip crowd, prefer to spend their free nights hitting the clubs. In general, most bars and clubs are tucked away and may take a while to discover. One of the more obvious places is known as the Bermuda Triangle; it is in the 1st district, bordered by Rabensteig, Ruprechtsplatz, and Seitenstettengasse, and is jam-packed with bars, clubs, and people. Bäckerstrasse, north of Stephansplatz, is also lined with bars. In the summer, head to the *Volksgarten* near the Hofburg, where music (from techno to classical) is broadcast into the park. Many people also head out to the *Donauinsel*, the island in the middle of the Danube River. The shore is lined with restaurants and bars. If heavy smoking bothers you, these open-air events are good options.

GAY LIFE

Vienna Gay Guide, a brochure issued by the city, is available at the tourist information center. It lists gay-friendly hotels, restaurants, bars, clubs, discos, saunas, travel agencies, cinemas, and stores. It also provides the names of gay groups, hotlines, and health centers. The Rosa Lila at 102 Linke Wienzeile in the 6th district provides a number of services to the gay community and is also a café.

GERMAN-LANGUAGE THEATER

You need a good command of German to enjoy one of the most celebrated German-language theaters, the *Burgtheater*. Located on the Ring, this theater is visually spectacular and boasts some of the best German plays and actors in the world. It is said that a German-speaking actor has not "made it" until he or she has performed at the *Burgtheater*. The *Akademietheater*, located at the *Konzerthaus*, is operated in conjunction with the *Burgtheater* and is also highly respected. The *Volkstheater* and *Theater in der Josefstadt* have a rich and long history performing great works in German.

A musical is easier to enjoy if your knowledge of German is limited. The *Theater an der Wien* has a very impressive history. Beethoven's *Fidelio* premiered here in 1805. Johann Strauss's *die Fledermaus* and Franz Lehár's *The Merry Widow* also premiered here, as did many of Johann Nestroy's pieces. Today, however, the theater is dedicated to staging musicals. More musicals can be seen at the *Raimundtheater*, also located in the 6th district. The *Ronacher* presents musicals and more abstract shows.

CABARET

Not only must your German be good, but your Viennese dialect as well, if you want to enjoy Vienna's cabarets. These shows, which comprise satirical sketches relating to a theme or a current political situation, offset by the occasional song-and-dance number, are popular among Viennese. Politicians are often the butt of the jokes, but they can be seen in the audience laughing with the rest.

ENGLISH-LANGUAGE THEATER

If you enjoy plays but lack the German facility to attend one of these theaters, there are three English-language theaters in Vienna. The English Theater in the 8th district stages plays with professional American and British actors. Two smaller theaters in the 9th district, the International Theater and Fundus, also give performances in English.

If you prefer to be up on the stage instead of in the audience, the VIC Players (a United Nations theater group) invites all English speakers who are interested to take part in the group's productions. Contact the United Nations office in Vienna for details.

CINEMA

Austria receives a good selection of international films, although most American films arrive well after they have premiered in the United States. Most Austrian cinemas show films that have been dubbed in German. Check movie listings for the following categories: *OmU*, original with subtitles in German; *OV*, original version, no subtitles; and *OmeU*, original version with English subtitles. Not many movies fall into the last category. Cinemas that show movies in their original language and have English-speaking staff are English Cinema Haydn on Mariahilfer Strasse, and Flotten Center, a couple of blocks down the same street. Votiv Cinema near Schottenring, Artis International Cinema near Hoher Markt, and Burg Kino on Opernring near the Hofburg also show English-language movies. The last runs the Graham Greene classic, *The Third Man*, every Sunday. This black and white mystery was filmed in occupied Vienna at the end of World War II and provides a glimpse into Vienna during that period. In Salzburg you can attend the *Salzburger Filmkulturzentrum Das Kino*. In Graz, go to the Royal English Cinema.

Every October brings the Viennale Film Festival, which showcases some fine international films. In November, children can enjoy the International Children's Film Festival. Films from across the world are shown in their original language with German translation available on a headset. During the summer, a huge screen is erected in the *Rathausplatz*, where concerts, operas, and ballets are all shown free of charge. To make the evening even more enjoyable, a number of stalls are set up selling food from many different countries. There are also open-air cinemas set up in the Augarten and the Prater.

VIDEO RENTAL

Video rental stores are everywhere, but once again, most of the movies are dubbed in German. You may be able to find an English-language section, but more often than not it will be very limited. In Vienna, for a small membership fee, you can rent English-language movies from *Pickwicks*, on Marc-Aurel Strasse 10–12 in the 1st district. It has videos in NTSC (American system) and PAL (European system). You can also rent a VCR. Just a block away at Salztorgasse 6, Austria Video has a sizeable selection of English-language videos. Video International on Gymnasiumstrasse in the 19th district also has English-language videos. For expatriates who work at the United Nations, there is a video rental store within the UN complex that offers movies in a number of different languages.

TELEVISION

Regular Austrian television has two channels, ORF 1 and 2, each presenting a mixture of news, sports, local programs, and shows and movies from other countries dubbed in German. Two popular local shows are *Kaisermühlen Blues*, a soap opera that revolves around the lives of a lower middle class family in Vienna, and *Kommisar Rex*, the adventures of a private investigator aided by his trusted German Shepherd. If you don't want to be limited to two channels, or are unable to understand German, consider installing cable or a satellite dish. A wide range of channels from many different countries are on offer (practically every country in Europe has a cable or satellite channel). If you are looking for English programming, there is news on CNN from the United States, and Sky News and BBC World from Great Britain. Televisions operate on the PAL system; if you bring an NTSC television or VCR from the United States, it will not work.

RADIO

Austria has about 10 radio stations, most of which play contemporary music. Stations focus on music from the 1980s onwards, with a strong preference for 1980s music. Susan still hears the songs that were popular when she studied here in 1985! FM4 at 103.8 in Vienna plays alternative music, and broadcasts mainly in English until 2 pm. From 6 am to 7 pm the news is read in English at the top of the hour. The Morning Show provides general information from 6 am to 10 am.

FM4 Update, a service-oriented program, is on from 10 am until noon. From 12 pm until 2 pm, news and features are discussed on Reality Check. For classical music, tune in to Ö1 or Radio Stephansdom. The latter is linked to the Catholic Church and broadcasts mass live from the cathedral every Sunday morning. The same radio stations can be heard at different frequencies in the provinces. News, weather, and traffic reports for the entire country are given.

PRINT

English-language Books

There is a good number of English-language bookshops in Vienna. Best known is *The British Bookshop*, which has a large selection for adults and children, and a very good section for instructive materials teaching English as a foreign language. The staff of primarily native English speakers can help you with any inquiries. *Shakespeare & Co.* is smaller and concentrates on the classics and academic works, with a focus on political science and history. It also has a nice selection for children and second-hand books. There are German-language book-shops that offer some English-language books. The *Buchhandlung Kuppitsch* store in the old *Allgemeines Krankenhaus* (AKH) campus offers books in several different languages. *Gerold & Co.* on the Graben in the 1st district also carries a number of English-language books. The large chain *Libro* has a small English-language section in its stores. *Amadeus* (part of the *Libro* group) is a chain of large multimedia stores that also carry English books. Do not count on native English-speaking staff in these stores.

If you prefer to borrow books, the British Council Austria Library (Schenkenstrasse 4, 1st district, near the *Burgtheater*, tel: 533 26 16) is open to the public. You register as a member for an annual fee of ATS 400 and a one-time new member fee of ATS 50. The library has an ample collection of books and videos. The public can also borrow books from the American International School Secondary Library

(Salmannsdorfer Strasse 47, 19th district, tel: 401 32 22) for a returnable deposit of ATS 400. It has an extensive collection of American periodicals. You can also find English-language and other non-German language books at the *Städtische Büchereien* (city public libraries). The main office is at Skodagasse 20, 8th district. Call 4000 8450, but be aware that the staff may not speak English.

German-language Books

If your German is good, there is a long list of works by top Austrian authors to choose from. Many of them have been translated into English, so even if your German isn't that good you can enjoy their work. Austrian literature was at its peak at the turn of the 20th century with authors such as Arthur Schnitzler, Hugo von Hofmannsthal, and Stefan Zweig, who accurately described life in fin-de-siècle Vienna. The break-up of the Austro-Hungarian Empire was addressed by Robert Musil and Joseph Roth. Following World War II, some authors continued writing in a traditional vein, while others, like those in the "Vienna Group," were more avant-garde. The best known contemporary author is Thomas Bernhard. Peter Handke is another popular author who wrote during the 1960s and 1970s. They have been joined by Elfriede Jelinek, Johannes Mario Simmel, Ingeborg Bachmann, Gerhard Roth, Peter Turrini, and Michael Köhlmeyer.

English-language Newspapers

Austria Today, issued weekly, publishes good articles on politics, business, and sports. Its website is www.austriatoday.at. The "Culture & Arts" section has articles on shows and events. It offers the listing entitled "What's on in Vienna," although it includes shows and performances throughout the country.

German-language Newspapers

Although the newspapers claim to be independent, some tend to lean in a certain direction. *Neue Kronen Zeitung* has the largest circulation.

It is published in Vienna, Graz, Klagenfurt, Linz, and Salzburg, and is somewhat populist and right-wing. The *Kurier* is published in Vienna and appeals to the masses. *Der Standard* is linked with the Social Democrats and *Die Presse* is a conservative newspaper tied to the People's Party (ÖVP). Both are read by businesspeople and the better educated. The *Wirtschafts Blatt* is a financial newspaper. Within Vienna, each district has a free newspaper, but they are loaded with advertisements.

Regional papers are published in Graz, Klagenfurt, Linz, Bregenz, and Tyrol. The *Salzburger Nachrichten* is targeted at the entire country, but is read primarily by people in the Salzburg area.

MUSEUMS

What should you do on Sunday with all stores and most restaurants closed? Spend all day at one of the many museums throughout the country! Entrance fees are not cheap, so choose your museum carefully. Often, children, students, teachers, and senior citizens pay a reduced fee. Many cities offer some type of card that provides access to museums over a specific period. In Vienna you have the option of purchasing an annual museum pass that lets you into many museums. If you have guests and plan on seeing a number of museums within 72 hours, purchase the Vienna Card which provides unlimited access to public transportation, and reduced rates at certain museums, shops, and restaurants.

National museums are free twice a year: National Museum Day on May 18 and Austria National Day on October 26. Within Vienna, certain municipal museums are free on Friday before noon, excluding public holidays.

Virtually all museums are closed on Monday. Tuesday through Sunday, they tend to be open from 10 am to 6 pm, although the hours may vary. Some museums stay open late one night a week. For detailed information on museums in Vienna, ask for the museum brochure at the Tourist Information Office.

Vienna

Vienna has so many museums that once you have taken in every permanent collection, the temporary exhibits will still keep you occupied. Vienna's most famous museums are the *Kunsthistorisches* (Art History) Museum and *Naturhistorisches* (Natural History) Museum. The former has one of the best collections of 16th and 17th century art by masters such as Brueghel, Rubens, Velázquez, Titian, Dürer, Rembrandt, Van Dyck, and Cranach. It also has an Egyptian and Near Eastern Collection, Greek and Roman Antiquities, and Sculpture and Decorative Arts. Do not try to see the entire museum in one day, but rather pick a section and stroll through it at a leisurely pace, then enjoy a coffee afterwards at the famous Museum Café.

The *Naturhistorisches* Museum, which faces the *Kunsthistorisches* Museum across the Maria Theresa Plaza, is best known for the Venus of Willendorf, a small statue of a woman representing fertility dating from 20,000–30,000 BC found in the Wachau region of Austria.

Among the more interesting museums in Vienna are the *Albertina* in the Hofburg. Founded in 1768 and well known for its extensive collection of graphic arts, it boasts a large number of pieces by the master Albrecht Dürer. The *Schatzkammer* (Treasury), also located in the Hofburg, houses priceless religious and secular objects. Here you can view the orb and scepter, and the imperial crown of the Holy Roman Emperor of the German Nation, dating from the 10th century.

The *Akademie der bildenden Künste* (Academy of Fine Arts), established in 1692, has a small picture gallery, its most famous piece being *The Last Judgement* triptych by Hieronymus Bosch.

The *Museum Moderner Kunst* (Museum of Modern Art) in the grand Liechtenstein Palace contains works by Andy Warhol, Pablo Picasso, Vassily Kandinsky, Paul Klee, Oskar Kokoschka, Ernst Ludwig Kirchner, Réne Magritte, Alexander Calder, and Christo, to name a few. The *Museum des 20. Jahrhunderts* (Museum of the 20th Century) houses more contemporary pieces of art and hosts temporary exhibitions as well.

Susan Roraff

Friedensreich Hundertwasser applied his whimsical style to many different projects, such as this rest stop on the A2 Autobahn.

The *Hundertwasserhaus* on Kegelgasse in the 3rd district is definitely worth a look. At first glance you may not realize that this unconventional, colorful, and creative building is a public housing block. Completed in 1985, it is the work of artist and architect Friedensreich Hundertwasser who has brought whimsy into Austria's rather austere, neutral buildings. Combining bold colors and wobbly geometric shapes using natural products such as tile, wood, and ceramics, he has invented a radically new way of living—floors full of soft bumps, for example, because in nature, the ground is not flat. He also designed the *Fernwärme* power plant, a church in Styria, a rest stop along the A2 Autobahn, and a fantasy-like spa. People live at the *Hundertwasserhaus* so entry is prohibited, but you can visit the small shopping mall across the street, which he also designed. If you'd like to see more of his work, visit the *KunstHausWien*, just a few blocks away on Weissgerberstrasse. This museum houses the permanent collection of Hundertwasser's paintings and also hosts temporary exhibits. The garden café is a fun place to relax.

The *Museum für angewandte Kunst* (Museum for Applied Arts), or the MAK, has a collection of beautifully designed objects used in everyday life. *Kunstforum Bank Austria* showcases important 19th and 20th century art. The *Kunsthalle Wien* in the 4th district presents temporary exhibitions of contemporary and modern art. It also has a great restaurant and café that looks out onto the museum.

The *Künstlerhaus*, which today displays contemporary art, was the official exhibition hall for artists studying at the Academy at the turn of the 20th century. In 1897 a group of 19 artists who deemed the academy too conservative broke away to form the Secession. The Secession building was used as a headquarters to exhibit their Jugendstil art. Completed in 1898, the building is beautiful and quite distinctive, with a large golden ball made up of laurel leaves at the top. It contains Gustav Klimt's *Beethovenfrieze* and hosts temporary exhibits of modern art.

You can feel a part of history at the Sigmund Freud Museum on Berggasse 19. This is where the psychoanalyst lived and worked from 1891 to 1938, although not many of his original possessions remain. You can also visit the Jewish Museum of the City of Vienna, the

Historical Museum of the City of Vienna, and the Austrian Museum of Folklore. The Museum of Military History traces the many years of Austrian military might and displays the car in which Franz Ferdinand was riding when he was shot.

Many former residences of the great composers have been turned into museums. While some may not have many original artifacts, you can see how they lived, and in many cases, enjoy their music as well. Entry to these museums is generally not expensive and if you particularly like the composer, you can spend your visit listening to recordings of his works.

Mozart, Austria's favorite son, was born in Salzburg, and the house of his birth is a popular tourist attraction in the center of the old city on Getreidegasse. Mozart lived in a number of places in Vienna, but the most famous is the Figaro House behind the *Stephansdom* on Domgasse, where he composed *The Marriage of Figaro*.

Beethoven, adopted by the Austrians as one of their own, was a somewhat unruly and loud tenant and changed residences often. In Vienna you can visit the *Pasqualatihaus*, *Heiligenstädter Testamenthaus*, and *Eroica Haus*, all former Beethoven homes. His apartment in Baden is also open to the public.

Johann Strauss's home is a museum, as are Schubert's birthplace and the house in which he died. Haydn fans should visit Eisenstadt to see Haydn's house and the Esterházy palace. The Haydn Museum in Vienna was his home later in life. In this house is a room dedicated to Brahms, who also lived in Vienna for a while. Brahms composed his fourth symphony in Mürzzuschlag, a small town in Styria about 2 hours from Vienna. This summerhouse has been turned into a delightful award-winning museum covering the many aspects of his life and work.

If you wish to pay your respects, visit the *Zentralfriedhof* (Central Cemetery) where Beethoven, Schubert, the entire Strauss family, Brahms, Schönberg, and Gluck are buried. Though Mozart is buried in an unmarked grave in *St. Marxer Friedhof*, there is a large memorial to the composer in the *Ehrengräber* (Tombs of Honor) section of the *Zentralfriedhof*, where other composers are interred. Gustav Mahler, who converted to Catholicism because of anti-Semitism, was buried in *Grinzinger Friedhof* in 1911. His tombstone was designed by Jugendstil architect and *Wiener Werkstätte* co-founder, Josef Hoffman. Another option is to take a stroll through the *Stadtpark* in Vienna, which is dotted with busts and statues of the great composers, as well as authors and painters.

There are three resting places for royalty. The Habsburgs lie in the Imperial Crypt at the *Kapuzinerkirche* on Neuer Markt, while their hearts are in the *Augustinerkirche*, and their organs in the crypt at *Stephansdom*. If you happen to enter the *Stephansdom* subway station, look for the lovely Romanesque *Virgilkapelle* (Chapel of St. Virgil) that was unearthed when work started on the subway line. For a more macabre look at Vienna, visit the Funeral Museum, or learn the history of torture in the Museum of Medieval Legal History.

If you prefer museums with a lighthearted theme, Vienna has an eclectic array: the Teddy Bear Museum, Circus and Clown Museum, Doll and Toy Museum, Clock Museum, and Globe Museum. You can also visit the *Fiaker* museum (*Fiaker* are horse-drawn carriages that make their way slowly through the old city), or Prater Museum (the local amusement park). If those aren't enough, try the Tram Museum, Soccer Museum, or even Schnaps Museum.

Salzburg

In addition to Mozart's birthplace, you can visit the Rupertinum Museum of Modern and Contemporary Art and Carolino Augusteum Museum. The Natural History Museum boasts the mummified body of an Ice Age rhinoceros. You can also experience firsthand the salt mines that produced much of the region's wealth. Stiegl's Brauwelt shows how beer is made, and the museum provides historical information on the beverage. In Salzburg, you can also see the tombs of the prince-archbishops in the crypt of the cathedral.

Innsbruck

The Museum of Tyrolean Folk Art has wonderful displays of Tyrolean costumes, living quarters, furniture, and tools—a great introduction to Tyrol. The Tyrolean Provincial Museum Ferdinandeum houses the largest collection of Gothic art in Austria. You can also find the old masters here as well as Baroque art. The Maximilianeum has original art pieces, weapons, and gold and coins from the treasury. The Tyrolean Regional Museum, located in Maximilian I's arsenal, offers a varied collection related to the history of Tyrol—cartography, music, hunting, avalanches, and the fire brigade. The Alpine Museum has Alpine art from two centuries, maps, antique mountain climbing equipment, and models of mountain refuges.

The Tyrolean Imperial Militia Museum has displays on regiments from World War I and the legendary regiments that guarded the old mountain borders of Tyrol. The *Kaiserjägermuseum Bergisel* (Military Museum) and Andreas Hofer Gallery pay homage to the heroes of the 1809 Battle of Bergisel against Napoleon's troops.

The *Hofkirche* (Court Church) contains the memorial tomb of Maximilian I (he is actually buried in Wiener Neustadt, south of Vienna). The marble sides of the sarcophagus are carved with scenes highlighting his reign. Surrounding the tomb are 28 larger-than-life figures (26 of them cast in bronze, the rest in copper) representing his ancestors and relatives by bloodline or marriage, and admired heroes. One of the best statues is of King Arthur, by Albrecht Dürer. The church also contains the tomb and memorial of the Tyrolean hero Andreas Hofer (1767–1810).

The world famous Swarovski crystal company is headquartered in nearby Wattens. Crystal Worlds, built to celebrate the firm's 100th anniversary, has some unique displays—a crystal dome, a wall made of 12 tons of crystal, and a simulated crystal rain shower. While in Innsbruck you can also visit the Bell Museum. The Grassmayr family has been making bells for 14 generations. At the museum you can see bells of all sizes being modeled and cast, and finally, rung.

Linz

In Linz, visit the Nordico City Museum, Francisco Carolinum Provincial Museum, "Linz-Genesis" Museum in the Old City Hall building, Adalbert Stifter House, and Linz New Gallery, an art hall opened in 1947. Every autumn, the Ars Electronica Center, a museum of the future, stages a festival of art and technology.

Graz

The *Zeughaus* (Arsenal) in this jewel of a city holds more than 29,000 weapons, armor, and even a horse. The Ancient Art Gallery's collection of medieval art includes altars, crucifixes, and stained glass. The Styrian Folklore Museum displays reconstructions of Styrian living quarters. About 16 kilometers outside of Graz, the Austrian Open Air Museum begins. Houses from the different provinces of Austria have been built over 100 acres to show how rural Austrians live.

Other Cities

Vorarlberg Museum in Bregenz has beautiful religious art from churches in the province. Also of note is the Jewish Museum *Hohenems*. Klagenfurt's regional museum, the *Landesmuseum*, exhibits Carinthian art and mineralogy. Here are both religious art, a fossilized rhinoceros skull discovered in 1335, and an open-air museum highlighting Roman stonework found throughout Carinthia. The Jewish Museum and the Jewish Quarter in Eisenstadt, capital of Burgenland, and once home to many Jews, are also worth seeing.

PALACES AND CASTLES

Austria boasts an incredible number of spectacular palaces and impressive fortified castles. No longer homes for nobility nor defense against a feared enemy, many of these palaces and castles can now be enjoyed by everyone. Some have been turned into fascinating museums, others welcome you with pleasant restaurants and hotels, and still others are the magical settings for summer concerts and operettas.

Except for those in Vienna, most palaces and castles are closed from November until April.

Vienna

Two of Vienna's most famous palaces are Schönbrunn and the Hofburg. The Hofburg contains the Imperial Apartments, Treasury, Church of the Augustines, Court Chapel (where the Vienna Boys' Choir sings), several museums (including the *Albertina*), Spanish Riding School, Esperanto Museum, Austrian National Library, and government offices. Some 20 rooms in the Imperial Apartments, the city residence of Emperor Franz Josef and Empress Sissi, are open to the public.

Schönbrunn Palace was the summer residence of the Habsburgs. Built on the grounds of a former hunting lodge, its gardens are as well worth visiting as its Rococo and Baroque apartments. Construction on the current building began after the Turkish siege of 1683, under the guidance of architect Johann Bernhard Fischer von Erlach, but it wasn't until the reign of Maria Theresa (1740–80) that the building was expanded to its present state. The gardens were also extensively developed at this time.

Two tours are available, the Imperial Tour and the Grand Tour. The former entitles you to see only half of the rooms open to the public. Invest in the second tour, and you will see some of the best rooms, which are excluded from the first tour. The Blue Chinese Salon, Porcelain Room, and Miniatures Room are among the finest on display, but the Millions Room is by far the best. Miniature 17th century Persian watercolors are set into the walls, although their simple beauty is overwhelmed by the accompanying decor. There is a great deal of information on Princess Elizabeth (Sissi), given Austrians' love for her, but it is somewhat ironic as she did not spend much time at Schönbrunn. The gardens include the Gloriette, Neptune Fountain, Palm House, Zoo (the oldest continuously working zoo in the world), Roman Ruins (replicas built for the gardens),

Butterfly House, Obelisk, and innumerable paths that wind through floral gardens, trees, and hedges. You may easily while away a beautiful sunny afternoon. Bring a picnic!

The Belvedere was built by architect Johann Lukas von Hildebrandt for Eugene of Savoy, a French prince who helped Austria repel the Turks in 1683. The palace was completed in 1723. Following his death, it became the property of the emperor. It was the home of Archduke Franz Ferdinand before he was assassinated in 1914. Its most important moment in history was on May 15, 1955, when the Austrian State Treaty was signed by the United States, France, Britain, and the Soviet Union, granting Austria independence and sovereignty. Austrian Foreign Minister Leopold Figl waved the treaty from a balcony, declaring "Austria is free!" to the crowd below.

The Belvedere (*belvedere* is Italian for "beautiful view") is actually two palaces, Upper Belvedere and Lower Belvedere, separated by beautifully laid out gardens. The admission fee allows entry into both. The Upper Belvedere houses Austrian works from the 19th and 20th centuries, including many pieces by the late 19th century artist Hans Makart. The museum is famous for its collection by Jugendstil artists, notably *The Kiss* by Gustav Klimt. See it to appreciate Klimt's unique style. Also on display are *Judith I,* other portraits, and some of his wonderful landscapes. Two rooms are devoted to Egon Schiele, a controversial artist whose works have been described as obscene. Two others devoted to Otto Kokoschka show mainly works he completed while living in Vienna in the early 1900s.

The Lower Belvedere contains Baroque art, but the rooms are interesting in and of themselves. By far the most intriguing is the Goldkabinett, a small room decorated entirely with gold walls, mirrors, and Oriental vases. Adjacent to the building is the Orangery and its Museum of Medieval Art. This museum has an impressive display of 12th to 16th century art.

Burgenland

As the name suggests (*Burg* means "castle"), this province just south of Vienna is home to an incredible number of castles. Built to protect Vienna from its enemies, they now house museums and offer open-air concerts and other musical events on warm summer evenings. Forchtenstein castle has an extensive collection of armory and other military items.

Salzburg

The first thing you see upon entering the city of Salzburg is the Hohensalzburg, a huge fortress atop the hill that overlooks and protects the city. Work on the castle began in 1077, and archbishops lived there until the end of the 15th century. A cog railway takes you to the top, where you can explore the castle, its chapel, the fortress, and puppet and regiment museums, then enjoy the view from the café.

The most photographed view is of the fortress from the Mirabell Palace and the Mirabell gardens. Archbishop Wolf Dietrich von Raitenau, who in spite of being a man of the church, married Salome Alt in the late 16th century, had this palace built for her and their many children. Even if you do not enter the palace, no trip to Salzburg would be complete without a walk through the beautiful gardens.

Construction of the *Residenz* in the town center also began under Archbishop Wolf Dietrich, in 1595. A young Mozart conducted many concerts in its Conference Hall. It now houses the *Residenzgalerie* (primarily 17th and 18th century art), the Modern Gallery and Rupertinum Collection of contemporary art, as well as hosting art shows and musical events. Tours of its state apartments are available.

Although not in the town center, Hellbrunn Palace is definitely worth a visit. This was the summer residence of Archbishop Marcus Sitticus. The gardens are full of the water tricks and games that were played upon his guests. The highlight of the gardens is a theater with 113 tiny mechanical figures, all powered by water. Go with a good sense of humor, and protect your camera.

Venture into the Salzkammergut and visit the Imperial Villa in nearby Bad Ischl. This is the small town where Emperor Franz Josef spent all of his summers. Franz Lehár also lived and composed a number of his works here.

Innsbruck

Innsbruck's Hofburg was built during the reign of Maria Theresa, and completed in 1777. The Rococo State Rooms can be viewed, and the gardens are a treat. The most impressive room is the Giant's Hall, which contains a ceiling fresco that glorifies the House of Habsburg.

On the edge of the city lies Ambras Castle, built in 1564 by Archduke Ferdinand II for his wife Philippine, a commoner who was never accepted by the royal family. It has some beautiful interiors—specifically the Spanish Hall—and lovely gardens. It became Austria's first museum in 1580 after Philippine's death. Today you can see some glorious treasures inside the Chamber of Wonders.

MONASTERIES

Driving along the Autobahn from Salzburg and Linz to Vienna, you can't miss the immense yellow Benedictine Abbey at Melk. Founded in 1000, it has an interesting library and an awe-inspiring Baroque church. Umberto Eco's *The Name of the Rose* takes place here. The Göttweig Benedictine Monastery perched on a hill is also a day trip from Vienna. After viewing the crypt and gatehouse dating from the Middle Ages, and the Imperial Wing built later, eat in the restaurant and enjoy the view of Krems and the Danube. Much closer to Vienna is the Augustine Monastery *Klosterneuburg*, on the other side of the Kahlenberg bordering Vienna to the north. It was founded in the 12th century and contains the famous Verdun altar and Gothic stained glass. Entrance to the museum allows you into the Baroque imperial apartments, still in their original state, and to a medieval art collection.

In Tyrol, you can stroll around the beautiful Stams Cistercian Monastery, founded in 1268. In Upper Austria, you can see the

199

observatory at the Benedictine Monastery in Kremsmünster and tour its science-related collection. The Benedictine Monastery in Admont, southwest of Linz, boasts the largest monastic library in the world. In Carinthia, the Benedictine Monastery of St. Paul is home to the largest monastic art collection north of the Alps.

SPANISH RIDING SCHOOL

Another of Vienna's trademarks is the *Spanische Reitschule* (Spanish Riding School), where tourists flock to see the performance of the legendary white Lippizaner horses. Commercialism aside, it is still enjoyable to watch these beautiful horses as they execute graceful, ballet-like movements. The horses received their name from the town of Lipizza in present-day Slovenia, where the line began during the time of Maximilian II by crossbreeding horses from Spain with horses from Italy and Arabia. Karl VI created the Winter Riding School, providing a home for the horses in a new annex to the Hofburg, built in 1735. It is difficult to obtain tickets and they are away on tour quite often, so plan this visit well in advance. It is easier to attend the training sessions which offer an entertaining show just the same.

In the wake of Slovenia's independence from Yugoslavia, the Slovenian government has filed a claim against Austria's use of the name "Lippizaner" before the European court, arguing that they hold the right to the name, since Lippiza is a town in Slovenia.

PRATER

Especially if you have children, don't miss the Prater in Vienna. This large green area and amusement park was hunting grounds for the aristocracy until Emperor Josef II opened it to the public. When the waltz was at the height of its popularity, the cafés here were crowded with people who came to dance. The relatively small amusement park has rides for thrill seekers of all ages. The park is famous for the over 65-meter tall *Riesenrad* (Ferris wheel), which has become a symbol of Vienna. Although there are no high-tech rollercoasters, the smaller,

Susan Roraff

The Prater in Vienna, formerly imperial hunting grounds, has an amusement park, restaurants, and plenty of green areas for sports.

older ones still provide an exciting ride. There are brand new slingshot and bungee-type rides for the more daring. Some attractions open year-round, but most close between November and March. The rides operate from morning until midnight. The *Hauptallee* is a pedestrian-only street full of people walking, rollerblading, and cycling. The large park is great for picnicking or sports.

If this seems like a lot of information, you need not be overwhelmed. A valuable resource is the Vienna Tourist Information Office at Maysedergasse 9-19. Be sure to grab their free copy of *Programm*, a comprehensive monthly guide to the cultural scene that provides essential information. Among other brochures, one lists the museums in the city complete with description, address, phone number, opening hours, and public transportation. Major landmarks such as the *Staatsoper* and *Musikverein* issue their own season and festival programs. The Resource Guide in this book gives contact information for principal venues and tourist offices in major cities.

Musical performances and art exhibitions are advertised on large round pillars in the center of Vienna, and on any available surface in every city. In general, venues are closed during July and August, when the official symphonies and ballet, opera, and theater companies are on vacation. Special festivals abound to make up for their absence.

OUTDOOR ACTIVITIES

River Cruises

An exciting way to see Vienna, Lower Austria, and some of the neighboring countries is to take a cruise along the Danube. The trip is short within Vienna, and not particularly captivating. A longer, more delightful journey takes you through the Wachau valley. A river trip allows you to see the castles that line the Danube, the way they were meant to be seen. You can travel from Vienna to Tulln, Dürnstein, or all the way to Melk and back. Alternatively, drive to Krems (where the Wachau begins) and travel by boat between Krems and Melk. You can even take your bicycle with you and explore the area that way. If you feel adventurous, take a *Schnellboot* (fast boat) to Bratislava or Budapest—Bratislava for the day, Budapest for the weekend. The trips take $1^1/2$ hours and $5^1/2$ to $6^1/2$ hours respectively. None of these journeys can be made during the winter.

Winter Sports

Austrians revel in the approach of winter because they know how to take full advantage of the season with skiing, snowboarding, ice skating, sledding, and Alpine style curling. So don't hide out in your heated home, but bundle up and venture out for some fun in the snow.

Skiing is second nature to Austrians, who grow up skiing and are among the best in the sport—not surprisingly, as Alpine skiing was first developed in Tyrol. On winter weekends, cities empty as every-one flocks to nearby resorts. If you ski, you'll be anxious to hit the slopes too, but keep in mind that some consider the runs here more challenging than those in the United States. Runs are categorized by color according to difficulty: beginners blue, intermediates red, and advanced black. Ski lessons are available for first timers and those who wish to brush up on their skills.

The Viennese frequent Semmering, Annaberg, Josefsberg, and Wechsel, all about one hour away in Lower Austria. On holidays and during winter vacation, they travel much farther to even better resorts, although they prefer to stay within Austria and rarely ski in the Swiss, French, or Italian Alps. Families tend to return to the same resort year after year. In Tyrol, Seefeld (near Innsbruck) and Ischgl are among the favorites, while Kitzbühel and St. Anton are popular with the wealthier set. In Vorarlberg, Lech and Zürs are by far the best known. They are expensive, but offer high quality infrastructure, such as helicopters, for ski trips. In Salzburg, Austrians head to Badgastein, Saalbach-Hinterglemm, Zell am See, and Obertauern. The World Cup race has been held in Schladming in Styria, another popular resort. Nassfeld in Carinthia is also a great place to ski.

Make reservations well in advance and be aware that every province has its own "ski week." As part of the school year, students take a week-long ski trip. Each province is assigned its own week so that the runs do not become overcrowded and every school in the province will go skiing that specific week. All Austrians learn to ski very young, so don't be discouraged by the kids' abilities.

Snowboarding is becoming increasingly popular, especially among the young. It is considered "cooler" than skiing. Snowboarding is permitted at all resorts, and some problems have arisen as snow-boarders and skiers must share runs. Some resorts hope to establish separate runs, but that is not expected to happen anytime soon.

Skiing is a social activity, and after a day on the slopes, Austrians enjoy a big meal and drinking *Glühwein* and *Schnaps*. On the down side, they often light up cigarettes as soon as the skis are off. Heavy smoke may be the only disadvantage to passing the evenings in ski lodges. Clothing and equipment play an important role. Everything the Austrians use are of high quality. This appears to be the one time they wear bright-colored, non-conservative clothing.

Summer skiing is possible in a few places in Tyrol, Salzburg, and Styria. The best known location for the sport is 40 minutes outside of Innsbruck, at the Stubai Glacier. Other areas in Tyrol are the Upper Tux valley and above Mayrhofen on the Gefrorne Wand glacier.

Cross-country skiing, although less popular than downhill skiing, is another great way to enjoy winter. If you live in Vienna you needn't go far to indulge in the sport. Besides a 4 kilometre trail in the Vienna Woods between Cobenzl and Kreuzeiche, there is also good cross-country skiing near Mariazell. Seefeld near Innsbruck has 200 kilometers of cross-country trails. Many other resorts, like Kitzbühel, are well equipped for cross-country skiing as well.

Public **ice-skating** rinks at the *Rathaus* and the *Stadtpark* in Vienna charge an entrance fee and rent skates. During carnival season the *Rathaus* rink offers shows complete with ice princesses and princes. At night the ambience changes with live bands and DJs playing dance and hip-hop music. If skating is not for you, you can try your hand at curling at the *Rathaus* rink. A cold-weather event would not be complete without something to keep you warm. Stalls surround the *Rathaus* rink selling food, coffee, and, of course, *Glühwein*.

If you feel like getting out of Vienna for the day, head to *Neusiedlersee* where there is plenty of skating and ice sailing on the lake. Every other major city and all ski resorts have ice-skating rinks, but the best is in Innsbruck, where you can skate at the Olympic rink.

All you need is a snow-covered hill to have fun, and this makes **tobogganing** the easiest sport to practice. It doesn't require lessons and kids love it. If you are searching for a somewhat substantial hill, there is a toboggan run near Cobenzl in the Vienna Woods.

Summer Sports

Wandern, a favorite pastime in Austria, combines hiking, strolling, and observing. With all the rural and scenic areas in Austria, a perfect setting can always be found. Thanks to the efforts of the Viennese in 1870, who launched a campaign to stop the sale and subsequent razing of the Vienna Woods, today's generation can enjoy the forest and all it has to offer. The Vienna Woods comprise about 80,000 acres of beech trees and conifers, with oak, elm, maple, poplar, and aspen commonly seen. They stretch from the foothills of the Alps to the Vienna city limits. Innumerable paths crisscross through the trees, the most famous passing through the *Helenental* near Baden. If you plan on doing a lot of hiking, get vaccinated for encephalitis, which is carried by ticks. Most Austrians have been vaccinated because bites are not uncommon. The woods provide ample opportunity for horse-back riding, swimming, fishing, and simply relaxing: many lovely *Gasthäuser* (inns) and *Heurigen* are located in the Vienna Woods.

The *Lainzer Tiergarten* on the edge of the 13th district is a large section of the Vienna Woods. It was once a royal hunting reserve and is currently home to native wildlife. Of numerous trails through the park, one leads to the Hermesvilla built by Franz Josef for his Sissi. It hosts exhibitions and has one of the park's many restaurants. There are two entrances to the park: the *Nikolaitor* on Himmelhofgasse, and the *Lainzer Tor* on Hermesstrasse. If you want to see wild animals like elephants and lions, you must visit the safari park in Gänserndorf, half an hour northeast of Vienna. It also has a petting zoo and playground.

Bicycling

As you walk through the cities you'll notice designated bicycle lanes everywhere. If you are driving or walking do take care because there is a significant number of bikes on the road, particularly in summer. A map of bike routes in Vienna is available at the tourist information office. Vienna has over 500 kilometers of cycling paths, 40 kilometers of which can be found on the *Donauinsel* (Danube Island). The Prater

Donauinsel on the Danube has 40 kilometers of bicycle paths.

is another good place for cycling. The *Donau Radweg* (Danube Bike Path) covers 305 kilometers and stretches from Passau in Germany to Hainburg near the Austrian border with Slovakia. The Wachau section is particularly pleasant. You can even cycle around Neusiedler Lake. It takes more than a day, camping is possible, and you need your passport because the southern tip lies in Hungary. If you are up to it, you can participate with 13,000 other riders in the 355 kilometer *Tour de Mur* that takes place every June in Styria. Of course, there are many paths, including some challenging ones, in Alpine areas.

In Vienna, bikes are allowed on the subway and trains, but with some restrictions: not during rush hours, with a half-price ticket for the bike, and confined to areas with a blue-and-white bicycle sign. If you don't own a bicycle, rent one at the following train stations: *Westbahnhof*, *Südbahnhof*, and *Bahnhof Wien Nord*. You can also rent bicycles on the *Donauinsel* and at the Prater amusement park.

Donauinsel

Not only can you ride your bike on *Donauinsel*, but there are also walking paths, large greens for picnicking or playing soccer, and a trampoline-like play area for children that floats on the river. You can rent bikes and rollerblades near the *Reichsbrücke*. The Viennese head to the island to sunbathe and swim in the river. After a day of sports, you can relax with a drink or a meal in one of the many clubs or restaurants. The *Donauinsel* is easily reached by taking the U1 subway, or you can park nearby and cross over to the island.

Water Sports

In the summer, Austrians take to the water, to swim, sail, windsurf, or canoe. Hundreds of lakes dot the country amid beautiful surroundings. Closest to Vienna is the *Neusiedlersee* in Burgenland, the only steppe lake in Europe. It averages 2 meters in depth, making it very warm in the summer, but is an incredible 30 kilometers long. If you go, plan a full day because you have to pay to enter the lake area. The lakes of the Salzkammergut are colder, but have a more romantic setting. Carinthia is another wonderful area with almost 200 lakes; the most popular is *Wörthersee*. The shores are lined with hotels and more affordable pensions. Less well known are the lakes of Tyrol. *Achensee* is the largest in the region and provides good facilities. Many resort areas also provide swimming pools.

If you are stuck in Vienna, follow the locals and swim in the Danube. The Strandbad Alte Donau has beaches and swimming pools. You can also rent rowboats and sailboats. The *Donauinsel* has beaches, a regular pool, and a wave pool. If you're walking along the river, don't be surprised to find little piles of clothes here and there. People tend to swim in their underwear, especially when they are trying to catch some sun on their lunch hour. At the far end of the island is a nudist beach.

If you don't want to swim in the river there are many indoor and outdoor swimming pools to enjoy. Brochures listing all the pools are available from the City Information Office at City Hall. Their quality is good and all have lifeguards on duty. Many pools offer classes for children and adults. The *Stadionbad* in the Prater has six pools and waterslides in addition to the big pool. The *Krapfenwaldbad* in Grinzing is set amidst vineyards and overlooks Vienna. The *Schafbergbad* sits high up in the hills of the 18th district. The *Hallenbad Döbling* has a fantastic children's pool, and for those living in the 13th district there is the *Hallenbad Hietzing*.

If walking and water sports are too tame for you, try rock climbing and hang-gliding. Hohewand, just south of Vienna, is a sheer cliff wall that is perfect for such activities. Rock climbing is possible in many Alpine resorts.

DANCING

Ballroom dancing will come in handy if you plan on attending a ball. There are many *Tanzschule* (dance schools), and some have private lessons in English. In Vienna, check out Ellmayer (Bräunerstrasse 13, 1st district), Immervoll (Hietzinger Hauptstrasse 6, 13th district), and Wiater (Martinstrasse 96, 18th district). The Vienna Tourist Information Office provides a list of dance schools.

FITNESS

There is an increasing number of health clubs in Vienna for those who enjoy working out. The most popular among yuppies is Manhattan Club in the 19th district. Club Danube, located in several districts, is popular with the average Viennese. A good gym frequented by the upper crust is John Harris in the 1st district. Oberlaa, in southern Vienna, is a resort area great for exercising, tennis, swimming, and spa therapy.

SPECTATOR SPORTS

Austrians are especially proud of their world champion professional skiers, including Hermann Maier, Toni Sailer, Franz Klammer, Karl

Schranz, Annemarie Moser-Pröll, and Renate Götschl. Austrian skiers consistently rank among the best in international competitions. Austria has played host to many world and European championships in a variety of disciplines, among them Alpine Skiing World Championships, Nordic Skiing World Championships, Ice Hockey World Championships, and ski jumping competitions. If you want to fit in, keep abreast of professional ski events; they are likely to come up in conversation.

Austrians also enjoy watching *Fussball* (soccer) matches, and their national team made it to the 1998 World Cup. Many Austrians are interested in motor and motorcycle racing. There is a Formula 1 track near Graz. Austria's most famous driver is Niki Lauda, who won the Formula 1 World Championship title in 1975, 1977, and 1984. Jochen Rindt, Franz Wurz, his son Alexander Wurz, and Gerhard Berger are other well known names. Austrians also enjoy betting on the horses races. Races take place at the *Freudenau* Track at the Prater on specific days. If you're only interested in betting, there are a number of places to do so, often located in train stations.

SPAS

Austria has a number of spa resorts that treat a variety of ailments and offer curative waters, curative mud treatments, kneipp cures, dietetic treatments, and acupuncture. Thermal baths are found all over the country, in Alpine resorts and in eastern Austria. Sulfur springs are said to be good for joints, muscles, the nervous system, and certain skin problems. Baden, near Vienna, is famous for its sulfur springs, as is Bad Goisern in the Salzkammergut. Iodized springs, such as Bad Hall in Upper Austria, are helpful in curing metabolic and circulation disorders, and vision and glandular problems. Salt springs are said to be good for gynecological and respiratory problems. Bad Ischl in Upper Austria and Salzerbad in Lower Austria are known for their salt springs. Bicarbonate-bearing waters, such as those at Bad Gleichenberg in Styria, are drunk to treat stomach, intestinal, and kidney ailments.

The waters at Badgastein are special because of their radon content, which is believed to help relieve rheumatic pain. Radon cannot be retained by the body and is eliminated within 2–4 hours. Many spas also use mud treatments to help those suffering from inflammation of the joints and certain skin problems. You can undergo such treatments at Grosspertholz and Bad Harbach in Lower Austria. As you might have guessed, *Bad* is German for baths, and any town with Bad in its name will have thermal baths. At Bad Vöslau, a special grape cure is offered during the grape harvest.

TRAVELING

In order to fully enjoy many of these activities, you'll need to travel throughout Austria. The roads are good and no destination is ever more than a day's drive away. The major cities offer a wide array of accommodations, from charming hotels to affordable pensions. If you are looking for a quiet weekend in a small town or rural community, there are many options. A good choice is a *Bauernhof*, or family farm. The lodgings are comfortable and you are always made to feel welcome. The homemade meals are another draw. Your hosts are especially nice if you have children because many are working farms, and the kids can help out. A weekend at one of these farms is extremely affordable. Another possibility for those with children is *Kinder Hotels* (Children's Hotels). They offer babysitting services and even full-scale play centers where you can leave your children for the day. Everything is geared toward the children, from activities to meals. It takes the pressure off you so you can enjoy the vacation as well.

Chapter Ten

FESTIVALS AND TRADITIONS

The succession of music festivals, balls, and traditional events is a central part of Austrian life. Many customs have their roots in pagan rituals, which were guided by the cycle of seasons and the movement of celestial beings. It was believed that both friendly and evil powers influenced the earth and its growth and fertility, powers so strong that they also affected people. The rituals served as a means of protection from things that people could not understand.

When the Church came to gain converts, missionaries embellished these traditions with Christian themes. Angels and devils, and the concept of good and evil, took on a central role.

BALLS (BÄLLE) DURING FASCHING

In January, Vienna celebrates the **New Year** with lavish balls. One would also call this time *Fasching*, which in essence is Fat Tuesday, the eve of Ash Wednesday (*Aschermittwoch*). *Fasching* is also a general term describing the period beginning on the 11th hour of the 11th day of the 11th month, and ending with Ash Wednesday.

Balls abound, hosted by various organizations. There are balls held for members of certain professions, for example: *Roter Herzenball* (Red Cross Ball), *Ball der Pfarre Floridsdorf* (Clergymen's Ball), *Installateurball* (Plumbers' Ball), *Technikerball* (Technicians' Ball), *Ärzteball* (Doctors' Ball), *Ball der Zollwache* (Customs Guards' Ball), *Zuckerbäcker ball* (Confectioners' Ball), and *Kanalwerkmeister Ball* (Sewer Managers' Ball). Some ethnic groups put on lively cultural dances at their balls, examples being *Ball der burgenländischen Kroaten* (Burgenland's Croatian Ball), *Russische Ballnacht* (Russian Ball Night), *Ball der Griechen* (Greeks' Ball), and *Roma Ball* (Rome's Ball). A ball with a twist is the *Rudolfina Redoute Ball*. Here, single women enter wearing masks, which they take off at midnight to reveal their identities to their dancing partners. High schools and dance schools also organize balls.

The Opera Ball is the highlight of the Viennese ball circuit. On the eve of Lent or *Fasching* (*Carnivale*), the opera house is magically transformed into a sumptuous dance hall. Rows upon rows of chairs are removed from the audience section, and in their place a dance floor emerges. Those who can afford a ticket (usually ATS 5,000 per person) dress in their best: a long evening gown for the women, and black suits with tails for the men. The attendees wait with bated breath to see which famous stars the self-made millionaire Richard Lugner will bring with him to the ball. Outside the opera house, as in decades gone by, people peacefully protest the extravagance of the event.

Another noteworthy event is the Life Ball, which raises money for AIDS research. This is an offbeat ball for those who like to make wild and crazy fashion statements for a good cause.

Debutantes in white gowns and their young tuxedoed escorts open each ball with a dance. They walk onstage in an orderly fashion, showing off their outfits, and then dance a waltz. When they go offstage, everyone else may begin to dance. If you are at a popular ball, it may be difficult even to dance, the dance floor is that crowded.

Anyone with a ticket can go to the balls. Prices differ based on whether you want to sit at a table, have a meal (if served), or just dance all night. Most balls are advertised with ticketing information included. A ball pamphlet, available at information centers, lists all the balls lined up for the year. As you buy your ticket, be sure to ask about the dress code. Not all balls require long gowns and suits with tails. Julie has been to several where women wore short dresses and men wore off-black or gray suits.

FESTIVALS AND CUSTOMS

Epiphany or Three Kings Day—January 6th

Epiphany on January 6th is a time to remember the manifestation of Christ's birth to the Magi. Catholic boys dress up in Oriental dress to represent the three wise men, Caspar, Melchior, and Balthazar. Led by a star bearer, they go from house to house seeking donations, singing traditional carols, and swinging their incense carrier. On each house, they chalk three crosses to banish evil spirits. The money raised is used to fund church projects around the world.

The **Glöckler of Ebensee** in Upper Austria is celebrated on the evening of January 6th, after evening prayers. In a tradition that dates to the 16th century, a group of 20 men from various villages of *Ebensee* run to farms or homes within a certain radius. They are dressed in white shirts and trousers, and wear belts hung with cowbells. On their heads, they wear gigantic *Lichtkappen* (lighted caps) of various shapes decorated with ornaments and symbols. The caps weigh up to 15 kilos and are illuminated from within. The purpose of the custom is to drive away the evil spirits of *Ebensee*.

213

Gerhard Krejci

The Glöckler of Ebensee, wearing exquisite lighted caps, get ready to dance in front of various homes on the eve of January 6th.

In the Rauris valley in Salzburg province, the legendary beaked *Perchten* **of Rauris** are out on the eve of January 6th, warding off mischief from house and farmstead, and ensuring that everything is clean. The half-bird, half-witch costume is worn chiefly by men. Their beaks are about 60 cm long, and their clothing includes overalls, headscarves, baskets worn on the back, wooden scissors, and brooms. If a home is found to be unclean, they threaten to open the stomach of the housewife. The stomach is considered a symbolic receptacle for the filth swept up by the Perchtens' broom. However, when they are entertained with food, wine, and gifts, they forget to look too closely in all the corners, and instead frolic and have fun with the owners of the households.

Easter Holidays

Shrove Tuesday (**Fat Tuesday**, *Fasching*, or *Carnivale*) is the day before Lent. More importantly, it is a time for many festivals throughout Austria, and the last day for drinking alcohol and feasting on certain foods before the abstinence of Lent begins.

A popular alpine festival is the *Schemenlaufen of Nassereith* in Tyrol, held once every three years, on the last Sunday before Lent. The *Scheller* symbolizes the male element, or winter, while the *Roller* is the female component, or spring. Three sweepers, beautifully dressed in carved wooden masks and wearing crowns made with feathers (a fertility symbol), finery, ribbons, and mirrors are assigned to the *Roller*, to sweep away the snow, or winter. Also included in the procession are *Kübellmajen*, or witches; *Engelspritzer*, the Moors who splash water according to the ritual of an ancient fertility cult; *Ruassler*, who instill respect in the crowd; *Sackner*, who keep order; and *Schnöller*, who drive away winter with long-handled whips. The highlight is the fight between the bear and the *Scheller*. The bear symbolizes fertility (spring) and must always win the fight against the evil *Scheller* (winter).

Bonfire Sunday in Vorarlberg celebrates a heathen ritual very

Susan Roraff

You can buy beautifully painted eggs at any Easter market throughout Austria.

likely started by the Celts. The bonfires can reach as high as 15 meters, and are lit several days before the first Sunday in Lent. Schoolchildren go around begging for wood and straw, and a bonfire master supervises the making of the bonfire.

Easter (*Ostern*), the day of Christ's resurrection, is heralded with more carnivals, processions, concerts, and costumes. Most towns and cities have Easter markets where Easter baskets, special breads, decorated eggs, and ornaments are sold.

Children in Austria love this holiday not only because it means two weeks off from school, but also because it is a time to look for colored eggs, eat a glut of chocolate bunnies and chocolate eggs, and receive gifts from family members. Many Austrians attend church on this day to have their Easter basket lunches blessed.

Every year, the farming community of Tressdorf in the Mölltal in Carinthia put on the ***Mölltal* passion**. This wordless play depicts Christ's last days on earth. There are only roles for men (Mary Magdalene and Mary do not appear); during both world wars, the women carried on with the play in the absence of their menfolk, as it was thought to be unlucky if the play was skipped.

The first Sunday after Easter, Catholic children in their second year of primary school receive Holy Communion for the first time. Girls wear white dresses and floral wreaths on their heads, and boys wear suits. In some areas of Austria, the costume is a bit different. In Höchst in Vorarlberg, the boys wear crowns of ivy leaves called the *Chappel*, showing that they are the children of God or of a king, while the girls wear garlands and veils.

Pentecost/Whitsun (*Pfingsten*), 50 days after Easter. Whitsun, or the festival marking the descent of the Holy Spirit, is celebrated in Arbesthal, near Bruck an der Leitha in Burgenland. An old custom there was recently revived: a young man and a schoolboy cloaked entirely in a framework of hazelnut branches and greenery both become the Whitsun kings. On Whit Monday, the Whitsun kings and the folk dance group walk through the town, stopping at various

217

Susan Roraff

Maypoles, which symbolize fertility, are centers of festivities in small villages.

locations where the townsfolk recite a special verse and sing the Whitsun king song. The procession ends behind the main church.

The second Thursday after Whitsunday is the feast of Corpus Christi (the Body of Christ, or Blessed Sacrament). There are festive processions and magnificent pageantry throughout the land. In **Deutschlandsberg in western Styria**, the processional route and four gospel altars are decorated with artistic and incredibly detailed carpets of flowers. The town of **Hallstatt in the Salzkammergut in Upper Austria** has celebrated a Corpus Christi procession since 1623. After mass, the crowd boards boats elaborately decorated with garlands and flowers. The priest boards a special boat, and the procession makes its way to various stops along the route. The most important stop is the Salzberg (salt-giving mountain), Hallstatt's livelihood, which the priest blesses. For the last three centuries, Hallstatt has been a key area for mining salt, which was highly valued in the past, much as gold is today.

The Sunday after Corpus Christi, a strong boy is elected to swing a large flag beautifully decorated with the coats of arms of both the house of Esterházy and the Holy Roman Empire in **Neckenmarkt, Burgenland**. The tradition hails back to 1620, at the beginning of the Thirty Years War, when the men from Neckenmarkt helped Count Nicholas Esterházy defeat Bethen Garbor, a Hungarian rebel king. A grateful Count Esterházy reduced their rent and allowed them to dress in full regalia during special festivals. The flag is a historical artifact that has been restored several times.

Maypoles and Labor Day

In May, it is common to see the **Maypole** in many parts of Austria; this is a pine tree put at the top of a pole up to 20 meters tall and decorated with ribbons. The Maypole is a symbol of fertility, happiness, and prosperity. It used to be erected for newly married couples so that they would be blessed with many children. Today, young men erect the Maypole on April 30th, then guard it as it is customary for boys from

219

other villages to try to steal it. Losing the Maypole embarrasses the owners, who then must search for it. In a part of Deutschkreutz in Burgenland, it is still the custom to place small Maypoles by wayside shrines and statues of saints the night before May 1st.

Unfortunately, Maypoles today are often used for political purposes. They are usually decorated in a political party's colors as an advertisement, and also to create a rallying point.

May 1st is **Labor Day** (*Tag der Arbeit*), a day off for all working people. It is also a favorite day of politicians, who make never-ending speeches at political rallies. Parades abound in all the major cities, so park your car and walk around to enjoy the festivities.

Summer Festivals

Bonfires all over Austria mark the **Summer Solstice**. Fire, as tradition has it, symbolized great power, warding off peril and pestilence in midsummer. Today, bonfires mark the sun's reaching its zenith, on the first Saturday or Sunday after 21st June. There are also bonfires marking saints' days: St. Vitus fires on June 15th, John the Baptist fires on June 24th, and fires for St. Peter and St. Paul on June 29th.

In two neighboring villages in the **Lungau region in Salzburg**, there are beautiful processions celebrating St. John (June 24th) and St. Paul (June 29th). Each procession is heralded with beautifully decorated poles called *Prangstangen*, 6–8 meters tall, weighing 45–80 kilos, and covered with garlands of 40,000 flowers. Only single, eligible men may carry the poles. They wear a traditional costume with a heavy white scarf tied around one shoulder, which the pole is then fitted into. After the procession, the poles are brought into the church and remain there until August 15th, Assumption Day.

The poles are made lovingly by farming families. A week before each procession, wildflowers such as daisies, arnica, pinks, gentians, and lady's mantle are collected. The women make up the garlands, and the men tie them around the poles. The origins of the tradition are not known. Some believe that several centuries ago, a plague of locusts and beetles destroyed the harvest and ate the trees. A vow was made soon thereafter to protect trees and crops forevermore from a plague of that nature; decorating the poles symbolized disguising the crops and trees from their destroyers.

August 15th is **Assumption Day** (*Maria Himmelfahrt*), when the Virgin Mary ascended to heaven. In parts of western Austria, it is also when the church blesses a variety of herbs. The bunch of herbs is composed differently from area to area, but in **Lofer in the Salzburg**, it should consist of 72 different herbs. Small bunches are more common, but they should contain at least the following herbs: arnica, goldenrod, camomile, brown gentian, mint, yarrow, woodruff, and horsetail—all sun-dried in the garden. Some are added to cattle fodder to make the animals more resistant to disease, and some burned at Christmas and New Year to bring good luck and prosperity.

Samson the Giant

In the **Lungau region in Salzburg** and around **Murau in Styria**, several villages have a giant they call Samson, as a symbol of strength. One man carries Samson, a figure usually 6 meters tall, made from wood and papier-mâché, wearing a cuirassier's helmet and a cloak over his striped tunic, and carrying a halberd. There are usually four helpers standing by in case Samson's bearer wavers and falls. Samson is usually seen after church festivals or processions, when he is taken from house to house to perform a dance before guests of honor.

There are different versions of how this figure originated. Some say Capuchin monks brought him in from Bavaria. Others, that Samson is a relic of Baroque-style processions. Yet others think the Celts used large figures for special celebrations. Lungau people believe, however, that he was built to frighten the raiding Turks.

Herds and Harvests

The ritual driving down of herds of cattle happens on September 15th in the **Schwarzenberg of the Bregenzerwald**, a mountainous area

221

outside Bregenz, the capital of Vorarlberg. The weather starts turning cold at about this time, and the cattle are driven down from the Alps into the warm valley. Tradition holds that to prevent demons and ghouls from noticing the long trek up and down, the cattle have to be "veiled." Today the cattle are decorated only on the way down with beautiful headdresses of pine, fir twigs, ribbons, and flowers, to show joyful and thankful celebration for the safe summer on the mountain. The townspeople give the cattle and cowherd a warm welcome in the middle of the square, and cowbells are then removed.

Harvest Thanksgiving, held between the end of September and the end of October, is the anniversary of the dedication of the local church. Although no actual harvest takes place, traces of days of yore are represented in the procession to the church. The women are usually in their local costume, the children carry sheaves or a basket of fruit to be blessed by the priest, and there is also the traditional harvest crown and harvest garland. The festivities, which are similar throughout Austria, include a street party with food, beer, and wine stalls, rides for children, farmers selling cheese and meat, and toys and clothes for sale.

National Day

October 26 sees much patriotic flag-waving throughout Austria to commemorate the day in 1955 when the last of the World War troops (English, American, Russian, and French) left. It is also known as "fitness day," and many people go out for long walks. Entrance to the parliament building and all national museums is free on this day.

St. Martin's Day (Martinmas)

In the **east of Austria** and **Burgenland**, where St. Martin is the patron saint, November 11th is a time to eat goose (*gans*) and drink wine. Legend has it that there was once a Roman soldier named Martin, who cut his coat in half with his sword to share it with a shivering beggar. This soldier was to become bishop of Tours. The eating of

a lantern, and the other a basket of cookies and fruit; a *Lotter*, the accordionist; and the *Litterin*, who begs for alms from spectators. They walk from house to house, and will only cross the threshold of a house if they are welcome. St. Nicholas asks about the children's behavior over the past year and distributes his gifts. In the meantime the *Lotter* plays a tune while the *Litterin* collects alms. Outside, the *Klaubäufe* make a terrible commotion as they also want to visit. St. Nicholas decides whether or not to let them in. In days gone by, the *Klaubäufe* would take the main table and bring it outside to dance on; if the table was damaged, it was a bad omen for the owner. St. Nicholas is supposed to have the ability to prevent bad things from happening, and to stop whatever raucousness may ensue.

Crib visiting in Tyrol is a tradition that became popular in 1223 when St. Francis of Assisi had a crib set up in a cave in Greccio forest to illustrate Christ's incarnation. The crèche (the tableau of Christ in his crib, with Mary, Joseph, the three wise men, and farm animals looking on) then became the symbol of Christmas, rather than the Christmas tree as we have come to know it.

Sculpted crèches became extremely popular during the 17th century Counter-Reformation in Tyrol. Some of the most exquisite and ornate ones date from that period. Today, famous sculptors create crèches that can be as large as a farmhouse room. Sculptured crèches can be found in the villages of Zirl, Rum, Götzens, and, above all, Thaus near Innsbruck.

Crèches can be viewed in Tyrol from December 26th until January 15th. Friends, acquaintances, and strangers are welcome to go through homes and view the crèches. A sign reading *Weihnachtskrippe* welcomes them into the home.

Christmas Eve (*Weihnachten*) is traditionally the evening when families get together, have a good meal, sing Christmas carols, and open presents around the Christmas tree. Many Austrian children don't believe in Santa Claus but in the Baby Jesus. Children write letters to him at the beginning of Advent (four weeks before) asking him for things they would like. The letters are left on the windowsill.

Christkindl in Lower Austria is an actual town made famous by its name. Children also send their Christmas wish lists there, and many people go to this town especially to have the postmark of the town on their Christmas letters.

New Year's Eve (Silvester)

Silvester is a huge celebration in the provincial capitals. Vienna's 1st district, for example, turns into a stage with many different bands performing live outdoors and people setting off fireworks. The highlight is when the bells of St. Stephen ring in the New Year. Beware, however, after the last bell has tolled: many crazy people throw their bottles of *Sekt* (sparkling wine) up in the air!

Many Austrians prefer to stay home and celebrate the night in a more relaxed way. They have their own fireworks display, eat decorated sandwiches (always open-faced), and drink *Sekt*. They also pass good luck to each other through the exchange of marzipan, ceramic, and cloth pigs, chimneysweeps, and four-leaf clovers. To foresee what luck the year will bring, many buy lead pieces especially made for New Year's. A piece of lead is put on a spoon, melted over a candle, then quickly plunged into cool water. Whatever form the lead takes reveals the character of the new year.

· Chapter Eleven —

THE HILLS ARE ALIVE

The mention of Austria conjures up images of a grand empire and world power, encompassing many lands and peoples, and governed by such famous rulers as Maria Theresa and Franz Josef. For many people, what is known of Austria was taught in history class. In fact, Austria itself promotes this image to boost tourism. Yet many people do not have a clear idea of what to expect from a modern-day Austria. What are the people like? What day-to-day conveniences are available to its residents? What role does Austria play in international politics? Indeed, Austria has retained much of its imperial charm, but it is so much more than that.

Austrians are a traditional and conservative people who have enthusiastically embraced the 21st century. Life in Austria is a wonderful mix of quiet cafés and mobile phones, leisurely strolls in the woods and speeding along the Autobahn, Mozart and jazz, tuxedos and green hair, Baroque buildings and the largest shopping mall in Europe with probably the shortest opening hours. It is a country that, although no longer an empire, is an active member of the European Union and the seat of several international organizations. Geographically, the country is much smaller than it was at the height of the empire, yet what remains contains some of the most breathtaking scenery, too many castles and churches to count, and one of the most vibrant, culturally rich capitals in all of Europe. You'll be hard pressed to take in all of the attractions that the cities have to offer, visit the picturesque villages tucked away in the mountains, and take advantage of the numerous world-class sports facilities.

GEOGRAPHY

The Habsburg dynasty ruled the Austrian Empire from 1273 until 1918. Under its rule, the empire grew and at various times included today's Czech Republic, Slovakia, Slovenia, Croatia, Bosnia-Herzegovina, Hungary, parts of Poland and Italy, and, for a short while, the Netherlands and Spain and its territories. Following World War I and the renunciation of Emperor Karl I, the Austrian Republic was established. The country was reduced to the German-speaking areas, the heart of the former empire. Today, Austria is a country of eight million people. Although 98 percent of the population is German-speaking, there are significant ethnic minority groups. They include Croats, Slovenes, Hungarians, Czechs, Slovaks, and Turks.

Bundesländer

Austria is a federal republic consisting of nine *Bundesländer* or autonomous provinces. Beginning in the west and moving in an eastwardly direction, the states are Vorarlberg, Tyrol, Salzburg,

Carinthia, Upper Austria, Styria, Lower Austria, Vienna, and Burgenland. These provinces have marked differences in topography, customs, dialects, traditional dress, and personality. Geographical and cultural differences have given rise to a strong sense of regionalism. People often consider themselves Tyrolean or Viennese first, and Austrian second.

Vorarlberg

Vorarlberg, Austria's most westerly province, lies between the *Bodensee* (Lake Constance) and Arlberg Pass. It could be argued that Vorarlberg resembles a Swiss canton more closely than an Austrian province. Before the 14-kilometer Arlberg tunnel was opened in 1978, linking this province with Tyrol, Vorarlberg was practically cut off from the rest of Austria during the winter months. Over the centuries it had forged close ties with neighboring Switzerland. Thus, clothing, customs, and food in Vorarlberg are similar to those found in Switzerland. In fact, the German they speak is much closer to Swiss German than to the German spoken in the rest of Austria.

Austria may be landlocked, but this province's capital, Bregenz, bursting with life along the shore of the huge lake, can play with your sense of reality. Bregenz is famous for its summer festival and the floating stage on which the performances take place. Just outside of Bregenz begin the *Bregenzerwald*, which literally means "Bregenz woods." In addition to the forests, this beautiful area encompasses rolling hills, green meadows, the Bregenzer Ache River, and rocky cliffs; not to mention the delightful towns that dot the scenery. The houses in this region are almost identical to houses found in Switzerland. The traditional dress, which is not commonly worn today, also differs from the *Trachten* worn throughout the rest of Austria. This is especially true of the hats, which include wide black straw hats, fur hats, and cone-shaped hats.

The *Kleines Walsertal* is also a favorite destination for tourists. It is a very small area that is virtually cut off from the rest of Austria by the Allgäu Alps, and it has always had close ties to Germany, both economically and culturally. The *Montafon* valley is another heavily touristed area noted for its green pastures.

Dornbirn is the most populous city in Vorarlberg and is also the economic capital. The textile industry has a long tradition in Vorarlberg, and every summer, Dornbirn hosts one of the most important textile fairs in central Europe. Feldkirch, another important town in Vorarlberg, has maintained its medieval charm. Although not the capital of the province, it has remained an administrative center.

The mountains of Vorarlberg have made this province, along with Tyrol, the center of Alpine skiing. Lech and Zürs top the list of ski resorts. Although they rank among the most expensive in Austria, these resorts do provide first-rate equipment and infrastructure such as ski lifts for four to five people and helicopters to reach choice skiing areas. In fact, Zürs was the site of the first modern ski tow in Austria.

Tyrol

When you think of skiing in Austria, no doubt it is the province of Tyrol that comes to mind. This is the heart of the Alps, where snowcapped mountains, glaciers, Alpine meadows, valleys, and farmhouses decorated with window boxes of red geraniums can all be found. It is a winter sports mecca that includes Kitzbühel, St. Anton, Ischgl, and Seefeld. Kitzbühel is best known as the site of professional skiing competitions, and like St. Anton caters to the wealthy. Innsbruck hosted the winter Olympic Games in 1964 and in 1976. Of course, skiing is not the only sport practiced here. In summer there is hiking and mountain climbing. In fact, Tyrol earns more money from tourism than any other province in Austria. The people of the Tyrol are very warm and friendly, making it a great place to visit.

The capital, Innsbruck, lies along the Inn River nestled between the Alps. The *Goldenes Dachl* (little golden roof) is the signature attraction. Contrary to the legend that it was built by "Fredriech the Penniless" to prove his wealth, it was commissioned by Maximilian

I. Dating from 1500, this small balcony on the former Ducal Palace is topped with 2,657 gilded shingles. It was built to commemorate Maximilian's second marriage, to Bianca Maria Sforza of Milan, in 1494.

In addition to all of the city's main attractions, you can visit the *Alpenzoo*. The zoo sits on a mountainside overlooking the city, and contains 150 species of Alpine animals. Although you can drive or walk up to the zoo, the best way to get there is to take the Alpenzoo-Hunger-Burgbahn cog railway.

West of Innsbruck lie the Upper Inn valley, the rugged Ötztal Alps, ancient Rhaeto-Romanic villages high up on the mountain slopes, and the primeval forests of Lech valley. Lying in the Inn valley just west of the city of Telfs is Stams Monastery. This impressive Cistercian Abbey with over 180 rooms was established in the 13th century. Its carved altar, designed in the shape of a tree, is breathtaking.

The Lower Inn valley lies east of Innsbruck and includes the Achen Lake area, the Ziller valley, and the Tuxer valley, where summer skiing is possible. Cattle and dairy farming are a major source of income for this area. The charming town of Kufstein with its fortified castle overlooking the valley lies at the border with Germany. Above Kufstein sits the Kaiser mountain range, which resembles the Dolomites, that spectacular mountain range in northern Italy that juts forcefully into the air.

Prior to World War II, Tyrol was a much larger area encompassing *Südtirol* (Southern Tyrol). Even though Austria was forced to cede this area to Italy in 1919, the region remains culturally closer to Austrian Tyrol than to the rest of Italy. Austria has always been concerned about the rights of the German-speaking community there and it has been a sensitive political issue between the two countries. After it became apparent that *Südtirol* would not be returned, Austria pushed for greater autonomy for the region. After long negotiations, the Italian government finally increased the area's authority.

Another result of the change in borders was that East Tyrol became geographically separated from the rest of Austrian Tyrol and it remained somewhat isolated until the Felbertauern tunnel was built in 1967. This region is blessed by a more temperate Mediterranean climate, and the Dolomites rise up along its southern border.

Salzburg

Salzburg the city is known the world over as the birthplace of Mozart and the setting for the classic movie *The Sound of Music*. Always overflowing with tourists, the city and its surroundings have much to offer sightseers. Salzburg was founded by a bishop who chose the site as a base from which to spread Christianity to most of present-day Austria. Prince-archbishops ruled the city and the province, which share the same name. After visiting the fortress and the Cathedral, most people meander through the streets of the small city. A must-see is Getreidegasse, a narrow lane lined with stores, each proudly advertising its business on a beautiful wrought-iron sign. Even McDonald's almost seems to fit in on this street.

Salzburg and the neighboring Salzkammergut region, noted for its scenic lakes and mountains, received their names from the very important salt trade. Salt has been mined here for centuries, bringing in much of the area's wealth. If you are looking for something different you can tour the mines. Another fascinating underground experience are the *Eisriesenwelt* caves south of Salzburg. As the name "World of the Ice Giants" suggests, massive ice formations can be viewed inside the caves.

Most of the province lies south of the city of Salzburg and north of the *Hohe Tauern* mountain range. By taking the cable car to the top of the *Untersberg*, just south of the city near the town of St. Leonhard, you can see the ice-covered mountains as well as the lakes of Salzburg's Salzkammergut region to the east and northeast. The Salzach valley stretches between Salzburg and the Krimml Falls, the largest waterfalls in Europe, in the far western tip of the province.

Susan Roraff

The Salzkammergut region, dotted with scenic lakes and mountains, is a favorite holiday destination for many Austrians.

These dramatic falls mark one end of the Gerlos Pass, which takes you into Tyrol amidst spectacular scenic views.

The two most popular skiing resorts in Salzburg are Bad Hofgastein and Badgastein. If you'd rather not take to the slopes, then spend a relaxing day in the spas. Zell am See is a picturesque town on a beautiful lake and the nearby glaciers allow year-round skiing. The spectacular Grossglockner Road begins just south of Zell am See in Fusch and takes you past some astounding scenery in the Hohe Tauern National Park on your way to Heiligenblut in Carinthia. The highlight of the journey is the close-up view of Austria's highest mountain, the Grossglockner, which rises 3,798 meters into the air, and the Pasterze glacier. The road was built from 1930 until 1935 and is only open from May through October, 5 am until 10 pm.

Carinthia

Carinthia (*Kärnten*) is another of Austria's Alpine provinces. The Nockalm Road between Innerkrems and Ebene Reichenau takes you into the breathtaking Nockberge National Park. Carinthia has some very good, though less famous, ski resorts. Many Austrians head to the province in winter, and Nassfeld, a ski resort close to the border with Italy, is a popular spot.

Yet, Carinthia might be more popular in summer because of its many lakes. Principal among them is the *Wörthersee* near the capital, Klagenfurt. This large lake, ringed by hotels, pensions, and summer homes, is great for swimming, boating, windsurfing, and sailing. Jutting out on a tiny peninsula on the lake is the town of Maria Wörth and its oft-photographed church. This picturesque town was a center for the area's conversion to Christianity. Summer vacationers also descend upon *Ossiachersee* near Villach, *Millstättersee* near Spittal, and some of the 200 other smaller lakes in the province.

The capital, Klagenfurt, lies on the eastern shore of the *Wörthersee*. Its most notable attraction is the dragon fountain erected in the main square in 1593 to honor the city's founding. The area north of Klagenfurt is rich with interesting historical sites. A trip to the top of the Hochosterwitz castle takes you through the 14 gates that once protected the castle. Roman ruins can be found in Virunum and remains from the Celtic capital of Noricum can be seen in nearby Magdalensberg. The stone chair from which the Carinthian dukes dispensed justice and issued land grants in the Middle Ages sits in the Zollfeld. The fortified Maria-Saal Cathedral is noted for its gothic "lantern of the dead" and "skeleton house." Gurk has a beautiful Romanesque basilica that dates from 1140. The tomb of St. Hemma, who used her wealth to found eight churches and a convent, is buried in the crypt. The frescoes in the Bishop's Chapel dating from 1230 and the Baroque high altar from 1632 are worth seeing.

In the eastern corner of the province is Bad St. Leonhard, proud of its Parish Church that has preserved its stained glass windows from

Bildstock, distinctive shrines featuring different religious scenes on each of their four sides, are common in Carinthia.

235

the 14th and 15th centuries. Wolfsberg is a large town at the base of a late Gothic fortress. The church within the castle dates from the 15th century and, remarkably, has never been altered.

Carinthia is Austria's southernmost province. It borders Slovenia and is home to a sizeable Slovenian population, particularly in the Gail, Rosen, and Jaun valleys in the southern part of the province. Although some Slovenian customs and traditional costumes remain, and the Slovenian language is sometimes heard, the Carinthians are all Austrian. In fact, following the breakup of the empire in 1918, they voted to remain part of Austria instead of joining with Slovenia in Yugoslavia.

Styria

Styria, or *Steiermark* in German, is lovingly called the "green province" of Austria. Forests cover about half the province and pastures and vineyards cover almost another quarter. This makes it a great place for *Heurigen* where fresh new wines are available. This beautiful region has a bit of everything. The town of Bad Aussee is the capital of the Styrian Salzkammergut located in the northwest corner of the province. From here you can venture to Altausseer Lake or Grundl Lake to take in their spectacular views of the Totes Gebirge and Dachstein mountain ranges.

The Benedictine Abbey of Admont is located in the nearby Enns valley. Founded in the 11th century by St. Hemma of Gurk, it is one of Austria's most famous monasteries and its extensive library makes for an interesting stop. Between Admont and Hieflau lies the Gesäuse, a wild gorge cut by the churning River Enns. From Hieflau you can follow the Eisenstrasse (Iron Road) to Leoben, going along the Eisenerz Alps, which are famous for the Erzberg (Iron Mountain). About 90 percent of the nation's iron ore comes from this mountain which towers above the city of Eisenerz. Here you can see the *Schichtturm* (shift tower), whose bell was rung to signal the changing of workshifts. In spite of being the green heart of Austria, Styria also happens to be the country's most heavily mined province. In addition to iron ore, lignite and magnesite are two of the other economically important minerals found here.

The Mürz valley and the surrounding area, known as *Waldheimat Mürztal*, is dotted with small villages and larger picturesque towns such as Mürzzuschlag and Kindberg. This beautiful valley is perfect for outdoor activities like hiking, cycling, and horseback riding. A fun yet affordable option is to visit a working farm for the weekend, a great experience, especially for children.

Graz, Styria's capital, is Austria's second largest city. The outskirts are industrial, but don't let that put you off. Graz's wonderful historic city center has been declared a United Nations Cultural Heritage Site. Strolling through the quaint streets takes you along the Mur River to the base of the Schlossberg. As the name suggests, a castle sat atop this large hill to protect the city from the Turks. It is also the source of the city's name, Graz, which is derived from the Slovenian *gradec*, meaning small castle. The city's most internationally famous son is Arnold Schwarzenegger, who returns often and helps promote tourism in the province. The nearby town of Piber is the home of the stud farm for the Lippizaner horses.

Quietly sitting in the mountains in northern Styria is the lovely town of Mariazell and its awe-inspiring pilgrimage church. A monk founded the church in 1157. Not long after, it was reported that its small Virgin Mary with Child statue could perform miracles. Soon people started visiting the church to ask for favors or to give a prayer of thanks, making it the most important place of pilgrimage in Austria. Prayers are directed at the Virgin and Child, who are now dressed in an elaborate gown and encircled by a finely detailed silver lattice.

Upper Austria

Upper Austria is primarily an agricultural region, but it also produces a significant amount of oil and natural gas, and has an important industrial center in the area surrounding Linz, the provincial capital.

The Danube flows through Linz, making it a center of trade since the Middle Ages. In contrast to its modern port and economic dynamism, the city has a number of historical sights. You can begin by taking the steepest railway in Europe (dating from 1898) to the top of the Pöstlingberg hill to visit the pilgrimage church or simply take in a wonderful view of the city. At the *Landhaus* in the city center, currently the seat of the Upper Austrian government, you can see where Johann Kepler taught and developed his theories. The astronomer and mathematician was a teacher at Linz College (formerly located here) from 1612 to 1626. On the outskirts of Linz is St. Florian Abbey. For a thousand years, people have traveled to the church to ask for help or to thank God for an answered prayer. Anton Bruckner, who composed majestic pieces of classical music in the 19th century, often played the organ here and is buried in the church's crypt.

North of Linz is the *Mühlviertel*, named for the Mühl River, which flows into the Danube. A trip through the *Mühlviertel* takes you past steep granite hills, dense forests, meadows, small towns, and farms. This area is a must for nature lovers who enjoy horseback riding, hiking, or cycling. Or follow the Museum Road, the highlight of which is the carved Gothic winged altar at Kefermarkt, or the Weaver's Road where you can visit workshops, artists' studios, and museums. The capital of the *Mühlviertel* is Freistadt. An important city on the salt and iron road, Freistadt has preserved its ring of fortifications, which date from the Middle Ages. Seeing the moat, gates, towers, and castles can stir up your imagination and transport you to a time long since past.

South of the Danube and east of Germany lies the *Innviertel*, named for the Inn River. With sprawling meadows and vast forests, this region boasts some of the richest farmland in Austria. The *Innviertel*'s two main towns, Braunau and Schärding, lie on the border with Germany. Braunau has the unfortunate distinction of being Hitler's birthplace, but it is a pleasant medieval town in its own right. Schärding has a lovely Baroque main square and is also known as a health resort where you can experience the hydrotherapy cure invented by Sebastian Kneipp. Halfway between the two is the thousand-year-old town of Obernberg, noted for its Baroque townhouses. If you're particularly impressed by Baroque architecture, travel down the Baroque Road.

Although the Salzkammergut region lies within three provinces, the heart of the region is found in Upper Austria. Some of the largest and most beautiful lakes, such as *Attersee*, *Traunsee*, *Mondsee*, and *Hallstättersee* can be found here. Austrians flock to these lakes in the summer to enjoy water sports, *particularly* boating. Since the 15th century, the town of Gmunden on the *Traunsee* has produced the colorful pottery that is used throughout the country. A large 1487 abbey overlooks the small town of Mondsee. The village of Hallstatt sits at the base of the Dachstein Mountain, alongside the lake of the same name. Many visitors have referred to Hallstatt as the most beautiful lakeside village in the world. Here you can meander through steep streets, visit the Gothic church and tour the oldest salt mine in the world. But these are not the only lakes in the Salzkammergut. The region is dotted with many smaller ones set amidst highly dramatic backgrounds.

Perhaps Bad Ischl can be referred to as the center of the Salzkammergut. Emperor Franz Josef spent his summers here, and his presence caused the aristocracy and other important people of the 19th century to make it their summer resort as well. All of the important artists, composers, writers, poets, and actors of the day were drawn to the town. Franz Lehár's home has been turned into a museum.

Lower Austria

Lower Austria, *Niederösterreich* in German, is the largest province in terms of area. More significantly, it is considered to be the cradle of Austria. This was the very place that was referred to as the *Ostarrichi* or Eastern Realm of Charlemagne's Frankish Empire. It is from this word that Austria's name in German, *Österreich*, is derived. The existence of over 400 castles in Lower Austria prove the historical weight of this province. The medieval dynasties of the Babenberger and the Kuenringer were seated here. Although it used to promote itself as "the province on Vienna's doorstep," Lower Austria is a fascinating area in and of itself.

The Danube valley has traditionally been the life source of the area, and a leisurely drive along the river will have your head spinning with ruins, castles, palaces, abbeys, and fortified churches. Perhaps the most spectacular section of the river is the Wachau, which runs from Melk to Krems. This stretch of the river is the most important valley in Central Europe both historically and culturally. This is where the Venus of Willendorf was found. "Venus," a statue of a plump woman said to represent fertility, is estimated to be at least 20,000 years old.

The Baroque Melk Abbey looks gracefully out over the town of the same name and the Danube River. Impressive as it is from the outside, a tour of the Emperor's Gallery, the Marble Hall, the library, and the church lavishly decorated in gold prove no less interesting. The restored medieval town of Krems with its cobbled streets lies at the other end of the Wachau. Stein, formerly a separate town but now part of Krems administratively, has not yet been restored, and provides you with a truer picture of its past.

The wonderful medieval town of Durnstein is the highlight of the valley. Leaving your car outside town in one of the special parking lots, stroll though the old walled city and, if you have the energy, climb to the ruined fortress high on the hill. This is where Richard the Lionheart was held captive in the 12th century. He was arrested for offending the Babenberg ruler, Leopold V, on his way back from the Crusades. Legend says that King Richard's minstrel Blondel wandered throughout the region singing until the king heard him and told him of his fate. This, however, is just another of the legends that Austrians hold dear. England did in fact have to pay a hefty ransom for the return of her king, and it was used to develop Vienna. Farther upstream are the Aggstein ruins. Climbing through the remains of this large castle is fun for both kids and adults, and the views are worth the effort. In addition to these historical sights, a drive through the valley takes you past vineyards and apricot orchards. Any restaurant or *Heurige* along the route would be a great place to stop for wine and a tasty snack.

Several other areas within Lower Austria are worth visiting. The *Waldviertel*, or wooded quarter, lies north of the Danube in the western portion of the province. The *Weinviertel*, or wine quarter, also lies north of the Danube, but to the east. There are ample opportunities to hike or cycle, but the slower pace and gentle sloping hills suggest a glass of wine instead. Sixty percent of Austria's wine comes from this area, most ranking among the best in the country. Not surprisingly, agriculture plays a major role in this province.

Surrounding Vienna is the *Wienerwald*, better known in English as the Vienna Woods. This is a large region of rolling hills, hiking paths, small roads, farms, vineyards, villages, and heavily wooded areas that were saved from development. Scenic towns and villages lie within the *Wienerwald*, such as Perchtoldsdorf, Mödling, Gumpoldskirchen, and Baden. Pass an afternoon at a *Heurige* in any of the first three wine villages. Spend a day or a weekend in the spa town of Baden. Relax at the baths or head into the casino for some action. You can either stroll through the city streets lined with shops, or through the Kurpark, a beautiful large park that begins near the town center, from which over 60 kilometers of marked paths into the woods begin.

The foothills of the Alps begin 50 kilometers west of Vienna. South of the capital is the Alpine region, where the Viennese head to hike and ski. The ski resort of Semmering is quite close, and always packed on weekends throughout the winter. The nearby Raxalpe is a favorite spot for mountain climbing. The Raxbahn cable car transports you to the top to wander along trails, and you can spend the night in one of several hotels there. Also in the vicinity is the *Schneeberg* or Snow Mountain. The Schneebergbahn (mountain railway), which operates from June to September only, takes you to the top. Close to Wiener Neustadt sits the Hohe Wand, a tall sheer cliff that is perfect for hang-gliding and climbing.

Vienna

The city of Vienna is both the capital of Austria and a federal province. Its history dates backs to the Celts and the Romans, but it only flourished in the 12th century when the Babenberg dynasty made it the imperial residence. The Habsburgs assumed power in the 13th century, and remained in control until 1918. Under their rule, the empire grew and the city blossomed along with it. Palaces, churches, museums, and gardens beautified the city. Austria's intelligentsia were drawn to it. Architecturally, culturally, and politically, Vienna became one of the most important capitals in Europe. Most of the city's architecture, art, and music were influenced by each other and by events within the empire. The Baroque period blessed Vienna with ornate palaces and churches. Biedermeier focused on comfort, simplicity, and function in architecture and furniture. Historicism saw the removal of the city wall and the building of the Ringstrasse and many parks and green areas. Jugendstil left its mark not only on architecture and art, but also on everyday household items. Add to this the architecture of Red Vienna, a period noted for its massive public housing projects, and you have a strange mixture of styles that can only be Vienna.

Today, Vienna is a curious mix of its imperial past, its ties with socialism, and its modern development. It promotes an image of emperors and palaces, but that is merely one level of a highly complex city. We have heard Vienna referred to as a capital without an empire, and that is true to some extent. But it remains an elegant and proud city, an integral member of the international community. Vienna is easily accessible, enjoyable, and safe. For a capital city, its crime rate is remarkably low. Visitors have commented that Vienna has all the culture and interests of Paris, but because of its smaller size, has a cozier atmosphere. It is a city that entices and enthralls without overwhelming or intimidating.

Burgenland

Southeast of Vienna, Burgenland was formed in 1921 from the German-speaking border areas of Hungary. The region was annexed by Austria in 1920, a development which resulted in sporadic fighting. A plebiscite was held the following year and the residents of the area's main city Sopron voted to remain with Hungary. When you look at a map, you'll see that Sopron sits on a little finger of Hungary that juts into Burgenland. In terms of geography, this province is quite different from the rest of Austria. This is where the Hungarian Plain or *Puszta* begins. The gentle landscape gives a sense of peace and relaxation. In fact, some Viennese complain that the pace is too slow, and joke that the clocks run slower there. The region produces a lot of wine, in particular red wine, and other agricultural products such as fruit, vegetables, and wheat. The ethnic mix of Burgenland is also somewhat different from that in the rest of the country. While the majority are German-speaking Austrians, there are significant Hungarian and Croatian minorities.

Eisenstadt became Burgenland's capital in 1925 and is the smallest of all the provincial capital cities. It was most notably the home of Joseph Haydn during the many years that he was chief conductor for the Esterházy dynasty. This very powerful and wealthy family (at times even wealthier than the Habsburgs) had palaces in Eisenstadt and Esterháza (in Hungary), and owned other property in the region. The imperial yellow Esterházy Palace stands proudly on a hill near the center of Eisenstadt, visible for miles around. The palace combines Baroque, Classic, and Biedermeier styles. A tour will take you through many of the rooms in which Haydn worked, including the large Haydnsaal concert hall. An even better option is to forego the tour and attend a concert at the palace. Not only is the concert room beautiful, with its ceiling covered in colorful frescoes, it is also one of the world's acoustically acclaimed concert halls. Big Haydn fans can also visit his home and mausoleum. Throughout history, Eisenstadt was home to a relatively large Jewish population. The Austrian Jewish museum and the Jewish quarter of Unterberg deserve a visit.

Burgenland was of great strategic value to Austria, and especially to Vienna. The Turks had to pass across these lands en route to the capital. Thus, many fortified castles were built high atop hills to stop the advancing armies. Hence "Burgenland"—land of the castles. One of the best castles to visit is Forchtenstein, 22 kilometers southeast of Wiener Neustadt. Built in the 14th century by the Counts of Mattersdorf, the castle was enlarged when it passed into the possession of the Esterházy family around 1635. It houses a very large collection of arms and armor (close to 20,000 items on exhibition in 32 rooms) used in the defense of Austria, as well as some Turkish items seized during the invasions of 1529 and 1683. It is the largest private collection in central Europe open to the public.

A pleasant way to pass a weekend is to meander from one castle to the next, following the *Schlossstrasse* (a route that will allow you to see fine examples of historic castles), which also passes into Styria. Some of the highlights along the road are Lockenhaus, Bernstein, Stadtschlaining, and Güssing. You can stop to tour the castles and small museums between April and November. Many castles offer lodging, and you can spend a quiet evening strolling around the grounds or nearby town, and enjoy a meal with a glass of the local wine. Another option is to attend one of the many musical perform-ances held in the castles.

Perhaps the most visited attraction in Burgenland is the *Neusiedlersee* (Lake Neusiedler). It is the only steppe lake in central Europe and has some odd characteristics. It is huge, about 30 kilometers long, but the maximum depth is only about 2 meters. There is no shore per se, the edge of the lake being full of reeds, and long

Burgenland may be Austria's smallest province, but it is full of castles like Burg Lockenhaus where you can stay overnight or attend a concert.

piers extend into the lake to provide access. No river water feeds into the lake, the source of which are underground springs. The Viennese flock to the lake in summer where water sports of all types are popular, especially windsurfing. The nearby village of Rust is famous for its wines and storks. Almost all of the chimneys in town are topped with a stork's nest and if you're there at the right time you can sit in a café and watch the storks fly overhead.

Romantic Road

One way to take in some of the best sights in Austria is to follow the Romantic Road. It begins in Vienna and winds westward through Lower Austria and Upper Austria, ending in Salzburg. The route is marked by brown signs and takes you on small winding roads. It's a lovely journey if you aren't in a hurry. Along the way you'll pass castles, monasteries, lakes, caves, and mountains. Be sure to stop at as many as you can. Beginning in Klosterneuberg, site of the oft-visited monastery and wonderful enameled Verdun altar, you then make your way to the beautifully restored town of Krems. At Spitz, a wine village, you leave the Danube and head up into the hills to see the simple church at Maria Laach, noted for its Late Gothic altar and the painting of Mary with six fingers.

You join the river again at Melk and continue to Artstetten Castle, the former residence and current resting place of Archduke Franz Ferdinand. The scenic road continues into Upper Austria, passing through Enns, the oldest city in Austria, and Steyr, with its remarkable town square. At the resort town of Scharnstein im Almtal at the foot of the Alps, the road turns south. If you are tired of buildings, head towards Grünau, a beautiful green valley that lies below snow-covered mountains where you can hike or just sit and stare at the scenery. The road then backtracks and leads into the Salzkammergut region. Gmunden, Traunkirchen, Bad Ischl, the health resort of St. Wolfgang, St. Gilgen, and Mondsee—so named because it has the shape of the moon—are all excellent places to stop, not only for an afternoon, but for a few relaxing days.

CLIMATE

The country can be divided into three climatic zones. The eastern part of the country, which includes Vienna, has average temperatures that range from –7°C in winter to 25°C in summer. Winters are cold and summers are short. Temperatures can be cool all the way into June, and in general, only July and August may truly be considered hot and humid. There are just as many gray, cloudy days as there are bright, sunny ones and this can have a negative effect on your disposition. The central Alpine region experiences high precipitation, long winters, and short summers. The rest of the country is part of the transitional central European zone. Summers average 14–19°C and precipitation levels are very high. Most of the weather comes in from the west and an imperfect but plausible way to predict the weather is to see what's happening in Munich.

FÖHN

You may hear Austrians blame the *Föhn* for their bad moods. These are warm, dry winds that come from the Alps. They are strongest in Tyrol but can be felt all the way in Vienna. If you're feeling out of sorts, or notice that people in general are more cranky than usual, it might be the *Föhn*. These winds are also said to be responsible for an increased number of suicides.

AVALANCHES

The heavy snowfall that improves the quality of ski slopes can become deadly. Avalanches hit with no warning and with horrendous results. There have been a number of deadly avalanches in recent years. In January 2000, nine people were killed in an avalanche in Galtür in Tyrol. This was close to the site where 38 people had been killed the year before in a massive avalanche. The February 1999 avalanche also hit the neighboring town of Valzur. In March 2000, 11 more people were killed in the ski resort of Kaprun in the province of Salzburg. Although those most at risk are thrill seekers who ski at very high altitudes on unstable powder, avalanches occasionally hit more populated areas. That was the case with the Galtür catastrophe in 1999, when tourists had to be airlifted to safety.

FLORA AND FAUNA

The flora and fauna of Austria are what you would expect to find in central Europe. If you spend any time driving around the country, you won't be surprised to learn that 46 percent of the total area of the country is forested. Oak, birch, and beech trees are found in the lower regions. Coniferous trees, including spruce, pine, fir, and larch, are found at higher altitudes. Many of the valleys are blessed with arable land. The small white *Edelweiss* flower, the symbol of Austria, is actually very rare and grows at higher elevations.

In the Alps live chamois, marmots, and other alpine animals. The ibex, which has been over-hunted, is making a comeback. Many of the animals native to central Europe are found in the lower-lying regions, including red deer, roe deer, hares, foxes, badgers, martens, squirrels, marmots, and pheasants. The reed beds of Neusiedler Lake in the east are home to a diverse bird population.

TIME ZONE

The entire country lies within the same time zone. Local time is GMT + 1 in winter during daylight savings time, and GMT +2 in summer. Clocks are moved ahead one hour in April, and back one hour in October.

NEIGHBORING COUNTRIES

If you have seen a great deal of Austria and want to experience something completely different, taking a weekend trip to one of the neighboring countries is always a good option. No matter where you are in Austria, you are never far from the border. Austria is surrounded by eight countries: Germany, the Czech Republic, Slovakia, Hungary, Slovenia, Italy, Liechtenstein, and Switzerland.

From Vienna you can reach Budapest in about 3 hours, and some smaller Hungarian towns are much closer. You can make a day trip to Sopron, a well-preserved medieval town on the border. In summer, head southeast to Lake Balaton, where you find the same water sports as in Austria, but at lower prices. Bratislava, the capital of Slovakia, is only 45 minutes away. Prague, the capital of the Czech Republic, is $4^1/2$ hours from Vienna and $2^1/2$ hours from Linz. Telc in Moravia and Ceske Krumlov in Bohemia are both cultural heritage sites protected by UNESCO and well worth a visit.

If you are in Vorarlberg, you're not very far from Switzerland; and if you don't drive too fast, you can see Liechtenstein. Germany is only minutes away from Salzburg. You can rest beside the *Chiemsee* or visit Munich, the capital of Bavaria. Innsbruck is located right between Germany and Italy. You can choose to travel across the Bavarian Alps and visit the fairytale castle of Mad King Ludwig or take the Brenner Pass south into the *Südtirol* which is now part of Italy. Just south of Villach in Carinthia is another gateway to Italy.

A day trip from Klagenfurt into Slovenia, to see Bled, the Triglav National Park, or the capital Ljubljana, is another wonderful excursion. Finally, although Croatia does not border Austria, Zagreb is relatively close to Graz (about 2 hours). You pass through the medieval town of Ptuj in Slovenia before reaching the charming countryside of northern Croatia. In most instances visas are not required, but do check with the consulate first. Crossing the border is normally easy, but you might experience delays during peak hours and on holiday weekends.

CULTURAL QUIZ

SITUATION ONE

You've been invited to a small dinner party by some new Austrian friends. Eager to make a good impression you:

A. Arrive about 15 to 20 minutes later in order to give the hosts enough time to get everything ready.

B. Quickly proceed to the living-room area where the other guests are, after saying hello to the hosts, and begin introducing yourself to everyone.

C. Arrive exactly at the hour specified, greet your hosts, hand the hostess a beautiful bouquet of flowers, and wait to be introduced to the other guests.

D. If you are a man and want to be truly European, greet each woman by taking her hand and raising it almost to your lips and say "*Küss die Hand*."

Comments

A. Never appropriate if the hosts are Austrians. Guests are expected to be on time and arriving late is considered rude. Susan was once reprimanded for arriving five minutes late. If you've run into some unforeseen problems or heavy traffic, you should call and notify your hosts.

B. If you are attending a small dinner party you should wait to be introduced to each of the guests. This actually makes it much easier on you if you don't know anyone there. If it is a large party the hosts probably won't introduce you to everyone, perhaps just a couple of people so that you can join in a conversation. You can then meet other people on your own.

C. Yes, this is the best way to impress your new friends. By arriving on time you show your hosts that the invitation is important to you. By giving the hostess flowers, or a bottle of wine, you are thanking her for all the effort she has put into the evening. It would also be a good idea to send a thank you note by mail the following day.

D. The *Küss die Hand* greeting is practiced only in certain circles and a foreigner can look especially stupid trying it out. Our advice is to leave it to the experts and just shake hands as most Austrians do. Only once you have established a close relationship can you greet each other by kissing on both cheeks, starting with the right one. This, of course, does not apply for greetings between men. You may never attain this level, however, and to avoid any embarrassment, you should wait for the Austrian to make the transition from a handshake. Don't assume that the time is right.

SITUATION TWO

You have just started working for an Austrian company. Your German is good but you are not aware of the formalities on the job. You greet your co-worker by her first name. She, in turn, greets you by your last name and asks you how you are doing by using the formal "you" or *per Sie*. What do you do?

A. Tell her that where you come from you are immediately on a first-name basis with colleagues.

B. Tell her not to be so stuffy, to hang loose.

C. Correct yourself and ask her a question by using her last name and use *per Sie* until further notice.

D. Look for another job.

Comments

A. You may appear rather ethnocentric. On the other hand, your co-worker might understand that things are different around the world. However, in Austria one greets another in a more formal manner.

B. Choosing *B* might make her react very negatively. As in *A*, formality is often a way for relationships to develop slowly and to be sure you know the person you are dealing with before revealing yourself.

C. The only way to go is with *C* if you want to keep in good stead with your co-worker. This behavior will win you points with every Austrian you meet.

D. This is the loser's way out. Every job you have will end the same way unless you work with your own kind at an embassy or consulate.

SITUATION THREE

After a long, tiring day on the ski slopes you decide to unwind in a hot steamy sauna. Knowing it to be mixed, you put on your one-piece bathing suit to hide any little imperfections and head off. When you open the door you gasp: everyone is stark naked. Do you:

A. Alert the management and tell them to call the police because there's an orgy taking place?

B. Sit down in the far corner, subject to puzzled stares?

C. Make a mad dash to the privacy of your room where you can enjoy a nice hot bath alone?

D. Strip off your suit, sit down, and join the conversation?

Comments

A. This is obviously not the correct answer. Austrians are comfortable being naked in the sauna or at a nudist beach and there is nothing sexual about the experience.

B. You could do this if you really want to be in the sauna but just can't take off your suit. The Austrians would think it very odd though, and wouldn't be able to figure out just why you are wearing your bathing suit.

C. This is a good option if being in the sauna makes you uncomfortable, but you have to settle for a bath instead of a sauna.

D. If you can, go ahead and join in. Nudity is not out of the ordinary for Austrians so they won't stare or pay any more attention to you than to anyone else. While they don't use their towels to cover up, you could drape yours strategically for your own comfort.

SITUATION FOUR

Your cupboards and fridge are bare and you need to go to a grocery store. You buy everything in sight, then load it all onto the conveyor belt. The cashier rapidly checks your items through but then you realize that your groceries are merely piling up next to the cashier's elbow as there is no rear conveyor belt. She is fuming and the people behind you are hemming and hawing. What to do?

A. Quickly, like a madperson, start piling purchased groceries back into your cart.

B. Stare at her with a look of amazement.

C. Ask her in your broken German for an explanation for the lack of rear conveyor belts and baggers.

D. Take your time; either put everything back in the cart or have some plastic bags ready and pack then and there.

Comments

A. This is the best answer, and what most people do to keep up with the cashier. Most Austrians shop several times a week to avoid making large purchases or go once a week to larger grocery stores where rear conveyor belts are found.

B. This would make matters worse and most likely end with the cashier swearing and people behind you adding odd comments.

C. Like *B*, this would confuse the cashier as most people never question the system. And the cashier most likely would not even know that rear conveyor belts exist.

D. Risky, but if you can handle the pressure, go for it! Julie used to bag groceries, so for her, there would be no other option but to do it right there and then!

SITUATION FIVE

You're celebrating a special birthday and have invited a few of your new friends to a Saturday night party. You have food, wine, and music and the party has been a great success, but by no means a big bash. Just after 10 pm, the doorbell rings. It's the police telling you that a neighbor has called to complain about the noise at such a late hour. Surprised, because the party is not especially loud, you:

A. Tell the police what they want to hear, close the door, and resume festivities.

B. Phone the neighbor you believe made the complaint, call her an "old cow" and tell her to get a life.

C. Offer the police a bribe so that you can continue partying.

D. Make sure to invite all of your neighbors to your next party so that they'll be at your place having fun instead of at home suffering.

E. Apologize to the police, turn off the music, and try to talk softly, or else end the party prematurely.

Comments

A. This is what many foreigners might choose to do, but it's really not a solution. The neighbors will continue to complain, the police will return, and the party might end on a sour note.

B. This childish response certainly won't help smooth relations with your neighbors.

C. Bribing the police could land you in big trouble.

D. Inviting your neighbors might work the next time, but then again it might not. Your neighbors may leave earlier than your other guests, and once home could turn around and call the police because they are now ready to sleep.

E. Unfortunately, this is the only option. You are living in a country where not only is loud noise late at night prohibited, but even reasonable noise levels (for a large group) can elicit calls to the police. Hopefully, you can still have fun with the noise level down. However, if a conversation between six people has brought the police, you might have to call it a night. Another option might be to have an afternoon barbeque that starts and ends earlier.

SITUATION SIX

You haven't yet registered with the police and you desperately need your *Meldezettel* to get your driver's license. It's 9 am and by the time you get to the proper room there are already 50 people waiting in line. You sit, waiting your turn. After 30 minutes you realize that only people with numbers are being called in. You finally see the number machine and, feeling stupid, take your number after many other people have strolled in behind you. You try and tell the people behind closed doors of your dilemma but are only barked at and told to wait your turn, with the remark, "Can't you read the sign that says 'don't come in unless your number is called?'" What do you do?

A. Demand proper attention.

B. Wait patiently for your number to be called.

C. Try and talk to someone with a number that is soon to be called to see if you can go first.

D. Go home and cry.

Comments

A. Choosing *A* will only make the civil servants scream louder. No one is special, and if you goofed, you must pay and learn from your mistake.

B. This is the wisest choice. You might have to wait a long time but you will eventually get what you need in order to get other important paperwork accomplished. In many cases, the *Meldezettel* acts like an identification card.

C. This will give someone a reason to laugh his or her head off but at least you will find out that Austrians have a sense of humor.

D. This will not get you what you need and you will only have to return another day. Better to conform and stay calm.

GLOSSARY

ESSENTIALS

Hello	*Grüss Gott/Servus/Guten Tag*
Goodbye	*Auf Wiedersehen/ Wiederschauen/ Wiederhören/Tschüss/Baba*
Thank you	*Dankeschön/Dankesehr*
Please, Welcome	*Bitte/Bitteschön/Bittesehr*
Excuse me, Pardon me	*Enschuldigen Sie/Pardon*
Where is…?	*Wo ist…?*
Where is the toilet or restroom?	*Wo sind die Toiletten?*
Where is the underground?	*Wo ist die U-Bahn?*
What is your name?	*Wie heissen Sie?*
What time is it?	*Wie spät ist es?*

* Words in bold are used more often in Austria.

IN A RESTAURANT

Do you accept credit cards?	*Nehmen Sie Kreditkarten?*
I'd like to make a reservation.	*Ich möchte einen Tisch reservieren.*
The menu, please.	*Die Speisekarte, bitte.*
I would like … (when ordering in restaurants, for example)	*Ich hätte gern…*
Something to drink?	*Zu trinken?*
The check, please.	*Zahlen, bitte.*
(Paying) together? or separately?	*(Zahlen Sie) Zusammen oder Getrennt?*

256

(You give exact amount plus tip) *Das stimmt schon or danke.*
To eat in or to go? *Zum hier-essen oder zum
mitnehmen?*

A doggie bag, please (Austrians *Können Sie mir das einpacken,
don't normally do this). bitte?*

SIGNS

Ausgang	Exit
Eingang	Entrance
Einbahnstrasse	One way street
Gleis	Platform
U-bahn	Underground
Drucken	Push
Ziehen	Pull
Rasen betreten verboten	Don't walk on the grass
Die Toiletten	Toilet
Leitungswasser	Water (from the tap)
Bankomat	Automatic teller
Kassa	Cashier
Apotheke	Pharmacy
Bäckerei	Bakery
Drogerie	Drugstore
Feinkost, Delikatessen	Delicatessen
Fischhandlung	Fish shop
Konditorei	Pastry shop
Lebensmittelladen	Grocery store
Papiergeschäft	Stationery store
Reformhaus	Health food store
Weinhandel	Wine shop

TITLES

Mag. (Magister)	Master's degree
Dr. (Doktor)	PhD
Frau	Mrs.
Fräulein	Miss
Herr	Mr.
Ing. (Ingenieur)	Engineering degree (5-year study in high school with two-year hands-on job)
Dipl. Ing. (Diplom Ingenieur)	Master's in Engineering

ABBREVIATIONS

AUA	Austrian Airlines
ÖBB (Österreichische Bundesbahn)	Austrian Federal Railway
EN	EuroNight (International and Domestic Train)
ÖAMTC (Österreichischer Automobil-, Motorrad- und Touring Club)	Emergency Road Service and Towing
ÖMV (Österreichischer Mineralölverwertung	Austrian Oil Company
ORF (Österreichischer Rundfunk)	Austrian Radio and Television Network
TA (Telekom Austria)	Austrian Telecom
FPÖ	Freedom Party
EU	European Union
ÖVP	People's Party
SPÖ	Social Democrats

GAS STATION

Full tank, please.	*Super volltanken, bitte.*
gas	*Benzin*
Diesel	*Diesel*

GEOGRAPHY

Berg	mountain
Bundesländer:	provinces:
Kärnten	Carinthia
Niederösterreich	Lower Austria
Oberösterreich	Upper Austria
Steiermark	Styria
Tirol	Tyrol
Wien	Vienna
Burg	castle
Gasse	small road or street
Haus	house
Österreich	Austria
Schloss	palace
See	lake
Strasse	street
Tal	valley
Wald	woods, forest
Weinviertel	wine quarter

RIDING A BUS OR TRAIN

Where do I buy a ticket for the bus (or train)?	*Wo kann ich einen Fahrschein kaufen?*
What time does the bus (or train) leave?	*Wann fährt der Autobus (der Zug) ab?*
Have you seen the conductor (train)?	*Haben Sie den Schaffner gesehen?*
Your ticket, please (train).	*Die Fahrscheine bitte.*

Is this seat reserved (train)?	*Ist dieser Sitz reserviert?*
May I sit next to the aisle (window)?	*Darf ich beim Gang (Fenster) sitzen?*
Is there a dining wagon?	*Wo ist der Speisewagen?*
Is this a smoking (non-smoking) cabin?	*Ist das ein Raucherabteil?*
Where is this train (bus) going to?	*Wo fährt dieser Zug (Autobus) hin?*
Is this my stop?	*Muss ich hier aussteigen?*
Do I get on here?	*Muss ich hier einsteigen?*
Can you show me on the map?	*Können Sie mir es auf der Karte zeigen?*
First Class	*Erste Klasse*
Second Class	*Zweite Klasse*

SHOPPING

Can you help me?	*Können Sie mir bitte helfen?*
I am just looking.	*Ich schaue nur.*
How much does it cost?	*Was kostet es?*
How much does that cost?	*Wieviel kostet es?*
Anything else?	*Ausserdem? Noch einen Wunsch?*

Grocery Shopping

Where are the fruits and vegetables?	*Wo finde ich das Obst und Gemüse?*
Do I need to weigh the fruits and vegetables?	*Muss ich das Obst und Gemüse abwiegen?*
Aisle 1	*Gang eins*
May I have a bag?	*Ein Sackerl, bitte.*
Could you open up a new counter?	*Kassa, bitte!*
Bottle receipt	*Flaschenzettel*
Shopping cart	*Einkaufswagerl*
Do you have change?	*Haben Sie Kleingeld?*

Clothing Store

Clothing	*Bekleidung*
Women's clothing	*Damenmoden*
Men's clothing	*Herrenmoden*
Boutiques	*Boutiquen*
Department stores	*Kaufhäuser*
Do you have a smaller (bigger) size?	*Haben Sie eine kleinere (grössere)?*
Can I try this on?	*Darf ich das anprobieren?*
How much does it cost?	*Wieviel kostet das?*

ACCOMMODATION

I'd like a single (double) room.	*Ich möchte ein Einzelzimmer (Doppelzimmer).*
How much is it per night/per person?	*Wieviel kostet es pro Nacht/pro Person?*
Is breakfast included?	*Ist Frühstück inbegriffen?*
Where is the bath/shower?	*Wo ist das Bad/die Dusche?*

IDIOMATIC EXPRESSIONS

I want to get to the bottom of this.	*Der Sache will ich auf den Grund gehen.*
I'll attend to that personally.	*Das werde ich selbst in die Hand nehmen.*
I'm on duty.	*Ich habe Dienst*
Off duty/not working	*Außer Dienst/Betrieb*
I came to Vienna specially to see you.	*Ich kam eigens nach Wien, um dich zu sehen.*
Kindly give me your attention for a moment.	*Schenke mir bitte kurz deine Aufmerksamkeit.*
For what reason?	*Aus welchem Grund?*
Not without reason.	*Nicht ohne Grund.*

To fight tooth and nail	*Sich mit Händen und Füßen wehren*
You scratch my back, I'll scratch yours.	*Eine Hand wäscht die andere.*
The actual crux of the matter	*Der eigentliche Kern der Sache*
You have done me a favour.	*Du hast mir einen guten Dienst erwiesen.*
Could you do me a big favour?	*Könntest Du mir einen großen Dienst erweisen?*
One good turn deserves another.	*Ein Dienst ist des anderen Wert.*
Can I avail myself of your services?	*Kann ich deine Dienste in Anspruch nehmen?*
I'm at your service.	*Ich stehe dir zu Diensten.*
I wouldn't be seen dead in that coat.	*Den Mantel möchte ich nicht einmal geschenkt bekommen.*
Shall we skip going to the museum?	*Wollen wir uns den Besuch des Museums schenken?*
To make fun of something	*Etwas lächerlich machen*
To make someone laugh	*Jemandem zum Lachen bringen.*

RESOURCE GUIDE

All phone numbers are listed as long distance calls within Austria. For international calls into Austria, dial the country code **(43)** + number, but dropping the first **0**. Drop the area code when you are making a call in the same area. When a number includes a hyphen or slash, this indicates a direct dial extension. **–0** will connect you with the main switchboard or operator, who can then direct your call.

In this section the postal code is preceded by an **A-**. This should be used when sending mail to one of the following addresses from outside of Austria (**A** denotes Austria). If you are sending mail within Austria, drop the **A**. For example, Zentrales Fundamt, Wasagasse 22, 1090 Wien.

Within Vienna, the district can be ascertained from the two middle digits of the postal code. For example, **1090** indicates the 9th district. Addresses may also be given (although not when sending a letter) in the following manner: 9, Wasagasse 22, i.e., 9th district, street name (Wasagasse), and street number (22).

ESSENTIAL DOCUMENTS

Bring:

Passport
Birth certificate
Marriage/divorce certificate
Children's school records
Diplomas/degrees
Medical records
Vaccination history
Proof of health insurance
Driver's license

Obtain in Austria:
Visa (*Sichtvermerk*)
Residence Permit (*Aufenthaltsbewilligung*)
Work Permit (*Arbeitsgenehmigung*)
Police Registration (*Meldezettel*)

EMERGENCIES
Police: 133
Fire: 122
Ambulance: 144

LOST AND FOUND
Zentrales Fundamt
A-1090 Vienna
Tel: (01) 313 44–92 11

TELEPHONE INFORMATION
Telephone Companies
For an updated list of new and possibly cheaper long distance service
providers consult the website www.savecall.at.

Area Codes
Vienna—01
Bregenz—05574
Graz—0316
Innsbruck—0512
Klagenfurt—0463
Linz—0732
Salzburg—0662
St. Pölten—02742
Eisenstadt—02682

Directory Assistance
For Austria and Germany—118 11
For other foreign countries—118 12
Technical service (if you have problems with your phone line)—111 20

TAXIS

In Vienna, call any of these numbers:
313 00
401 00
601 60
814 00
910 91

C & K Airport Taxi
Tel: (01) 17 31 or 44 444
Fax: (01) 689 69 69

TRAIN STATIONS

Franz Josef Bahnhof
9, Althanstrasse 10

Südbahnhof
10, Wiedner Gürtel 1B

Westbahnhof
15, Europaplatz (on the Gürtel)

Train Information
Tel: (01) 1717

MEASURES

Austria uses the metric system.
220 volt electrical appliances only

INTERNET PROVIDERS

Chello (UPC Telekabel)
Erlachgasse 116
A-1100 Vienna
Tel: (01) 960 60 600
www.chello.at

Netway
Hollandstrasse 11-13
A-1020 Vienna
Tel: (01) 217 19–100
www.netway.at

UTA Telekom AG
Alserstrasse 34
A-1090 Vienna
Tel: (01) 9009–5045
www.uta.at

X Point
Am Spitz 7
A-1210 Vienna
Tel: (01) 275 20–0
www.xpoint.at

POST OFFICE

Main branch
Fleischmarkt 19
A-1010 Vienna
Tel: (01) 515 09–0

NEWSPAPERS

See Chapter Nine.

TELEVISION AND RADIO

See Chapter Nine.

GERMAN CLASSES

Berlitz School of Languages (main office)
Graben 13
A-1010 Vienna
Tel: (01) 512 82 86
Fax: (01) 512 82 86–4

Interlingua Language Services
Gusshausstrasse 14
A-1040 Vienna
Tel: (01) 505 97 44–0
Fax: (01) 505 19 45
E-mail: ILS@interlingua.co.at
www.interlingua.co.at

International Language Services (ILS)
Getreidemarkt 17
A-1060 Vienna
Tel: (01) 585 53 47
Fax: (01) 585 53 47–11
www.dolphin.at

Internationales Kulturinstitut (IKI)
Opernring 7
A-1010 Vienna
Tel: (01) 586 73 21
Fax: (01) 586 29 93
E-mail: iki@ikivienna.at
www.ikivienna.at

Talk Partners
Fischerstiege 10/16
A-1010 Vienna
Tel: (01) 535 96 95
Fax: (01) 533 30 73

University of Vienna (*Universität Wien*)
Wiener Internationale Hochschulkurse
Ebendorferstrasse 10/4
A-1010 Vienna
Tel: (01) 405 12 54–0
Fax: (01) 405 12 54-10
www.univie.ac.at/WIHOK

PRESCHOOLS

Arche Noah Wien International Privatkindergarten
Van-der-Nüll-Gasse 29
A-1100 Vienna
Tel: (01) 641 94 95
www.archenoah.vienna.at

Heidi Neuroth's
Schiffmühlenstrasse 59
A-1220 Vienna
Tel: (01) 269 09 00

Internationaler Montessori Kindergarten—The Children's House
Julius-Payer-Gasse 9
A-1220 Vienna
Tel: (01) 263 10 56
Fax: (01) 263 66 16
www.montessori-vienna.at

United Children Internationaler Kindergarten
Stumpergasse 49-51
A-1060 Vienna
Tel: (01) 597 00 06

SCHOOLS

American International School
Salmannsdorfer Strasse 47
A-1190 Vienna
Tel: (01) 401 32 22
www.ais.at

Danube International School
Gudrunstrasse 184
A-1100 Vienna
Tel: (01) 603 02 46

Japanese School in Vienna
Prandaugasse
A-1220 Vienna
Tel: (01) 204 22 01–0

Lycée Francais de Vienna
Liechtensteinstrasse 37a
A-1090 Vienna
Tel: (01) 317 22 41

Vienna International School
Strasse-der-Menschenrechte 1
A-1220 Vienna
Tel: (01) 203 55 95

Vienna Islamic School
Am Hubertusdamm 17-19
A-1220 Vienna
Tel: (01) 263 21 39

INTERNATIONAL, CULTURAL, SOCIAL, AND VOLUNTEER ORGANIZATIONS

American Women's Association (AWA)
Mahlerstrasse 3/7-8
A-1010 Vienna

Australian Women's Association
Australian Embassy
Mattiellistrasse 2-4
A-1040 Vienna
Tel: (01) 512 85 80

Austro-American Institute of Education (*Amerika-Institut*)
Opernring 4
A-1010 Vienna
Tel: (01) 512 77 20-0

Austro-American Society
Stallburggasse 2
A-1010 Vienna
Tel: (01) 512 39 82-0

Befrienders (English speaking crisis hotline)
Tel: (01) 713 33 74

British Community Association
British Embassy
Jaurèsgasse 12
A-1030 Vienna
Tel: (01) 716 13 00

British Council
Schenkenstrasse 4
A-1010 Vienna
Tel: (01) 533 26 16

Contact
This group welcomes new people to Austria.
Tel: (01) 714 67 20

United Nations
Wagramer Strasse 5
A-1400 Vienna
Tel: (01) 26060–0
Fax: (01) 263 33 89
www.unvienna.org

United Nations Women's Guild
Vienna International Center
Wagramer Strasse 5
Room F0919
A-1400 Vienna
Tel: (01) 26060–4276

EMBASSIES AND CONSULATES

Australian Embassy
Mattiellistrasse 2-4
A-1040 Vienna
Tel: (01) 512 85 80–0

British Consulate
Jaurèsgasse 10
A-1030 Vienna
Tel: (01) 716 13–5338

British Embassy
Jaurèsgasse 12
A-1030 Vienna
Tel: (01) 71 61 30

Canadian Embassy
Laurenzerberg 2
A-1010 Vienna
Tel: (01) 531 38 30–00

Indian Embassy
Kärntner Ring 2A
A-1010 Vienna
Tel: (01) 505 86 66

Irish Embassy
Landstrasser Hauptstrasse 2
Hilton Center, 16th floor
A-1030 Vienna
Tel: (01) 715 42 46–0

Japanese Embassy
Hessgasse 6
A-1010 Vienna
Tel: (01) 531 92–0

Malaysian Embassy
Prinz Eugen-Strasse 18
A-1040 Vienna
Tel: (01) 505 10 42–0

South African Embassy
Sandgasse 33
A-1190 Vienna
Tel: (01) 320 64 93–0

U.S. Consulate
Gartenbaupromenade 2 (Marriott Hotel building)
A-1010 Vienna
Tel: (01) 313 39–0

U.S. Embassy
Boltzmanngasse 16
A-1090 Vienna
Tel: (01) 313 39–0

BUSINESS ORGANIZATIONS

American Chamber of Commerce
Porzellangasse 35
A-1090 Vienna
Tel: (01) 319 57 51

British Trade Council in Austria
Laurenzerberg 2
A-1010 Vienna
Tel: (01) 533 15 94

Career Services
Women's Career Network
Contact the American Women's Association

HOSPITALS AND CLINICS

VIENNA

Allgemeines Krankenhaus (AKH)
Währinger Gürtel 18-20
A-1090 Vienna
Tel: (01) 40 400–0

Doctors-on-call Service (Ärztefunkdienst)
Tel: (01) 1771 Mon–Fri 7 am–7 pm
Tel: (01) 141 Mon–Fri 7 pm–7 am, Sat, Sun & holidays
You may use the service line 1771 to find a doctor in your vicinity.

On Duty Pharmacy Service (Apothekenbereitschafsdienst)
Tel: (01) 1550 (If you need to locate a pharmacy after hours)

Sozialmedizinisches Zentrum Ost (SMZ)
Langobardenstrasse 122
A-1220 Vienna
Tel: (01) 28 802–0

St. Annakinderspital (Children's Hospital)
(If an emergency, take the child to the AKH)
Kinderspitalgasse 6
A-1090 Vienna
Tel: (01) 401 70

Dental Clinics
Dr. Marcus Kolbeck
Hörlgasse 6
A-1090 Vienna
Tel: (01) 317 46 60

Dr. S. Weinländer
Boltzmanngasse 12/2, Vienna
A-1090 Vienna
Tel: (01) 317 99 99

Dr. Christian Zinn-Zinnenburg
Altgasse 25A
A-1130 Vienna
Tel: (01) 877 55 42

Medical Services

Vienna Medical Association: Service Department for Foreign Patients (*Ärztekammer für Wien: servicestelle für ausländische Patienten*)
Weihburggasse 10-12
A-1010 Vienna
Tel: (01) 51 501–213

EISENSTADT

Krankenhaus der Barmherzigen Brüder
Esterhazystrasse 26
A-7000 Eisenstadt
Tel: (02682) 601–0

GRAZ

Krankenhaus der Barmherzigen Brüder
Marschallgasse 12
A-8020 Graz
Tel: (0316) 7067–0

INNSBRUCK

Allgemeines öffentliches Landeskrankenhaus Innsbruck
Anichstrasse 35
A-6020 Innsbruck
Tel: (0512) 504–0

Privatklinik Triumphpforte Innsbruck
Leopoldstrasse 1
A-6020 Innsbruck
Tel: (0512) 5909–0

KLAGENFURT

Krankenhaus der Elisabethinen
Völkermarkter Strasse 15–19
A-9020 Klagenfurt
Tel: (0463) 5830–0

LINZ

Krankenhaus der Barmherzigen Brüder
Seilerstätte 2
A-4020 Linz
Tel: (0732) 7897–0

Krankenhaus der Stadt Linz
Krankenhausstrasse 9
A-4020 Linz
Tel: (0732) 7806–0

SALZBURG

Allgemeiner öffentlicher Landeskrankenanstalten
Müllner Hauptstrasse 48
A-5020 Salzburg
Tel: (0662) 4482–0

Krankenhaus der Barmherzigen Brüder
Kajetanerplatz 1
A-5020 Salzburg
Tel: (0662) 8088

INSURANCE

Allianz
Hietzinger Kai 101-105
A-1130 Vienna
Tel: (01) 878 07–0

Generali Versicherung
Landskrongasse 1-3
A-1010 Vienna
Tel: (01) 515 90–0

Wiener Städtische
Main Office (there are branches in most districts)
Ringturm, Schottenring 30
A-1010 Vienna
Tel: (01) 531 39–0
Fax: (01) 535 34 37
Vienna International Center (UN)
Tel: (01) 2600 22982

BANKS

Bank Austria
Am Hof 2
A-1010 Vienna
Tel: (01) 711 91–0

Creditanstalt
Stephansplatz 7a
A-1010 Vienna
Tel: (01) 534 25–0

Erste Bank
Graben 21
A-1010 Vienna
Tel: (01) 531 00–0

SHOPPING

VIENNA
(**1010**, **1060**, etc. refer to the postal code. For an explanation of what the code represents, see page 263.)

1010: Kärntner Strasse, Graben, & Kohlmarkt

These two streets are filled with exclusive clothing boutiques, china and silver shops, lingerie shops, and wonderful stationery and bookstores. The Dorotheum, also in the first district, is an upscale auction house/pawnshop that specializes in quality antiques. It's fun to browse even if you can't afford to buy anything.

1060 & 1070: Mariahilfer Strasse

Along this extremely long street between the outer Ring and the Westbahnhof are funkier clothing stores, large department and home furnishing stores, large book and music stores (often combined with coffee shops), discount clothing stores, toy stores, etc.

1110: Simmeringer Haide

This complex has a large Media Markt (electronics), Metro (bulk food warehouse where membership or diplomatic card is required), and other stores.

1200: Millennium Mall

Departments stores and boutiques are found on the lower levels of a skyscraper alongside the Danube on Handelskai.

1210: Shopping Center Nord

This mall has all the main stores selling clothes, shoes, stationery, books, toys, houseware, sporting goods, and pet supplies, and a sandwich shop.

1220: Donauzentrum

This two-story, two-sectioned mall found across from the U-1 Kagran stop houses the same selection of stores as the Shopping Center Nord mall, and includes two grocery stores besides.

2334: Vösendorf-Süd, Shopping City Süd

This is Europe's largest mall and the parking situation on Saturday can be frightening. It is divided into sections; the largest houses the same stores as a regular mall plus a food court and the Swedish houseware megastore, Ikea. Other sections include a multimedia complex filled with one of the largest movie theaters, small restaurants and cafés, a variety of electronic and houseware stores, and Toys 'R' Us. Interio, a funky houseware store, stands alone across from the complex. Across the highway, but still considered part of this mall, is Media Markt (electronics), Baumaxx (hardware), and Kaindl (houseware and appliances).

McArthur Glen Outlet Mall
Parndorf (near the border with Hungary) on the A4 Autobahn
Replica of an American outdoor factory outlet mall built alongside the highway—plenty of brand-name stores with lower prices. Considering the size of the mall, there is only a tiny food court and one café.

All-purpose Stores

VIENNA

Ikea
Shopping City Süd
Shopping Center Nord

Interio
1210: Brünner Strasse 73A
Shopping City Süd

Kika
1190: Kreilplatz 1
1220: Donauzentrum
2334: Vösendorf, Dr.-Robert-Firneis-Gasse
Shopping Center Nord

Leiner
1070: Mariahilfer Strasse 18
Shopping City Süd
Shopping Center Nord

Lutz/Möbelix
1210: Brünner Strasse 57A
1030: Kelsenstrasse 9 (Möbelix)
1150: Hütteldorfer Strasse 23 (Lutz)

Michelfeit
1100: Favoritenstrasse 130
1100: Laxenburger Strasse 145/Raxstrasse
1160: Sandleitengasse 26-30

Möma
Shopping City Süd area

EISENSTADT
Main street near Esterhazy Palace

INNSBRUCK
Maria-Theresien-Strasse, easily recognizable by the Triumphal Arch

KLAGENFURT
Main streets of Bahnhof St. and Alter-Platz

SALZBURG
Most of old city center, but primarily on Getreidegasse and Linzer Gasse.

REAL ESTATE AGENTS

Hans Schöll
Tigergasse 6
A-1080 Vienna
Tel: (01) 402 75 61–0 or 408 15 05
Fax: (01) 402 75 61–44

R.D. Kalandra
Franz-Josefs-Kai 33
A-1010 Vienna
Tel: (01) 533 32 69
Fax: (01) 533 82 43

Relocation Service Erika Strohmayer
2320 Schwechat, Am Concorde-Park 1/B6
A-2320 Schwechat
Tel: (01) 70 13 24 40
Fax: (01) 70 13 24 41
E-mail: reloserv@netway.at

ReMax
Singerstrasse 4/7
A-1010 Vienna
Tel: (01) 512 03 21
Fax: (01) 512 03 21–20

HOTELS

Children's Hotels
Postfach 10
A-9580 Villach
Tel: (042) 54 44 11
E-mail: office@Kinderhotels.or.at
www.Kinderhotels.or.at

Pension Cristina
Hafnersteig 7
A-1010 Vienna
Tel: (01) 533 29 61
Fax: (01) 533 29 61–11

Pension Domizil
Schulerstrasse 14
A-1010 Vienna
Tel: (01) 513 31 99
Fax: (01) 512 34 84

www.hotels.or.at
www.austria-hotels.co.at
www.familienhotels.org (children-friendly hotels and apartments)
www.schlosshotels.at (to stay at a castle)
www.tiscover.com (under hotels, search for *Bauernhof* to stay on a farm,
a very nice and inexpensive way to see Austria)

TOURISM

Austrian National Tourist Office

E-mail: Info@oewnyc.com

www.anto.com

An excellent website on tourism in Austria, giving detailed information on the cities of Salzburg, Vienna, Innsbruck, Linz, Graz, and Klagenfurt. See its sister website especially designed for the North American market: www.austria-tourism.at

The Austrian Press and Information Service

3524 International Ct. NW

Washington, D.C. 20008 (USA)

Tel: (1-202) 895 67 75

Fax: (1-202) 895 67 72

www.austria.org

Provides valuable practical information on many topics including visa regulations and business climate.

The Austrian Travel Network

www.tiscover.com

Somewhat difficult to navigate, but useful for finding accommodation and information on current events. Especially fun are the live cams of current weather conditions. Most provinces have a link from this website.

Tourism Websites

www.austriaguide.com

A great expat guide for people who live or plan on living in Austria.

www.help.gv.at

Only in German but it tells you everything you need to know to help you glide through the bureaucracy.

www.tourist-net.co.at

VIENNA

The Vienna Tourist Board
Tel: (01) 211 14–444
E-mail: wtv@info.wien.at
E-mail: rooms@info.wien.at
www.info.wien.at

Vienna Tourist Information Office
Albertinaplatz/Maysedergasse 9-19
A-1010 Vienna
Tel: (01) 513 40 15 or 513 88 92

Provinces and Regions

BURGENLAND
Schloss Esterhazy
A-7000 Eisenstadt
Tel: (02682) 633 84 28
Fax: (02682) 633 84 20
E-mail: info@burgenland-tourism.co.at
www.burgenland-tourism.co.at
www.tiscover.com/burgenland

CARINTHIA
Tel: (04274) 521 00
E-mail: info@carinthia.com
www.tiscover.com/carinthia

LOWER AUSTRIA
Walfischgasse 6
A-1010 Vienna
Tel: (01) 513 80 22–0
Fax: (01) 513 80 22–30
E-mail: tourismus@noe.co.at
www.tiscover.com/loweraustria

SALZBURG
Tel: (0662) 6688
E-mail: info@szgtour.co.at

SALZKAMMERGUT
Wirerstrasse 10
A-4820 Bad Ischl
Tel: (06132) 286 67
Fax: (06132) 286 67–71
www.tiscover.com/salzkammergut

STYRIA
Tel: (0316) 40 03-0
E-mail: tourismus@steiermark.com or Info@steiermark.com
www.steiermark.com

TYROL
Tel: (0512) 7272
Fax: (0512) 7272–7
E-mail: tirol.info@tirolwerbung.at
www.tiscover.com/tirol

UPPER AUSTRIA
Tel: (0732) 60 02 21-0 or 77 30 24
Fax: (0732) 60 02 20 or 77 30 25
E-mail: info@upper_austria.or.at
www.tiscover.com/upperaustria

VORARLBERG
Tel: (05574) 425 25–0
Fax: (05574) 425 25–5
E-mail: info@vbgtour.at
www.vorarlberg-tourism.at

Cities

Graz
Herrengasse 16
A-8010 Graz
Tel: (0316) 8075–0
Fax: (0316) 8075–15
E-mail: info@graztourismus.at
www.graz.com
www.tiscover.com/graz

Innsbruck Tourist Office
Burggraben 3
A-6021 Innsbruck
Tel: (0512) 598 50
Fax: (0512) 598 50–7
E-mail: info@innsbruck.tvb.co.at
www.tiscover.com/innsbruck

Klagenfurt
Rathaus, Neuer Platz 1
A-9010 Klagenfurt
Tel: (0463) 53 72 23
Fax: (0463) 53 72 95
E-mail: tourismus@klagenfurt.at
www.tiscover.com/klagenfurt

Linz Tourist Office
Old City Hall Building
Hauptplatz 1
A-4020 Linz
Tel: (0732) 70 70 17 77
Fax: (0732) 77 28 73
E-mail: linz@upperaustria.or.at
www.tiscover.com/linz

Salzburg Tourist Office
Auersperstrasse 7
A-5020 Salzburg
Tel: (0662) 88 98 70
E-mail: Tourist@salzburginfo.at
www.salzburginfo.at

Boat Trips on the Danube

Brandner Schiffahrt GmbH
Ufer 50
A-3313 Wallsee
Tel: (074 33) 2590–0
Fax: (074 33) 2590–25
E-mail: schiffahrt@brandner.at
www.ms-austria.at

DDSG Blue Danube Schiffahrt GmbH
Friedrichstrasse 7
A-1010 Vienna
Tel: (01) 588 80–0
Fax: (01) 588 80–440
E-mail: info@ddsg-blue-danube.at
www.ddsg-blue-danube.at

CULTURAL EVENTS

Bregenz Festival
Platz der Wiener Symphoniker 1
A-6900 Bregenz
Tel: (05574) 407–0
Fax: (05574) 407–400
E-mail: info@bregenzerfestspiele.com
www.Bregenzerfestspiele.com

Brucknerhaus
Untere Donaulände 7
A-4010 Linz
Tel: (0732) 77 52 30 .
Fax: (0732) 761 22 01
E-mail: kassa@liva.co.at
www.tiscover.com/linz

Haydn Performances
Schloss Esterhazy
A-7000 Eisenstadt
Tel: (02682) 719 30 00
Fax: (02682) 719 32 23
www.schloss-esterhazy.at

Haydn Festival
Tel: (02682) 618 66
Fax: (02682) 618 05
E-mail: office@haydnfestival.at
www.haydnfestival.at

International Theater/Fundus
Müllnergasse 6A
A-1090 Vienna
Tel: (01) 319 62 72
Fax: (01) 310 89 97

Marionette Theater
Schloss Schönbrunn
Hofratstrakt
A-1130 Vienna
Tel: (01) 817 32 47
Fax: (01) 817 32 47–4
E-mail: Marionette@vienna.at

Musikverein
Bösendorferstrasse 12
A-1010 Vienna
Tel: (01) 505 81 90
E-mail: tickets@musikverein.at
www.musikverein.at

Salzburg Festival
Hofstallgasse 1, Postfach 140
A-5010 Salzburg
Tel: (0662) 804 55 79
Fax: (0662) 804 57 60
E-mail: Info@salzburgfestival.com
www.salzburgfestival.com
(Program, history, ticketing, and other information)

Spanish Riding School
Michaelerplatz 1
A-1010 Vienna
www.srs.at/english
Detailed information, history, and performance schedules

Staatsoper
Herbert von Karajan Platz or Hanuschgasse 3
A-1010 Vienna
Tel: (01) 514 44–7880 (information)
Tel: (01) 514 44–2950 (last-minute tickets)
Tel: (01) 514 44–2613 (tours)
Fax: (01) 514 44–2969 (written requests for tickets from outside Vienna)
www.culturall.com, www.wiener-staatsoper.at

Vienna English Theater
Josefsgasse 12
A-1080 Vienna
Tel: (01) 402 12 60

Volksoper
Währinger Strasse 78
A-1090 Vienna
Tel: (01) 514 44 29–60
www.volksoper.at

Wiener Festwochen
Tel: (01) 589 22 22
E-mail: festwochen@festwochen.at
www.festwochen.or.at

ENTERTAINMENT
Vienna Tourism Office on Albertinaplatz has brochures on cafés, *Heurigen*, musical performances, theaters, and museums.

CINEMAS
Artis
Schultergasse 5
A-1010 Vienna
Tel: (01) 535 65 70

Burg Kino
Opernring 19
A-1010 Vienna
Tel: (01) 587 84 06

Flotten
Mariahilfer Strasse 85-87
A-1060 Vienna
Tel: (01) 586 51 52

Haydn English Language Cinema
Mariahilfer Strasse 57
A-1060 Vienna
Tel: (01) 587 22 62

BOOKSHOPS

British Bookshop
Weihburggasse 24-26
A-1010 Vienna
Tel: (01) 512 19 45–0

Shakespeare & Co.
Sterngasse 2
A-1010 Vienna
Tel: (01) 535 50 53–0

LIBRARIES
See Chapter Nine.

PHYSICAL FITNESS CENTER
See Chapter Nine.

MUSEUMS
See Chapter Nine.
Vienna Tourism Office publishes detailed brochures.

MUSIC
See Chapter Nine.
Vienna Tourism Office publishes monthly guides to musical events in
Vienna.

ALTERNATIVE LIFESTYLES
See brochure issued by Vienna Tourism Office.

Rosa Lila
Linke Wienzeile 102
A-1060 Vienna
Tel: (01) 586 81 50

RELIGIOUS INSTITUTIONS
Christ Church (Anglican/Episcopalian)
Jaurèsgasse 17-19
A-1030 Vienna
Tel: (01) 714 89 00

Islamic Center Vienna
Am Hubertusdamm 17-19
A-1210 Vienna
Tel: (01) 263 21 20–0

Jewish Welcome Service
Goldschmiedgasse 2
A-1010 Vienna
Tel: (01) 533 88 91 or 533 27 30
Fax: (01) 533 40 98

United Methodist Church
Sechshauser Strasse 56
A-1150 Vienna
Tel: (01) 893 69 89

Votivkirche (Roman Catholic)
Rooseveltplatz 8
A-1090 Vienna
Tel: (01) 402 18 30
(Mass in English at 11 am every Sunday)

FURTHER READING

GENERAL INFORMATION

Living in Vienna: A Practical Guide for the English-Speaking Community.
American Women's Association of Vienna, Vienna, 2000. A must-have
for anyone who will be living in Vienna. It provides priceless information
on every imaginable topic from education to recycling, and lists essential
addresses and phone numbers. The book is updated regularly and may be
purchased from the AWA directly and also at the UN.

The Xenophobe's Guide to the Austrians. Louis James. Ravette Books,
London, 1994. This little book offers amusing commentaries on who the
Austrians are and why they do what they do.

HISTORY AND POLITICS

The Austrians: A Thousand Year Odyssey. Gordon Brook-Shepherd.
Carroll & Graf Publishers Inc., New York, 1997. This comprehensive
book offers a good non-academic review of Austria's history. While the
title implies detailed information on all eras in Austria's history, the book
is biased towards the history of the 20th century.

The Viennese: Splendor, Twilight and Exile. Paul Hofmann. Anchor
Books Doubleday, New York, 1988. A critical and insightful look into
Austrian mentality through analysis of the country's history. Much of the
book focuses on political aspects of Austria, but it also devotes much
space to the country's cultural history and how it was affected by politics.

Twilight of the Habsburgs: The Life and Times of Emperor Franz Josef.
Alan Warwick Palmer. Grove Press, New York, 1995. Franz Josef's
personal life is analyzed within the context of much larger political issues.
The book looks at the political side of a crucial era in Austrian history that
has been the subject of much discussion.

Sissi: Elisabeth, Empress of Austria. Brigitte Hamann. Taschen, Cologne
and New York, 1997. This easy to read biography of one of Austria's

favorite personalities is neatly written and contains some lovely photographs. It's fun reading for fans of royalty.

A Nervous Splendor: Vienna 1888/1889. Frederic Morton. Penguin, New York, 1980. This is an entertaining read if you are interested in what led to the break-up of the empire and the end of the Habsburg dynasty.

Fin-de-Siècle Vienna: Politics and Culture. Carl E. Schorske. Vintage Books, New York, 1981. As the name suggests, this book takes an in-depth look at the close relationship between politics and the arts during this fascinating time in Vienna's history.

Freud: A Life for our Time. Peter Gay. W.W. Norton, New York, 1998. This critically acclaimed book provides insight into Freud's private life and theories.

The Interpretation of Dreams. Sigmund Freud. James Strachey (ed.) Avon Books, New York, 1983. If you're not clear on what Freud was all about, his most definitive work can be read without prior knowledge of psychoanalysis.

The Austrian Mind: An Intellectual and Social History 1848–1938. William M. Johnston. University of California Press, Berkeley, 1983. This award-winning book looks at the intellectuals behind the academic, scientific, and artistic achievements of this period in Vienna's history.

Alma Rosè: Vienna to Auschwitz. Richard Newman with Karen Kirtley. Amadeus Press, Portland, OR, 2000. An interesting biography tracing Alma Rosè's early life in a well-to-do Viennese Jewish family. The daughter of Justin Mahler, Gustav Mahler's younger sister, music was an important part of her life. She helped other Jews to leave Vienna after Austria was annexed by the Nazis, but wound up in Auschwitz where she conducted the only women's orchestra to be formed in a concentration camp.

Guilty Victim: Austria from the Holocaust to Haider. Hella Pick. I.B. Tauris, London and New York, 2000. The original German version received much praise. The author focuses on how Austria has been perceived abroad since World War II ended, and provides much interesting information on modern Austria.

The Haider Phenomenon. Melanie A. Sully. East European Monographs, Distributed by Columbia University Press, New York, 1997. Although this was written before the 1999 election, it still provides relevant information on the leader of the right-wing Freedom Party who continues to play a big role in Austrian politics.

TRAVEL AND TOURISM

Frommer's Austria, 8th Edition. Darwin Porter. Macmillan, New York, 1999. One of the better travel guides if you plan on seeing a lot of this beautiful country. It has lots of practical information for the tourist.

The Rough Guide: Vienna. Rob Humphreys. Rough Guides, London, 1997. Probably the best guidebook on Vienna, full of history, anecdotes, and valuable practical information.

Viennawalks. J. Sydney Jones. Boxtree, London, 1994. Four lovely walks through the heart of Vienna. Contains such wonderful and detailed information, you'll never be able to ignore this city's fascinating history.

Austrian Country Inns & Castles. Karen Brown. Harrap Colombus, London, 1996. This is a guidebook for the romantic who doesn't want to see all of Austria in five days. The author's itineraries take you along back roads, with fascinating stops at quiet little inns where you are tempted to stay for more than one night. All of the same information may be found at her website: www.karenbrown.com/austria.

Danube, A Sentimental Journey from the Source to the Black Sea. Claudio Magris. The Harvell Press, London, 1986. This book cannot and should not be read quickly. The author takes you on a slow journey down the Danube, stopping here and there with a fascinating tale. He explains much of life along the river, not only in Austria.

Walking Austria's Alps Hut to Hut. Jonathan Hurdle. Cordee, Leicester, 1999. This guide contains 11 walking tours. Each hike begins with a good introduction and is supported by detailed information.

Mountain Walks in Austria. Cecil Davis. Cicerone Press, Milnthorpe, Cumbria, 1986. This author has grouped Austria's mountains into 25 groups and 98 different walks. While the variety of walks is extensive, there isn't an overabundance of information.

293

THE ARTS

Some of the nicest books on the arts may be found in museum gift shops.

Music

The Illustrated Lives of the Great Composers. Haydn. Neil Butterworth. Omnibus Press, London and New York, 1987. This biography of Haydn's life includes his early years as a choir boy at St. Stephen's, working for the Esterhazy family, his relationship with Mozart and Beethoven, his travels to London, and finally his death in Vienna.

Mozart: A Cultural Biography. Robert W. Gutman. Harcourt Brace, New York, 1999. A sensitive look at the life and personality of Austria's most loved musical composer that also explains how his work fits in with the music of his time.

Beethoven. His Spiritual Development. J.W.N. Sullivan. Vintage Books, New York, 1960. This poignant and intense book on Beethoven's life follows his creative path and describes how his music was affected by his social being, affairs of the heart, deafness, failing health, and spirituality.

Schubert's Vienna. Raymond Erickson (ed.). Yale University Press, New Haven, 1997. Various scholars focus on Vienna during the Biedermeier period. They do not just examine developments in music and the other arts, but link them with the political repression of the day.

Second Viennese School. Oliver Neighbour, Paul Griffiths, and George Perle. Norton, New York, 1983. If you'd like to know more about Arnold Schönberg, Anton Weber, and Alban Berg, and their revolutionary style of music, this short book offers an explanation as well as biographical accounts of the three men.

Art

Vienna: 1890–1920. Robert Waissenberger. Wellfleet Press, Secaucus, 1984. This coffee-table book offers more than just beautiful photographs and reproductions. The politics, arts, architecture, music, and literature of this period are explained in detailed essays complementing the illustrations.

Art in Vienna: 1898–1918, Klimt, Kokoschka, Schiele and their Contemporaries. Peter Vergo. Phaidon Press Ltd., Oxford, 1975. This large illustrated book captures the essence of the ideological movement of the Secession toward the end of the 19th century and how paintings, architecture, and the applied arts were all affected. Paintings of Klimt, Kokoschka, and Schield are explained in detail, as are the architecture and applied arts of Wagner, Olbrich, Loos and Hoffman.

Gustav Klimt. Gottfried Fliedl. Taschen, Cologne and New York, 1991. This large illustrated book of the life and works of Klimt is an easily read account of the progress and changing nature of his work from Historicism to Jugendstil (Art Nouveau), his influence with members of the Secession, and his fascination in depicting the female nude in his search for a female image of the world.

The Applied Arts

Viennese Design and the Wiener Werkstätte. Jane Kallir. Galerie St. Etienne–George Braziller, New York, 1986. With both black and white and color illustrations, this book showcases the items that came out of the *Wiener Werkstätte*, including furniture, utensils, glass, and clothing. Ample information explains the workshop, its goals, and its products.

Thonet: Classic Furniture in Bent Wood and Tubular Steel. Alexander von Vegesack, with text by Brigitta Pauley and Peter Ellenberg. Rizzoli, New York, 1997. This book on the furniture of Vienna's internationally famous Thonet firm explains the principles and ideas behind their designs. Old and new photos show original pieces both then and now.

Architecture

Vienna 1900: The Architecture of Otto Wagner. V. Honrat Pintaric. Dorset Press, New York, 1989. A beautifully illustrated book of the works of Otto Wagner that were either built or submitted for competitions. Wagner was known as the father of architecture. His influence on Vienna's railroads, banks, churches, and residential buildings is still seen today.

Hundertwasser Architecture: For a More Human Architecture in Harmony with Nature. Friedensreich Hundertwasser, Angelika Muthesius, and Angelika Taschen (eds.). Taschen, Cologne and New York, 1997. A coffee-table book of beautiful pictures and interesting information on this wonderfully creative artist and architect. This book is a must for any fan of the artist.

FESTIVALS

Festivals and Traditions in Austria. Werner Schneider, Hella Pflanzer, and Erik Pflanzer. Pinguin-Verlag, Innsbruck, 1985. A comprehensive and beautifully illustrated book about the varied wealth of traditions and festivals in Austria. Each tradition and festival is explained in full detail, from the clothes the people wear, to how the tradition evolved, and its relation to pagan or Christian beliefs.

CUISINE

New Austrian Cookbook. Rudolf and Karl Oberbauer. Zabert Sandman, Munich, 1999. If you'd like to try your hand at some traditional Austrian meals, this is your best bet, with over 100 recipes using American measures and great photos showing how the dishes are supposed to look.

Austrian Cooking and Baking. Gretel Beer. Dover Publications, New York, 1975. A simple book providing very good recipes without fanfare.

A Little Book of Viennese Pastry. Illustrated by Aislinn Adams. Appletree Press, Belfast, 1995. A charming little book of recipes and drawings that makes a great gift.

The Wines of Austria. Philipp Blom. Faber and Faber, London, 2000. If you're into wines, this book is for you. It gives a history of Austrian wines, discusses the different wine-growing regions, and has several maps to guide you in your search for the perfect wine.

Essen & Trinken in Österreich. Bund Österreichischer Gastlichkeit (BÖG), BÖG, Vienna, 1999. This detailed guide to restaurants and cafés is divided by the nine provinces. Introductory information is given in English, but just a little knowledge of German is needed for specific information on each locale. Published annually in Austria, you can order a free copy by calling (01) 545 44 09-0 or fax (01) 545 22 50. You can also write to Bund Österreichischer Gastlichkeit, Embelgasse 59, A-1050 Wien, or e-mail your request to office@boeg.at. The website is at www.boeg.at.

FICTION

The Road into the Open. Arthur Schnitzler. University of California Press, Berkeley, 1992. Reprint of the 1908 edition. One of the richest portrayals of fin-de-siècle Vienna ever written. Following a group of Jewish intellectuals, the author captures the spirit of Vienna as Europe's cultural and intellectual center, and relates how it came to be threatened by an anti-Semitism that presaged the rise of fascism decades later.

Tale of the 1002nd Night. Joseph Roth. Picador USA, New York, 1999. Reprint of 1939 edition. Written fairy-tale fashion and filled with characters from old Vienna—civil servants, merchants, prostitutes, and soldiers. Yet the tale is not a happy one. Taking place in the 1870s, Roth's story is a metaphor for the Austrian Empire's fear of modernity and slow decline during the latter stages of the 19th century.

Correction. Thomas Bernhard. University of Chicago Press, Chicago, 1979. Although the author's style of writing may be dense and difficult to follow at times, this book is worth the effort. One of Austria's best modern authors, Bernhard addresses several philosophical issues in this story of a suicide.

The Piano Teacher. Elfriede Jelinek. Serpent's Tail, London, 1989. A dark and disturbing story about the relationship between a mother and daughter set in Vienna. Jelinek is one of Austria's critically acclaimed modern writers.

ABOUT THE AUTHORS

Susan Roraff was born in Chicago, Illinois, in the United States. She received a Bachelor of Arts in International Studies and German and spent part of her junior year studying at the University of Vienna. Later, she received her Master of Arts in Latin American Studies from Georgetown University and moved to Chile. With her husband, she moved from Chile to Singapore, and then returned to Vienna. She is also a coauthor of *Culture Shock! Chile*. Susan is responsible for Chapters 1, 2, 5, 9, and 11.

Julie Krejci was born in Roswell, New Mexico, also in the United States. She moved several times within the US and Europe during her adolescence. She received a Bachelor of Arts in International Relations at Syracuse University and a Master of Arts in Humanities at California State Dominguez Hills. After pursuing a teaching degree, she taught in Spanish in the Los Angeles School District and then went overseas to teach at the American International School in Vienna, Austria. Now married to an Austrian, she calls Vienna her home. She is responsible for Chapters 3, 4, 6, 7, 8, and 10.

INDEX